DO IT

Cycling around the world for a laugh

Bikes, music, judo, pizza, kangaroos, sex, football,
nurses, Greek fascists,
snow, *Britain's Got Talent*, castration, The King of
Thailand, monkeys and a sore arse.

By

Adrian Besly

also known as

"Oi, you" or "That's him, officer!"

Published by No Pasaran Printworks

All text and photographs copyright © 2016 by Adrian Besly. First published in 2016.

The right of Adrian Besly to be identified as the author of this work has been asserted by him in accordance with the Copyright, Designs and Patents Act 1988.

ISBN: 978-1-5272-0466-9

Dedicated, with love, to my wife Sharon
(Shazzabazzabingbong),
my son Kevin (Kev the Rev the dirty old
Dev),
and my daughter Laura (the Queen of
Shimpunku).

Thanks to my sisters Juliet and Shiel for their
unwavering encouragement, help and
sound advice, in my life. They have
continued in that style as my morale-
boosting back-up team on this little cycling
jaunt.

Contents

1 – Home

"...these last two weeks I've dealt with armed muggers, a spectacular crash, explosive diarrhoea and been admitted to hospital with heat exhaustion. Who knows what excitement the next few weeks will bring – maybe I'll get struck by lightning or abducted by aliens. Let the good times roll, baby!"

That was my diary entry for 4th October 2015.

My trip wasn't all doom and gloom though. I had the time of my life and some great fun getting drunk with Aussie cowboys, meeting the Only Gay in the Village in Andorra, nearly running over a dildo in Argentina, dancing with a pirate in Gibraltar, eating dog and cat in Vietnam, ending up on stage with drag queens in Sydney, doing a bungee jump in New Zealand and staying in a Brazilian brothel. Between those and many of other little dramas I cycled about 14,000 miles and developed possibly the world's sorest arse.

But let's backpedal to 2014, when a vague idea became a firm decision. Over a pint in the King Harold with Larry Ralph, aged 81, survivor of the Blitz, 6th Dan in judo, World Masters bronze medallist and fit as a fiddle, I discussed cycling around the world.

Without hesitation Larry said "Do it!"

Of course the best plans are invariably hatched over a few beers, never over a salad. The problem was that "doing it" would be financially bonkers.

Nevertheless, I'd been working in the NHS for over 14 years and I decided to cash in my pension – I'd get a lump sum of about £13,000 – and use that money to cycle around the world (RTW). Sensible folk no doubt shake their head at such a reckless decision. However, I saw people every day at Southend Hospital with life-limiting illnesses, and often they were younger than me. Frequently I'd met older people who, having saved all their lives for retirement, accumulating plenty of money in the bank, then were too poorly to enjoy it. You just don't know what tomorrow will bring.

"…if you can make one heap of all your winnings
And risk it on one turn of pitch-and-toss
And lose, and start again at your beginnings
And never breath a word about your loss…"
                                        Rudyard Kipling

The idea to cycle RTW had actually been at the back of my mind for over twenty years. I was 55 and felt that if I delayed any longer then something big might force me to cancel altogether. I wished I was Peter Pan, but I'm not. I get occasional chest pain. My teeth had started to fall out. Shoulders, elbows, knees and neck ached from repetitive judo injuries. So that was the plan – Now or Never – but as Mike Tyson said "Everybody has a plan, until they get punched in the face". You'll have to wait and see on that one!

As for the mode of transport, I feel there is something groovy and egalitarian about cycling. No matter how much money you have available to spend on an expensive bike you still have to push those damn pedals. Having said that, I'm not actually a massively keen cyclist, and I've noticed reading books by other RTW cyclists that they are not either. However, cycling does tick the boxes for getting lots of lovely fresh air, seeing new places and experiencing the whiff of adventure.

The truth is I'd only done four hours of actual cycle training for the trip over the previous six months, although I did keep fairly fit with judo and running every week, giving me a resting pulse of 45, which I could take up to 170. The charge nurse at work, Peter Allen, said I was "as fit as a butcher's dog," which I thought was pretty funny.

Equipment-wise, my wife Sharon bought me some proper cycling shorts and a shirt. The boys from the judo club bought me a solar phone charger to strap onto the back of the bike. My kids Kevin and Laura bought me a camera. I got a tent for £35, sleeping bag for £20, a cycling helmet for £8 from Aldi, and a toolkit from Tesco. I bought a commuter bike for £260 in Benfleet. I told the manager, who was also called Adrian, that I was going to cycle around the world. Rolling his eyes, he said "Yeah, right".

There was, of course, the distinct possibility that I could die on the journey, so I prepared psychologically and financially in case of my own death. It is a sobering experience realising that you might never see your family and friends again. Deadly tigers, bears, wolves, crocodiles, spiders and snakes still roam many of the places I would be travelling through. Malaria from infected mosquitoes kills about half-a-million people every year. Then again maybe I'd get hit by a truck. I could freeze to death in the snow. Or perhaps I'd have a heart attack pedalling up some of those crazy mountains. But more of a worry would be the human dangers.

There are wars and armed uprisings all over the world especially, in the Middle East, South America, Africa and South-East Asia. There is rape, pillage, murder and mayhem. Some places are even worse than Romford.

If you Google 'bike-jacking' you will see cyclists being held up at gunpoint in Brazil. I spoke to a South African man who had a friend who was attacked by a mob throwing rocks while out cycling. An Argentinian doctor at work told me not to cycle in certain parts of his country or I would definitely be killed. He also told me to say I was Australian or Irish. (Bollocks to that, *Soy Ingles!*) An Indian doctor at work said because I am European I would be a high-risk target for kidnappers in rural parts of his country.

You will probably notice that the opinions on politics, religion and kangaroos expressed in this book are not always consistent, and sometimes even contradictory. I don't care. It's my party and I'll cry if I want to. If I have upset every reader at least once, or prompted you to disagree, then my work is done. Raising awkward questions has its own intrinsic value. I don't have all the answers, and there is not much in this life that is pure black and white. I have nothing to lose so I talk about shitting and pissing and sexing because I can. I suspect this is the travel diary Michael Palin wants to write, but can't.

Lots of people asked which charity I was doing this for. Well... er... none. I've never quite understood that concept of asking your friends and family to cough up to partially pay for your adventures to, for example, climb Kilimanjaro or do a parachute jump.

Even if you passed on every penny you collected to the charity it still doesn't sit well with me. The boss of Save the Children has a salary of £234,000 (save the children, my arse, save the boss more like), and the boss of the British Red Cross gets £184,000, Christian Aid £126,000 and Oxfam £120,000. Quote these figures to the next 'chugger' (charity mugger) who accosts you on the high street asking you for a direct debit to their charity. Also consider that charitable donations of clothing have destroyed African textile production, and donations of food undermine Third World farmers trying to earn a living. Quite interestingly, *QI* claimed that for every £1 raised for charity by people doing extreme sport challenges it costs the NHS £13 to fix their resultant injuries and illnesses. Irony of ironies is that 60% of the charities are health-related.

Perhaps I should be less hostile to charities, because my

daughter works for Macmillan, an organisation that provides excellent nursing care. I know, because the lovely Macmillan nurses helped my first wife when she was very ill. However, those Macmillan nurses are on the same pay scale as me, £21-27,000 p.a., whereas the bosses of Macmillan earn many times more than that, have swanky offices in central London, and often rent out venues such as the Savoy Hotel for their 'charridee' fundraisers. Doesn't that just seem wrong to you?

OK, that's my whinge over. It's time to get down to business. So, with the following motivational axioms in mind ...

"Do it" – Larry Ralph
"If not now, when?" – Primo Levi
"You don't need a reason, you just need gas" – Jack Kerouac
"It is not a tragedy to fail, but it is a tragedy not to try" – anon
(on life) "This is not a practice" – Sharon B
"Carpe diem" – some Roman geezer
"Don't dream it, be it" – *The Rocky Horror Show*

...I started pedalling...

2 – Away

D-Day was planned for the 9th of May 2015, but I nearly delayed my leaving date because I was on *Britain's Got Talent*. I'd done *Southend Hospital's Got Talent* at The Palace Theatre in Southend, sodding about in fancy dress, playing the harmonica, and absolutely loved it. The organiser, Michael Daley, said I should have a go at *BGT*. So I did.

I passed an audition, then the big day came at the Dominion Theatre in London's West End. I was really excited, but not very nervous, it's only a bit of fun. They miked up Kevin and Laura, who were in the audience. In the wings Ant, or Dec, said "So did you win *Southend Hospital's Got Talent?*"

"No," says I. They thought that was hilarious, so I laughed along to keep them happy. Anyway, I went out in front of David Walliams, Amanda Holden, Simon Cowell and the other one and really got stuck into it. I was doing some groovy blues music, the crowd were clapping and cheering (or jeering, I'm still not sure which) then I got into some of my comedy routine, which among other things involved a rubber chicken, a pair of incontinence pants and some unusual dancing. That's when the very loud rejection buzzers blasted out and the big 'X''s all lit up behind me. I saw that Simon Cowell hated me so much that he pressed his own buzzer then reached over and pressed Amanda Holden's buzzer as well! Clearly that man does not have an eye for original talent. I bowed and walked straight off.

I'd never watched the whole show on TV before, so I didn't know you were supposed to stay on the stage after you've finished your performance to receive the judges' compliments and criticisms. I'm not sure I would want to listen to those smug bastards anyway. Nevertheless, we watched eagerly every Saturday when the new series started. They showed Kevin and Laura shouting and cheering, but edited out me, although I was briefly on the ITV2 companion show, *Britain's Got More Talent*. Never mind, it was a super-good day out and I enjoyed every minute of it. Needless to say, I was not invited back for the semi-finals, which meant I could start the RTW cycle trip on my original date!

*

Next item on the agenda was having a leaving do, well, two to be precise. Having a leaving do is a bit like attending your own funeral. You want to see who turns up. Some people you expect to be there don't show, others you are delighted to see have made the effort, and some express emotions almost as if it really is your funeral.

Sharon organised a blinding party in The Plough, Southend. The wonderful Tezza, the MC, got everyone involved in rowdy pub games, which, among other things, involved ladies from The Plough licking strawberries and cream from the navel of one of the judo boys. The Spanish nurses from work did a blow-yer-socks-off version of 'Highway to Hell' (which I privately hoped was going to prove to be inappropriate!), to which we pogoed like crazy. I was honoured because The Plough's resident pervert, 'Michael Jackson', even made an appearance. He's a little bloke with a pony tail who wears a bra, gropes all the girls and loves to dance like Michael Jackson, hence the name.

The following night, Laura and Kevin organised another fantastic party at Dagenham Football Club. I got a dazzling cake

9

in the shape of a *judogi* (judo suit). We were still doing the Macarena into the small hours. We invented a fun game called Dog of Truth which resulted in quite a lot of blushing. Laura's friend Justine rounded the evening off by puking down my arm, but frankly, my dear, by that stage, I didn't give a damn.

Prior to departure it was funny some of the advice people gave. If I'd taken all the equipment people recommended I would have needed a medium-sized lorry. One workmate said I should cycle with thick leather knee-high boots as protection against snakes. Someone else suggested I should cover the mileage on an exercise bike in the gym. That way there'd be no need to leave Essex. What was really useful was a little survival kit of needle and thread, string, rubber bands, safety pins, cable ties, matches etc. that Larry's wife Anna made up for me. Larry said those little kits were known in the army as a housewife. Several people said I should go by motorbike, and some said I should just fly. Another work colleague insisted I wouldn't have been around the world unless I went through Nigeria. (I pointed out that if I left heading west, and reappeared next year from the east, that was, by definition, going around the world, whether I ever went to Nigeria or not!) They all meant well, but sometimes it's best just to follow your own instincts, and do your own thang, man.

I asked Kevin to shave my head in preparation. It seemed like a good idea at the time. However, when I came to look in the mirror I realised I looked like a total bell-end.

On my last day at work at the Southend A&E Sister Betsy got everyone together to give me a card, vouchers, a round of applause and to wish me luck. I'd worked in the NHS for a long time and was hoping to come back. Considering that the NHS is the fifth biggest employer in the world (after the US Defence Department, the Chinese Red Army, Walmart and McDonald's) I was quite optimistic that they'd be able to squeeze me in somewhere. I had a very good attendance record. Working in a hospital you can develop an immune system that is almost bulletproof. In fact, the last time I'd phoned in sick was over eight years previously, and that was only because I needed to do some home decorating. (Keep that bit under your hat please).

The evening before I left Kevin and Laura cooked up a huge and tasty meal. I felt quite subdued, being very aware that this was the Last Supper. Then we sat down and watched *Marvellous*, a touching and hilarious film about Neil Baldwin, the kit man at Stoke City Football Club, which I highly recommend. Gary Lineker has a cameo role. I keep a close eye on Gary Lineker, Jeremy Clarkson and Simon Cowell because all four of us are exactly the same age. Obviously Lineker looks the best and is a good bloke, Clarkson is a bit of a knob and looks knackered, and I've gone right off Cowell since *BGT*.

Next morning, I woke up bright-eyed and bushy-tailed. Kevin said I was the Michael Palin of Basildon. The kids thought it was hilarious that my entire stock of spare clothes for nearly a year fit into a bag the size of a loaf of bread. Gleefully, they posted photos onto Facebook, whatever that is.

I started to faff about, going to the library, stroking the cat, packing and unpacking, washing-up, scratching my bollocks, etc. To the casual observer it must have looked like I was delaying and delaying and that I didn't really want to leave. If truth be told part of me didn't want to go, but by about lunchtime I realised I had to get going, so I gave myself a kick up the backside, loaded the bike, dropped it, loaded it again and set off for my 'official' starting point. This was just one mile down the road: the Hollywood-style BASILDON sign that greets motorists on the A127. There Kevin, Laura and Laura's boyfriend Lee met me and we clambered over the giant letters and posed for a few photos. Notices said anyone found climbing on the letters would be prosecuted. But I thought, "Sod it, they'll have to catch me first!" Maybe it would be like Detective Fix chasing Phileas Fogg all around the world!

Finally, after some more hugs and kisses, it really was time to go, and the serious matter of cycling 14,000 miles got started.

Within twenty minutes I was nearly taken out by a truck on the A128. Phew, close shave.

I carried on pedalling though Essex, heading for the Tilbury to Gravesend Foot Ferry, which also takes bikes. In Chadwell St. Mary I stopped to check the map and some kids asked me for a light. They had one cigarette between three of them. I told them I was too young to smoke. Their little brains took a few moments to process this information, then they wandered off to ask someone else. (My favourite smoking story was when my friend Vince asked someone for a light. The other person told him they were trying to give up, to which Vince replied "I wanted a light, not the story of your life.")

I arrived in Tilbury but just missed the ferry. It only takes five minutes to cross to Gravesend, but I could see it sitting over there, going nowhere. So, after about an hour, and wondering whether I should abandon my world trip on the first afternoon, I asked someone "Why isn't it coming back?" I was told the captain stops for his lunch about now.

When the ferry did eventually come back over I got chatting with one of the crew and told him I was cycling around the world and he said I could cross for free. Result!

It was raining so I was wearing my waterproofs which say Peter Storm (a brand) on the chest. The ferryman asked if that was my name, as if I was famous or something. He also told me, incidentally, that Pocahontas is buried in the little churchyard of St. George's there in Gravesend.

On through Kent I went heading for my first night away, staying with my nephew Jon and his lovely Argentinian wife Melisa in Brockham, Surrey. Since I'd dropped the bike that morning the gears were all buggered up and the chain kept slipping and coming off and I couldn't seem to adjust it correctly. So my hands were covered in oil, Kent and Surrey has dozens of steep hills, and I was wet, cold and hungry. It was getting dark. Occasionally idiots would shout abuse out of their car windows, as some young men are prone to doing. I was totally fed up.

Eventually I arrived over 3 hours later than predicted, but I cheered up considerably after a great big barbequed steak, home-made lager, *Jäger* shots and a session of table tennis in the kitchen. I'm not sure if Chris Hoy (Britain's most successful cycling Olympian) has that type of training preparation, but it was just what I needed. Jon and Meli told me they were going to Buenos Aires in July to see her family, so with a bit of luck I'd catch them there too.

After a fry-up the next morning and yet more hugs and kisses I jumped on the bike and got going through the Surrey countryside. Some of the woods looked really pretty with their carpets of bluebells.

Is Surrey the cycling capital of England? The country lanes had scores of individuals and teams zooming about training like mad. Also during the day I saw a dog grooming van called Short Bark and Sides and a pest control van called Drop Dead Gorgeous. Even better was a plumber's van which read, I think, 'Rajpinder Singh – you've tried the Cowboys, now try the Indians!'

Pushing on through Sussex was a trip down memory lane for me. I cycled past Brinsbury, near Pulborough, previously the West Sussex College of Agriculture, where I did a Youth Training Scheme course in farm work when I was 16. We had a right laugh mucking about in the fields and crashing the tractors. Among other skills, we learnt to save new born lambs when they were not strong enough to break through the foetal membrane. In such cases you had to act quickly, tear open the membrane and give the lamb the kiss of life. As fate would have it, I was out in the fields early one morning and came across that exact same situation. With mummy sheep looking on, I tore open the membrane and did mouth-to-mouth just like we'd been taught. The lamb died. I believe I did everything correctly, so it must have been my halitosis that finished the poor thing off.

However, my biggest memories from Brinsbury are of castration. We put tight rubber bands around the goolies of the lambs to cut off the circulation, so their doomed bollocks went necrotic and after a few weeks fell off. We held piglets between our knees, spread their back legs and sliced through their testicles and pulled them out. The mantra was "cut the white (the sperm duct) and tear the red (the blood supply)." We would do 50 or more with the same scalpel. As for the tool we used to castrate the calves, that would not look out of place in the dungeons at The Tower of London. Poor sods.

When we were finished with their nether regions we would clip the piglets' incisors using pliers to stop them biting each other, and chop off their tail to prevent other pigs from chewing it. We would cut off the horns of the calves using bolt croppers so they wouldn't damage fences. All of these procedures involved plenty of bright red blood spurting all over the place, and of course there was no anaesthetic. The pain and trauma those animals suffered must have been excruciating. I don't know if farming is still done that way.

*

Heading south you cannot fail to be impressed at the grandeur of Chichester Cathedral. Shame all the best buildings are wasted on religion. It is nearly 1000 years old and peregrine falcons nest in the spire.

Pub quiz question: Which are the only two English cathedrals that can be seen from the open sea?
Answer: Chichester and Liverpool.

Chichester was my hometown, so as a youngster I knew every nook and cranny. One day when I was about 12, I decided to cycle to the next town, Bognor Regis. The front wheel of my bike went into a pothole, and I went flying over the handlebars, landed on my head and was knocked out cold. A passing motorist stopped and came to my assistance by slapping me around the face. When I regained consciousness I dusted myself down and carried on to Bognor. These days I would definitely have been sent to A&E, but back then people only went to hospital if they were really ill.

My first judo club was in Chichester. I would have a bath on Friday evening, (my only bath of the week – we lived in different times) and on Saturday morning walk or cycle the five miles into Chichester for judo training. The warm-up consisted of running around the streets in our *judogi's* barefoot to toughen our feet. Ouch!

Anyway, next stop, heading west is the village of Southbourne, where we lived from 1967. I stopped at our old house and chatted to the man who was renting it, and he kindly took a photo for me.

Dad was a teacher and the headmaster of the local comprehensive school, where I was a pupil, which made life difficult. The judo came in handy.

*

So there I was, pedalling towards the car ferry terminal at Portsmouth. I had been dreading tackling the approaches to Pompey because it's a tangle of motorways, fast dual carriage ways and speeding juggernauts. However, the fine people of Hampshire had set up some dedicated cycle ways around the coast and straight into town. Perfect.

Sharon had come to see me off from Blighty for the final time. We booked into the Travelodge then went out to look for a restaurant. Instead we found a dishevelled man with wild, asymmetrical eyes busy head-butting a bus stop. As we passed he turned and blurted out "Got any weed? Got any pills?" When I said that we hadn't he carried on head-butting his bus stop.

15

Further along the pavement were some men so drunk they could barely stand up. Their speech seemed to consist of long words such as sshhwaaarropoolafinjoe and frallowzeebip which may or may not have been English. As Sharon and I were commenting to each other that Portsmouth seemed to be a very interesting place a man passed us wearing a T-shirt that said "I don't have Tourettes, I really think you're a pile of shit". On the bright side, the people of Portsmouth do love an Indian – we found three curry houses next to each other on London Road, so just for the *craic* we had a starter in the Massala Room, our main course in the Indian Cottage and dessert in the Shalimar.

Sharon had also prepared me a poem:

Cheerio, but come home soon
Cheerio, but please be careful
I love you Bes that is why
It's cheerio and never goodbye.
As you cycle having fun
Think of me while you're in the sun
Watch out for snakes and spiders too
Even the rats and the Kangaroos!
I know you my Bes so please be careful
I know that you're strong and never fearful
So cheerio but come home soon
Where my love awaits for you.

Have fun my babe
Your Wifey XX

There were more hugs and tears next morning as Sharon got on the train back to London from Portsmouth Harbour Station. Things had not been easy at home for the last few years, but Sharon was always so positive and cheerful, and a sexy minx, which is why I love her.

16

Before I get on to the ferry to France, please let me digress (again!) to tell you one of my favourite stories, one which happened to take place at Portsmouth Harbour station.

My anarchist mate Jamie, a mad-keen Millwall supporter, had been to one of their games one Saturday afternoon, then afterwards had a few beers and fell asleep on the wrong train. He woke up to hear the British Rail announcement "This is Portsmouth Harbour. The next train to London will be the 21.10 from platform 3."

Jamie looked at his watch, which said 21.09. He thought if he got out of the train, ran to the end of the platform (because Portsmouth Harbour is a terminus) then ran round to platform 3, he would miss the train back to London. Bear in mind that before electric doors you could open train doors yourself on either side of the carriage. So using his initiative, Jamie climbed out of his train on the wrong side, nipped across the tracks, and climbed into the train waiting on platform 3.

Kushty! No problem!

Anyway, 21.10 came and went, as did 21.15. By about 21.20 Jamie was wondering why the train wasn't moving, so he leaned out of the window and had the following conversation with a British Rail employee.

Jamie: "Excuse me, is this the 21.10 to London?"
BR man: "Yes, it is."
Jamie: "It's 21.20 now, so how come the train hasn't left?"
BR man (wearily): "We've had reports of some c*nt on the track!"

3 – France

The person sitting next to me on the car ferry from Portsmouth to St. Malo was obviously also a cyclist. He asked where I was going.

"Round the world" says me.

"So am I!" says he.

We chatted and got on really well. His name was Jack. He was 25, and had quit his job as a cameraman on the Shopping Channel ("Selly Telly" he called it), and strictly speaking said he might not cycle all around the world but might just go to India and back.

So, there I was on the overnight ferry, using my stinky trainers as a pillow, stretched out on the floor along with everyone else who hadn't got a cabin. French port workers at Caen and Le Havre were on strike so the ferry to St. Malo was extra busy. (Later I saw bus workers on strike in Toulouse and factory workers on strike in another town. The French are still good at bucking the system – a talent the English have almost lost.)

It was a smooth crossing, which would not have pleased my father. My Dad was always happier crossing the Channel when it was choppy. He liked the ship rolling, the rain lashing, the wind howling and the deck awash with vomit. He believed it created a better sense of adventure to leave England like that, or as he put it "more value for money".

18

*

Bonjour et allons-y!

Arriving in France, Jack and I decided to cycle together for a while. In fact we rode together for three days. You couldn't meet a nicer bloke than Jack. He had been working up to 70 hours per week for years, and now loved the freedom of cycling. Before leaving the Shopping Channel one of his workmates asked, with deep concern, "What if you get lost?" Jack, who had no particular desire to go one place any more than any other cheerfully replied "I can't get lost!" That is the true spirit of travelling!

Jack reminded me of a fellow I met in 2003 in Northumberland while I was cycling from Land's End to John O'Groats. That man was well over 60, a Geordie ex-miner. He had a rusty old bike, a few belongings in a leather saddle bag and wore an Australian-style bush hat. He gently pedalled around Northumberland and Cumbria, stopping and chatting as the whim took him. After a lifetime working down the mines, he clearly relished the open air, the sun, the green fields, the birds singing, the pretty flowers and even the rain. Perhaps he is still gently pedalling around Northumberland and Cumbria as we speak.

So here we were going across the beautiful French countryside, which is just as pretty as Northumberland. If you want a lovely cycling holiday you should make a beeline for France. The weather is usually better than England, the roads are first class, there's hardly any traffic, the scenery is picturesque, the small towns are delightful, but best of all is that France has given a mainstream, feel good and glamourous image to cycling.

France has also given the world French Kisses and French Letters. Bit of a theme going on there. Then there is French Toast, always affectionately referred to in Besly households as PMO (Poor Man's Omelette). Finally, there are French Fries. These have nothing to do with France. When I worked at McDonalds in Shepherd's Bush in 1978 another member of the staff told me they were not allowed to call their chips potato fries because they didn't contain enough potato. Their main ingredients are flour, fat, salt plus some other exotic chemicals. Consequently, my colleague said, McDonalds had to invent a new name to call that crap. *Et voila*! They came up with the cute-sounding term French Fries. What's more, during the 'McLibel' trial in the 1990s the very well-paid McDonald's lawyers had to big-up the nutritional value of their products. Hilariously, the best they could come up with for their Cola drink was "It contains water". As, of course, does urine.

Jack and I cycled on and came across a large formation of menhir stones, not dissimilar to Stonehenge, and at Monteneuf, a re-creation of an ancient village. We were the only ones there. I had to stop and check it out, having been raised on *Asterix* books. We took photos and jumped about from stone to stone. It was not quite Parkour, except in our heads.

Ten miles further on I stopped for a 'jimmy riddle' and mentioned that I'd never seen Jack pee before, then had to immediately apologise because that sounded a bit wrong! Another time, way out in the countryside, I was going like a horse when a young lady appeared from nowhere and jogged past. Being mid-stream all I could do was wish her a cheery "Bonjour". I couldn't even wave to her, because I had my hands full. Ooh, Matron!

En route we came across a bed and breakfast at Réminiac run by an English couple, the lovely Ken and Lesley, who especially welcomed bikers. The table rules were that it was forbidden to talk about politics, religion or motorbikes, because those three subjects caused too many arguments. They provided supper as well. The food was delicious and we had a lively evening chatting over a few beers.

Among other subjects Ken and Lesley told us about Bastille Day. Each *mairie* (local mayor) organises fireworks and celebrations every year and a good time is had all. You may have seen glorious paintings from the original Bastille Day, 14th July 1789, when hundreds of valiant revolutionaries filled the streets waving the French tricolour. Actually there were only seven prisoners in the Bastille at the time. There were four forgers, two lunatics and the Comte de Solanges who was inside for sexual deviance (don't ask!). These seven could hardly be described as the vanguard of the proletariat. Never mind, it makes a good legend, and the truth is they've got a lot of things right in their society under the banner of liberté, égalité, fraternité, so *Allez Les Bleus!*

Jack and I continued on the next day, and being cyclists in France it was not long before the subject of *Le Tour de France* came up. It is the largest annual sporting event in the world. Me and about two million other English people watched it come through Yorkshire and Essex last year. *Le caravan* precedes the riders by an hour or two. This is not like a caravan where you spend a wet week in Clacton, but a fabulous razzamatazz of speeding cars, motorbikes and lorries with pumping music, sexy girls and loads of freebies chucked out to the spectators. Then, with a whoosh, the cyclists in the *Peloton* zoom by. That was a really wonderful day out. The French have turned a potentially dull sporting event into a wonderful carnival of excitement and glamour.

The very best of modern technology goes into the *Tour de France* bikes. Their chain rings are not even round, but elliptical, to reduce the 'dead spot' while pedalling. They have electric gear-changing. *Tour de France* bikes weigh less than 7kg, whereas mine was 20kg, plus 15kg of luggage – five times heavier!

I would never have had a chance racing against the *T. de F.* boys, or, to be honest, even cycling against the world's best runners. I try to maintain a pedalling cadence of about 80 revolutions per minute, which gives me an average speed of about 10-12mph. At this speed Dr Roger Bannister would flash past me, even though he's only wearing some baggy shorts, his Dad's old vest and a pair of plimsolls. He could only do it for a mile though. Likewise, Paula Radcliffe and the Kenyan marathon runners would also overtake me because they run at about 13 mph, but only for 26 miles. I cover three or four times that amount every day, so I suppose I

21

would have the last laugh. Remember, the tortoise won the race, not the hare!

So Jack and I carried on pedalling through the gorgeous French countryside, and as afternoon rolled on we started to think about where to stay the night. We each had tents but I prefer a cheap *chambres d'hotes* (bed and breakfast) or hostel in order to get a bed and shower after a day of sweating-yer-nads-off. We found Nantes youth hostel, checked in, met a German cyclist called Tobias and cooked up a huge spag bol with him.

Tobias asked "Do you like football?"

"Yes" I said.

Then Tobias asked, "Do you like beer?"

Again I said "Yes."

"Ah, typically English" says he.

I thought about this afterwards, considering the fact that both me and Jack had quit our jobs and were traipsing off into the unknown, and thought we were not typically English at all.

Next day, as we cycled on our merry way Jack related a story about a girl who told her parents she was going on a gap year, then just Photoshopped herself onto a load of backgrounds like the Pyramids and the Taj Mahal. Apparently she never left England. I thought, if things get tough on this trip I might try something like that myself, once I find out what Photoshop is.

The following morning the weather was really bad. We were having a tough time cycling. At one stage I shouted, back to Jack, above the wind, "Cold! Wet! Windy! And uphill!"

Jack, being a half-full kind of guy, replied between breaths, "Living the dream!"

That day reminded me of one of Billy Connolly's quintessentially-Scottish quotes – "There is no such thing as bad weather, only the wrong sort of clothing. Get yourself a natty little raincoat and live a bit."

After three days together Jack wanted to go west to explore the Atlantic coast and I wanted to go south because I'd arranged to meet Sharon in Gibraltar on the first of June. I felt it was a bit emotional saying goodbye to Jack, and I was sorry we were going our different ways. If we were women we might have cried. I missed his company. A really nice guy. After he had gone it was a bit boring and lonely to be cycling alone.

Nevertheless, I pedalled on to the charming and impressive city of Angoulême. Incidentally, the Duchess of Angouleme was Queen of France for just twenty minutes on the second of August 1830. Imagine, if she had popped out to powder her nose, she could have missed it!

The tourist office in Angoulême directed me to an oldy-worldy *chambres d'hotes* run by an elderly couple who seemed so happy and comfortable together. It was sweet to see them. They didn't speak a word of English but we had a lot of fun via sign language and my schoolboy French. They provided a six-course meal in the evening, washed down with plenty of wine and beer. They had never been outside France but I was impressed by their Internationalism and concern for Africa and elsewhere. They reminded me of a night in a comedy club in London a few years before. The comedian, Lee Hurst, got chatting to a loved-up couple in the front row.

Lee asked, "How long have you been married?"

They replied, "Twenty-five years."

Seeing as they were clearly very happy together, Lee enquired, "So what is the secret of your happy marriage?"

The husband replied, "Well, I make all the big decisions, and she makes all the small ones."

Lee, being a modern sort of bloke thought this sounded a tad sexist, so he quizzed the husband a bit more – "So what big decisions have you had to make?"

The husband replied, "None, yet."

Next day I carried on to Cadouin. I passed the endearingly-named Hotel Bastard. I cycled about 110 miles over dozens of punishing hills and, excuse my French, but I was effing bolloxed.

It was worth it though. I've stayed at some stunning youth hostels over the years, including medieval watermills, remote lighthouses and Scottish castles, but Cadouin's hostel is one of the best. It's actually part of a 12th century abbey, but with all mod cons. My bedroom was previously one of the monks' rooms, which had a 'secret' shuttered window to look down on the cloisters. One night there, then back on the road.

All over south-west France you can find little memorials to the French Resistance. On the way out of Cadouin was a memorial plaque commemorating where the Resistance had killed 'The Premier Nazi in The Dordogne'. (Actually, many of the French Resistance's bravest and most experienced fighters were in fact Spanish anarchists, battle-hardened from the civil war in Spain.)

Keep pedalling Besly! Next stop, Toulouse, which is a beautiful city, with beautiful people. Back home in Southend there is a trendy French restaurant converted, as is often the case these days, from two public toilets. Its name – Toulouse. Two Loos! Sharon, me and some good friends went there for a meal. My friend had a dodgy oyster, and projectile vomiting and uncontrollable diarrhoea in their car on the way home. But the city of Toulouse really is lovely. Spectacular, in fact.

Whether the cities and scenery where lovely or not, my butt was really starting to hurt.The year before my trip I'd read Edward Enfield's (Harry's dad) funny book *Downhill All the Way*, about his cycling trip around France. In it he recommended getting a wide (ladies') saddle. I took his advice, so had a wide, sprung, gel-lined saddle. On top of this I had an additional gel cover. Also, I was wearing cycling shorts with a gel padding on the backside, which looked like I was wearing a massive sanitary pad, but, hey ho. Nevertheless, all day cycling does bring its aches and pains. I texted my judo mate Marshall to say I had sore legs, sore feet, sore arse and sore balls.

He replied "Sore arse and sore balls? What have you been doing, Sir?"

I was nearly at the border with Andorra. It was pouring with rain, I was soaked through, and I got my first puncture way out in the sticks. *Merde*, and double *merde*. I got the bike upside down amid plenty of cursing to get the rear tyre repaired. Characteristically, a kind French motorist stopped and offered to help.

Puncture fixed and off cycling again, I became aware that my right hamstring was very painful, and I was forced to do most of the pedalling with my left leg. I decided that at the next hotel I see I'll stay two nights, partly to dry out and partly to rest my leg. It was going to make it more of a rush to meet Sharon, but I didn't have many options.

I found a cheap hotel in Tarascon and the view out of the window of the Pyrenees was like a picture postcard. Cliffs, forests, raging rivers, an old castle and even an eagle circling high in the sky.

Two days later, my leg had improved so I hit the road again. Overall France had been a pleasure, so I wished her *Au Revoir, Merci et à Bientôt!*

4 – Andorra

Top of the world
I'm on top of the world

'Top of the World (Olé, Olé, Olé)'
Chumbawumba

Do you know where Andorra is? Not many English people do. It's a small country, less than a quarter the size of Essex, high up in the Pyrenees mountains between France and Spain, 1257 km from London. It's too mountainous to even have an airport. When you are there you really feel you are on top of the world.

I cycled uphill for miles through France climbing to 8000 feet, which is nearly double the height of Ben Nevis, to the border at Col d'Envalira. The road zig-zagged even more than the varicose veins in my left leg. (Varicose veins are the price of nursing - long hours on your feet.) There was snow everywhere, with sub-zero temperatures. I had to wear my entire stock of clothes, including two pairs of socks on my hands, but the views were worth it.

After the forests and quiet country roads of France, it's a bit of a shock getting into Andorra. Right from the frontier it becomes a shopping bonanza. I was greeted by neon, malls, flash cars, luxury hotels, restaurants and extensive construction work. It's a boomtown place, like a freezing cold Las Vegas. Andorra is tax-free so petrol, cigarettes, electrical goods and all the usual vices are dirt cheap. The citizens don't even pay income tax. They've also got Europe's highest golf course, although you would need a bloody good coat to play there.

I thought the people would speak French, but they only wanted to talk Catalan. In fact, it's the only country in the world with Catalan as its first language. When Gary Lineker played for

Barcelona (in Catalonia) he learnt Catalan rather than Spanish. (In fact when he played for Nagoya Grampus Eight in Japan he learnt Japanese. See, I told you he was a good bloke.) It was a bit startling to see 'Bombers' written on a big red truck zooming down the road towards me, until I discovered that is the Catalan word for fire brigade.

I found a cheap hotel in the only town, Andorra la Vella, turned on the TV and was pleasantly surprised to discover they had judo coverage for an hour. Can't be bad. I was warming to the place already.

I went out for a meal and had a delicious *Paella Valenciana* as recommended by my friend Alberto who comes from Valencia. It was the best meal I'd had for a week, because in France I'd normally get something cheap from the supermarket and, seeing as I didn't carry any cutlery, I would eat it with a screwdriver and a pair of pliers. After that lovely paella I sat at the bar and had an interesting chat with a dead ringer for Little Britain's 'The Only Gay in the Village'.

Andorra has had some quirky history. For example, in 1914 they declared war against Germany but nobody really noticed because they only had ten part-time soldiers. Consequently, at the end of World War One, when the Treaty of Versailles came to be signed in 1919 nobody remembered to invite Andorra, so officially they remained at war with Germany. This anomaly was not resolved until 25th September 1939, when Andorra made peace with Germany and so finally brought an end to the First World War. By which time, of course, the Second World War had already started, and everyone was far too busy to notice the end of the First.

There are parallels between Andorra and Berwick-Upon-Tweed. Berwick, a small town between Scotland and England, had independent status two hundred years ago. Subsequently England, Scotland and... er... Berwick declared war against Russia and battled it out in the Crimea. The Crimean War ended, and as with what happened to Andorra, the main warring parties forgot to invite Berwick to the signing of the peace treaty. Therefore, the little town of Berwick, on the Scottish border, remained at war with Russia until 1966, when they finally kissed and made up.

At 9655 feet Coma Pedrosa is the highest mountain in Andorra. Originally Kevin and Laura were going to meet me there, and we would climb it together. We conquer the highest mountain in a different country every year. We have conquered England, Wales, Scotland, Northern Ireland, the Republic of Ireland, Luxembourg, the Netherlands and Belgium. Actually our family mountain climbing career started when we conquered the highest point in Essex – a field near Harlow. There is a distinct feel good factor in climbing to the highest point in a country, almost like you own it, as if you're the king or queen, at least for a day. I'm glad we didn't climb Coma Pedrosa on this occasion though. It was too damn cold and covered in thick snow. We'll save that particular delight for when it's hotter in July or August another year.

Next day, I had the pleasure of cycling for miles downhill, towards the border. My ears 'popped', something normally associated with air travel, not cycling. I wondered why my water bottle kept falling out of its holder on my bike frame. Then I remembered that I had had a drink at Col d'Envalira at 8000 feet, where the air pressure must be so much lower. When I unscrewed the top, the bottle expanded back to normal size, with a hiss, and didn't fall out of the holder again.

It was time to leave Andorra. The sky was blue. The forests were green. The snow on the mountains looked heavenly. The town was a pleasant surprise. It was damn hard work pedalling to get up there, but it was worth it.

Adios Andorra.

5 – Spain

Vamos! Sporting a wide, happy grin I went over the border and into Spain. Ten minutes later my front tyre got a puncture. Bollocks, or perhaps I should say *Cojones*.

Spain is such a beautiful country, with wide open spaces, forests, mountains, pretty rivers and small rocky hills, with castles, churches or villages perched dramatically on top. The roads are fast, smooth and often deserted. They're a wet dream for fans of *Top Gear*. If the only thing you had known about Spain was from reading *Don Quixote* (nearly pronounced "Donkey Oatey") you would still recognise the place, even though that book was written 400 years ago.

For years I'd struggled to learn Spanish with books, CDs and the Open University. Fortunately, Southend Hospital had recruited 200 Spanish nurses the year before, because not many English people want to do nursing. (Nursing seems to be too hard work mentally and physically for most English people. A fact that really depresses me!) Anyway, the Spanish nurses, male and female, taught me the most important part of the Spanish language, i.e. how to swear. In that I am now fluent. So, if there is something you don't like in this book, you can *comeme la polla, coño!*

About twenty miles into Spain I came across a Chinese man on a very heavily-laden bike which even had a trailer. He was 29, and his name sounded like Tiler. He had ridden from Macao, via

Mongolia, Russia, Eastern Europe, Holland, Britain, France etc. He was a bubbly, happy-go-lucky sort of fellow. He had left home two years ago and thought he'd be away for another two.

We were standing in the car park of a smart restaurant and I mentioned that I'd been having trouble with my gears. Without batting an eyelid, he got stuck in trying to help me. He had every tool imaginable in his panniers, plus camping gear, loads of fruit and biscuits, saucepans, a fishing rod, a notebook where he kept pressed flowers, and even speakers on the handlebars so he could listen to music.

Tiler rolled up his sleeves and in a whirlwind of activity adjusted my gears, spokes, tyres and wheels, which made a great improvement. It took over an hour. Midway he walked over to one of the restaurant's flower pots, which had a small tree growing in it, and had a piss, calm as you like. Then he came back and carried on working on my bike. He instantly became my hero.

Tiler camped because he said hotels and youth hostels were too expensive (they were only about £10 per night). He would put his tent up anywhere – fields, parks, even graveyards, or he would sleep under bridges. To eat he would catch fish or get some fruit and veg from the fields. He had walked into McDonald's once, seen the prices, and walked straight out again. I've done the same in Starbucks.

I asked how he survived for money. Amazingly, he said he was sponsored by his old employer, a casino in Macao, where he had been a croupier. This was when I noticed the faded and torn T-shirt he was wearing which had the casino logo printed on it. He had greasy jogging pants and large leather boots. He wasn't a smart 'MAMIL' (Middle Aged Man In Lycra) like me. In fact, he was a scruffy bugger who looked like he'd just been dragged through a bush backwards. But he was a happy chappy, so good luck to him.

He said newspapers had covered his cycle trip four times in China, once in Latvia and once in Scotland. Each time he got newspaper coverage he would email his casino and they would send him money for the publicity it gave them. I'm not sure if they really want publicity about pissing in plant pots, or the hobo chic look, but Ad Men do say all publicity is good publicity.

Tiler described the people in England as very helpful, but he hated the weather. Not surprising really, camping in winter, probably in a graveyard. His favourite country was Lithuania because the girls were so pretty.

After fixing my bike the least I could do was buy him a meal. So we went into the restaurant whose flower pot he had pissed in. Immediately, without the least sign of embarrassment, he set up camp inside. He plugged in half a dozen electrical gadgets to charge. He went to the toilet for a wash and brush up. He plonked a load of his own food on the table and got tucked in, sharing it with me.

I ordered seafood paella for two. The food arrived and it was really tasty. With the meal we each had a large prawn (langoustine?) about the size of a banana. I carefully deshelled mine and ate the white meat inside. Tiler, chuckling, ate the whole lot – shell, body, legs and head!

It was time to go our separate ways. I thanked him. He was going north to Andorra, so I warned him about the 8000 feet of uphill pedalling. He just laughed and said "I've been to Tibet!" I suppose all mountains are small compared to the Himalayas. He had a keen desire to go to Bulgaria, Turkey, Syria and Africa. I felt properly humbled because he was seeing the world at a leisurely pace, not like me racing around. It didn't bother him that there was a war in Syria. He'd seen the TV news – "It's all lies", he said cheerfully. He was either mad, brave, foolish or had a wonderfully optimistic view of the goodness of human beings. Or, for all I know, maybe he was right, and it is "All lies".

So I waved goodbye to Tiler and hit the road again. Look out for him. I carried on across the almost deserted countryside of rural Spain. Some of the windswept viaducts and cliff edges do test your nerves as a cyclist, because if you got blown over the

31

edge probably no-one would find you for weeks. Travelling through such a remote place I was reminded of Stephen Fry who has a neat phrase to describe his upbringing in rural Norfolk "I was miles from the nearest lemon." Presumably that has a double meaning. (I met Stephen Fry once when I was a motorcycle dispatch rider. I had to deliver a script to his house in West Hampstead.)

*

Progressing across Spain's vast landscape one day I was really busting for a pee, or as Glaswegians say "Ma' back teeth are floatin' here." So I stopped the bike in the middle of a dusty plain. I couldn't see any people or buildings for miles, so I thought I might as well go there. Bear in mind that in those temperatures you need to drink 6-10 litres of water per day, so peeing can take a while. I was happily standing there when a large and very angry buzzing insect (a hornet?) started to take a distinct dislike to me. It was coming at me from all angles with a vengeance. My arms were swinging like windmills to shoo it away. I was swearing in English and Spanish. But that winged bastard was persistent. I felt the only thing I could do was jump on the bike and pedal away faster than it could fly. Remember, I still had my wedding tackle out and was still pissing like a buffalo, so wee went all over my legs, shoes and the bike. Damn that hornet.

The other thing you see in the Spanish countryside, sometimes on the approaches to towns, are the prostitutes. They sit or stand beside the road waiting for tricks. The weather is warm so I suppose it's okay to wear skimpy clothes. Incidentally, the police in the Casa de Campo, the prostitute area in Madrid, tried to force the girls there to wear more clothes, but that matter went to court and the judge ruled that wearing basques, miniskirts, suspenders etc. was the uniform of their trade, so they could carry on. If you delve I'm sure all these girls have a sad backstory of childhood abuse, violence, rape, drugs or poverty. Let's face it, all we want is to love, and be loved.

If truth be told, I went to a prostitute once, when I was 17. At the time I was working at a pickled onion processing factory in Holland. (By coincidence, my brother Paul was in *The Guinness Book of Records* in 1971 as world champion pickled onion eater). As you probably know, every Dutch town has a legitimate red-light district. So I went to the one in Eindhoven. I was a teenager desperate to lose my virginity. I found one of the ladies of the night and we went upstairs, to a grubby bedroom. This was before euros, and she asked for a fairly small amount of money in Dutch guilders, which worked out at about £5 I think. I thought "That's cheap". So we sat on the edge of the bed half-dressed and I started rubbing her breasts. Then she put on a big polythene glove, almost like she had a Tesco carrier bag on her hand and starting pumping my John Thomas. First of all, I thought she must be getting me ready before full sexual intercourse. But as you probably know it doesn't take long before young men reach the point of no return, so before you could say "Cruyff Turn," it was all over. She removed her Tesco-style glove, got dressed and showed me the door. No wonder it was only £5. I had arrived as a virgin and I left as a virgin.

Back to Spain. It was a bit daunting to see a road sign saying 1159 km to Cadiz, which was basically where I was going next. It was especially daunting battling in first gear against a strong headwind. I was on the road 8-12 hours every day, averaging about 90 miles. That's like the London to Southend Bike Ride twice, every day.

Spain is a wonderful country in nearly every respect but what I don't like is the bottles of piss, boiling in the sun, every few metres all along the main roads. Truck drivers pee in a plastic bottle then throw it out of the window. There are millions of them. It's gross.

Monday, 25th May was a day of highs and lows. I left Benicassim and the back wheel buckled. That's was a LOW. I went to *Decathlon* in Castello and their super-efficient mechanics made my bike as good as new. That was a HIGH. I pedalled on, but 20 miles outside Valencia I inadvertently got onto the *Autovia*, the motorway. Trucks and cars were hooting. I heaved my bike over the *Armco* onto a country lane and soon got lost in an orange grove. I thought "This is not the quickest way around the world." That was a LOW. Eventually made it into the centre of Valencia. The city seemed to be built around two rivers, neither of which had any water in them. Never mind, it was a beautiful place, so that was a HIGH. I tried to head out of town, but Spanish cities are a nightmare of motorway junctions unsuitable for bikes. Instead I ended up down a dusty suburban lane, then got lost in some rice paddy fields. That was a LOW. Eventually I made it south out of the suburbs to Sueca and asked the local alcoholic for directions to a hotel. He sent me to the charming Hotel Ciudad de Sueca. That was a HIGH. I went to a bar in town later, had a meal, even a few Foster's, and bumped into my alcoholic friend again and shared a few beers. Thereby ending the day on a double HIGH.

*

In Valencia I had passed the impressive Plaza de Toros - the bullring. That jogged my memory about when I cycled to Spain and went to see a bullfight in Madrid eleven years before. Like most English people I'm not that keen to see animals suffer, but that does not stop us eating chicken curry or bacon sandwiches. So I thought I would go and see what a bullfight was all about.

First consider that the bulls are raised in virtual cow luxury for four years, then get to fight a man dressed like a doll, wearing ballet slippers and trousers so tight the whole world can see his lunchbox. Also consider that the bulls can run faster than Usain Bolt, can turn on a sixpence and have lethally sharp horns.

Now perhaps you can appreciate the bravery of the matadors who go in to fight them. I really admire their courage. Within twenty minutes of the battle starting the bull is normally dead, and

34

on its way to the dinner table. But just occasionally the bull wins and kills the matador, although more usually only causes horrific internal injuries as he gores the Matador up the arse while he tries to run away.

The chicken in your curry and the pig in your bacon sandwich had absolutely zero chance of getting one over on the human race, but the bull in a bullfight just might. So don't criticise unless you are a vegetarian, and even then you should admire the bravery of the matadors. Ernest Hemingway said "There are only three sports – motor racing, mountaineering and bullfighting. All the rest are games." I don't really agree with him but I can understand where he's coming from.

Back to the present. It was election day, so the TV was full of the familiar guff. It appeared compulsory for Spanish politicians to wear blue jeans. I thought it was funny that one of the parties is called the Compromise Party. British political parties normally pretend to hold the high moral ground, either left or right. It's anathema to their self-image to suggest that they are a bunch of compromisers. Yet there in Spain was a party who relished the image of being middle-of-the-road. Politicians who are middle-of-the-road in Britain get, metaphorically, run over.

That afternoon, after a sweltering pedal uphill on a very long straight road, I decided to have a rest in the shade of a solitary tree at the top. I wasn't too sure if I was on the right road so I thought I would check with the next person who came along. In the distance appeared a dot. The dot got bigger, until I realised it was a man on a bike. After an age the man on the bike arrived, sweating profusely, at the top of the hill. Using my best Spanish, which features atrocious grammar, I said "Hola. Quiero voy a L'Olleria. Es correcto aqui?"

He replied, and I detected Spanish wasn't his first language.
I asked "Do you speak a little English?"
He said, "I speak a lot of English, because I am English!"
So I said, "Well, nice to meet you!" And we got chatting.

His name was Peter. He'd moved to Spain with his family fifteen years before, but his business had gone tits up. Now he was stuck there, couldn't sell his house, and didn't know what to do.

I said "Come with me!" But he felt he couldn't do that. To add to his woes, Peter had spent years learning Spanish, then moved to that area where they only speak *Valenciano*. What a bummer.

Among other things Peter mentioned that cycle helmets are compulsory in Spain, although I noticed he wasn't wearing one. The Guardia Civil only enforce the law when they are in the mood.

For over thirty years, cycle helmets had been my pet hate. They make you look like a dipstick. They look so naff I'm convinced they put kids off cycling for life. Admittedly, the original cycle helmets, as worn by the *Tour de France* boys, looked like you had a string of sausages on your head. In the event of a crash they probably gave you about as much protection as if you had … er … a string of sausages on your head.

Since then cycle helmets had improved in both style and protective ability, but I still didn't like them. What changed my mind was working as a nurse in Southend Hospital Accident & Emergency Department. Almost daily someone came in with a bike injury, and no matter if the cyclist had hurt their arm, leg, or any other part of their anatomy, the doctor's first question was always, "Were you wearing a helmet?"

If they were then you could pretty much rule out a serious head injury, which of course would be a big concern. Wearing a helmet also shows the cyclist has taken some measures towards road safety, and is not just a plonker on two wheels. So I had to eat my words and put my cycle helmet on, although privately, between you and me, sometimes now I quite like wearing it!

So there I was riding across the huge open spaces of southern Spain. The air was so clear and the light so bright. It was blistering hot but I could see snow on top of the Sierra Nevada mountains ahead. I went past the Hotel Malena which must be a shit place to stay (Sorry – that's a nurses' joke.) There were vast fields growing wheat, apricots, figs, nectarines and peaches. It was like being on the moon, but with fruit trees.

When you are there you really notice that Spain is the least populated country in Western Europe. Hollywood producers took a fancy to the area to shoot the Clint Eastwood spaghetti westerns, and Harrison Ford's *Indiana Jones* films were partly shot just down the road in Almeria.

I passed Huescar, where there are caves and a museum displaying the oldest evidence of humans in Europe. I would have loved to visit these places if I had had time, but I didn't regard myself as being on a sightseeing holiday, but on a cycling challenge. To be honest, I needed to increase my pace in order to meet Sharon in Gibraltar the next week.

Apart from small groups of stocky South Americans harvesting the fruit, there is hardly anyone for miles in Andalucia. In England, we have Poles and Indians doing the backbreaking jobs working in our fields. It's a mixed up world.

When planning the trip I budgeted for about £30 per day. So far I'd been spending £40-50 per day on food and accommodation, but I was hoping to cut that down to less than £30 a day in South America and Asia. The night before was good though - I stayed at a truckstop near Granada and had a massive three course meal including four beers, a lovely en suite room and double breakfast all for 42 euros (about £30).

*

I was on a fast dual carriageway (not an *Autovia*) when the Guardia Civil flagged me down and told me to get off, saying no bikes were allowed on that road. I was forced to spend the next four hours on dirt tracks bumping through fields and farmyards which would have tested any 4x4 jeep to the limit. I eventually reached civilisation in Guadix, found a gorgeous hotel for 33 euros, had a long soak in the bath then went for a wander around town. That region is often so hot it's not unusual to live in a cave. They have all mod cons. In fact, I saw a cave for sale. I think if I lived in a cave it would be fun to change my name to Flintstone and really relish the experience.

I'd seen lots of interesting creatures by the road, all dead, all run over. Rats, mice, cats, dogs, birds, rabbits, a pine martin, lizards, a deer, three wild boar, some snakes longer than my bike, and other furry animals I didn't recognise. The boars had those distinctive upward pointing incisors. There is a pub near us in Brentwood called The Boar's Head, which is a gift to lovers of spoonerisms and innuendo, such as me.

Cycling is popular in France, but it seemed even more so in Spain, perhaps because of the pleasant combination of good weather, good roads and good drivers. That is the Dream Team for a happy cycling life. I could count the number of joggers I'd seen on one hand, but there had been literally thousands of cyclists. Some were relaxed, cheerful individuals, others were head down, arse up teams pounding out some serious mileage.

Safety worries a lot of people about cycling. With the introduction of compulsory seat belts in the UK in 1983 the fatalities in cars went down, but cyclist fatalities went up. Maybe the motorists felt more secure wearing a seat belt, and so drove more recklessly, killing more cyclists. (My brother's plan to reduce crashes would be to remove all seatbelts and fit all cars with a hefty metal spike in the middle of the steering wheel.)

Apparently, cycling in Britain is increasing in popularity in direct relation to the decline in golf. This may have been encouraged by the fabulous medal-winning successes of British cyclists in the Beijing and London Olympics. Or it may be that golf, as Oscar Wilde is often reputed to have said, is "A good walk, wasted." Apologies to my brother-in-law Roy and other golf-lovers!

Back to Spain. Some days it felt as if all of Spain was uphill. It's a very mountainous place. While in the familiar process of

38

slogging up another steep hill in first gear I came across an oldish hippy coming down.

I said "Hola."

He replied, and from his accent it was clear he was English. His name was John. He reminded me of Bill Nighy in *Love Actually*. He swayed a bit and smelt of strong liquor because he was walking home from an all-night party something which they have a predilection for in Spain. His leg was all cut and bruised, from where he'd fallen into a storm drain. He blamed poor Spanish road design for that. Nothing to do with the drink then.

John told me he was a *pensionista*, living in Spain thanks to his British state pension and a private pension from his previous employer, Weetabix. Therefore, I think it might be more accurate to call him a *Weetabixista*. We discussed the economy and he said Spain is doing very well, which was the opposite of what British news reports said. I had to admit, that after travelling the length of the country, their standard of living seemed better than ours. I've seen more poverty just in Southend than in the whole of Spain.

John moved to Spain 14 years ago from Faversham, so I told him my sister was deputy mayor there and knew nearly everyone and probably knew him. He said he was going to start Spanish classes the next week. After 14 years that sounded like a classic case of *mañana!*

I pushed on and eventually reached the sparkling Mediterranean at Torres del Mar. I passed the Burger Kings, Irish bars, a man in a QPR shirt, and the pole-dancing clubs. Nice of those ladies from Warsaw to come all that way. There were several *playas nudistas*, which seemed quite popular, but couldn't be as popular as the Cap d'Agde nudist beach in France which gets 60,000 visitors every summer. That's a lot of willies.

In Benalmádena I checked into a hotel then found a bar just in time to see Arsenal thrash Aston Villa in the F.A. Cup Final. Then, a bit tipsy, I went next door to an Indian restaurant for a proper British meal of chicken curry and pilau rice. You think I'm joking?

Chicken curry is the most popular meal in the UK. Chicken tikka masala was even invented in Glasgow in 1960. What was funny though was that there was a large English-Indian family on the table next to me, and they all ordered pizza!

I'd been here before. We actually came to Benalmádena in 1997 after my Mum died. My Dad asked to come with us. Kevin and Laura were about 7 and 5 years old.

I like travelling light, but my Dad had it down to a fine art. For that week in Spain he just took a medium-sized shoulder bag. Not only that but every day, for seven days, he would take out a new toy for the kids, maybe a pack of cards, a book, a small jigsaw puzzle. It was a proper Mary Poppins bag. He was a very good grandfather. There was a bottle of Spanish sherry in the bag too, which he occasionally had a swig of, strictly for the purposes of appreciating local culture, you understand.

One evening we went for a walk along the promenade. Dad and Kevin were walking along ahead, chatting. They walked past some warning signs and straight across some wet concrete. Some workmen started shouting using rather colourful language and making several highly expressive continental hand signals. My Dad, either oblivious or trying to style it out, smiled and happily waved back to the friendly locals.

I slogged it down to La Línea, which is on the border near Gibraltar. The cycling and the hills I didn't mind in Spain. What was really annoying was pedalling along and having the road turn into *Autovia* (motorway) without warning. Mapmakers put in errors on purpose to combat plagiarism, but in this case the roads were upgrading too fast for the cartographers to keep up, and there were no easy alternative routes for me on my little bike. Consequently, the last leg in Spain from Benalmádena to La Línea took about four hours longer than expected because of the dirt tracks, dead ends and wild detours that put me in a bad mood. Take ten deep breaths Besly and say *Adios* to *Espana. Hasta la vista*, baby!

6 – Gibraltar

I don't care how you get here
Just get here if you can

'Get Here'
Anita Baker

It was such a relief to arrive in Gibraltar, rest and meet Sharon. We booked a luxury hotel – The O'Callaghan Eliott. So what? You only live once. The crew of a British nuclear submarine in port were staying there as well. Perhaps they were given rooms in the basement to make them feel at home. The submariners seemed like a cheerful bunch of lads. Apparently the captain of each of Britain's four nuclear subs are given a hand-written note from the incumbent prime minister with instructions on what to do in the event of a surprise nuclear attack against the UK. The options include:

1: "Retaliate"
2: "Put yourself under the command of the US government, if it still exists"
3: "Use your own judgement"
4: "Go to Australia" (Jim Callaghan's instruction was "Retaliate" apparently)

I met Sharon at Gibraltar International Airport. It seems kind of funny that they call it the International Airport, because Gibraltar is too small to have any domestic flights. The nearest you could get to a domestic flight is if you crashed a plane into the Gibraltar mountain, as the Polish Prime Minister, General Sikorski, did in mysterious circumstances.

Sharon said a man on her flight couldn't get his suitcase to fit into the EasyJet sizing frame at Gatwick. So, in the middle of the departure lounge he started jumping up and down on it, breaking bits off such as the handle and the wheels. Eventually he smashed it small enough to squeeze into the frame. However, when he got aboard it was still too big for the overhead locker, so the crew insisted it had to go in the hold, and they still charged him £32 extra.

Sharon thought my tan was hilarious. I had been in the hot sun continuously for three weeks, always wearing the same shorts and T-shirt, so my tan looked like I was wearing dark brown stockings and long brown gloves. My feet and body were as pale as a pint of milk.

I'd been to Gibraltar half a dozen times. First time, when I was about 18, I was skint of course, so each night I just slept on the beach at Catalan Bay. One of the Gibraltarians offered me a job as a house painter. How my life would be different if I'd accepted and stayed. At that time the Spanish had the land border closed, so you had to get the ferry to Tangiers to get in and out of Gibraltar.

It is cosmopolitan, sunny and friendly in Gibraltar. The locals speak a mixture of English and Spanish called *Yanito* or *Spanglish*. For a couple of hours every day, because Gibraltar is tax-free, the main street is jammed with tourist shoppers from cruise liners.

John Lennon and Yoko Ono got married there, as did Sean Connery, twice. In 1988 the SAS shot dead three Irish people on the street who they suspected were in the IRA. Part of the Bond movie *The Living Daylights* was filmed there. Nelson's navy fought the Battle of Trafalgar in the next bay, and some of the sailors who died in the battle are buried in a little cemetery on Gibraltar.

The Gibraltar peninsular is the centre of European internet gambling and various other hooky financial activities. The local hero is Kaiane Aldorino who won Miss World 2009. To top it all, there are the semi-wild monkeys, which try to nick your sandwiches and climb onto your head and shoulders if you stand still. Apart from these details, Gibraltar is more British than Britain in many ways – there are still the classic red phone boxes, *Marks and Sparks*, coppers with a tit on their head, that kind of thing.

A few Spanish people get quite worked up that Gibraltar is British. On the mainland I have seen graffiti saying '*Gibraltar Español!*' although plenty of Spaniards have no qualms about coming over the border for the cheap cigarettes, booze and petrol. There is a whiff of hypocrisy about the subject because Spain has two similar enclaves, Ceuta and Melilla, on the African Coast. Pot, kettle!

Sharon and I had a lovely few days in Gibraltar eating, drinking and catching up, particularly in the romance department. Sharon's suggestion to help keep me cool while cycling was to shave all over, if you know what I mean. It sounded a bit pervy to me but apparently lots of blokes do it. Really? I'm not too sure how Sharon knew this information, but she's right on most things so I just trusted her with this idea. Anyway, I'll try anything once. (Well almost anything – I don't think I would like sex with a kangaroo, or Victoria Beckham.) Afterwards, I don't know why, but all I could think about was a couple of snooker balls, and a bald rabbit frozen in the headlights. A one-eyed rabbit.

On our first evening in Gibraltar we went to a bar where they had a band playing. The joint was jumping. The frontman and harmonica player was a man called Paul, who owned a glass blowing factory. It was a terrific night and Paul got everyone a-whooping and a-hollering along to everything from the Rolling Stones to the Wurzels. But at eleven o'clock the police arrived and shut the place down, saying it was too noisy.

The following lunchtime, while we were in our favourite pub, The Gibraltar Arms, we bumped into one of the lads from the band. He said, gloomily, that the police stopped all their gigs.

I said, "Wow! That's street cred! I bet loads of bands in England would love to be able to say that. It would really boost their bad boy image." Maybe only the Sex Pistols came close.

On the second evening Sharon and I went to a karaoke bar in Casemates Square. That was fun and we joined the locals for some dancing. Also strutting their stuff and throwing some shapes in the bar was a man dressed as a pirate and a man dressed as a banana. The pirate informed us that "To *err* is human, but to *arr* is Pirate." That was a great night out, although I don't believe my twerking deserved quite the level of derision it received.

On our third evening there was a blues/rock jam night at the Lord Nelson pub. By this time, the Gibraltarians were treating us like family. I took along my harmonica so I could dazzle them with my talents, but the musicians were all Premier League and I'm only Division Two, so I kept my harmonica in my pocket and enjoyed their greater skills. True to form, the police arrived at eleven o'clock and closed the place down.

In preparation for what lay ahead I managed to get my bike serviced. Tomas, a Polish mechanic, trued the wheels and fitted a new chain set. He worked happily in what must have been the world's smallest workshop. He could hardly turn around. I'm sure he would need to step outside just to scratch his bollocks. Amazingly, he even had an assistant in there. As they were getting on with their repair bicycle work it looked like they were playing Twister. They would communicate, and pass spanners and oily rags to each other, under their armpits, behind their heads, and between their legs. Somehow they did a fine job on my bike though, so, *Dziekuje* Tomas!

The Nazis devised a plan to conquer Gibraltar during WW2 called Operation Felix. If they had gone ahead they might have won the war in North Africa and Malta, prevented the Allies from landing in Italy and changed the course of the rest of the war. The British knew an invasion was imminent. Most Gibraltarian civilians were evacuated to Northern Ireland, Madeira and Jamaica. British army engineers and miners built the best defences they could, though in reality a few thousand German assault troops could have conquered little Gibraltar by lunchtime.

We know Churchill expected Gibraltar to be conquered, maybe after a fight, or maybe the Germans would just have taken it, as they did Jersey and Guernsey. We know this because just a few years ago, someone climbing through one of the more inaccessible areas near the top of Gibraltar noticed several slits in the rock hidden by thick undergrowth. An investigation discovered that the British had excavated some secret rooms during WW2, long since forgotten. If Gib was occupied by Germans the rooms were to have been home to six men, who would have been walled in, remaining silent and hidden for years. Their job would have been to observe German troop and ship movements, and to report to London by radio.

Back to 2015. Gibraltar were recently accepted to play in the European Football Championships. Who did they draw? Germany, the world champions. However, the Victoria Stadium in Gibraltar only seats a couple of thousand people. If the German team are like the England football squad they would need to have brought hairdressers, beard specialists, diving coaches, coke dealers, WAGS and some poor sod like Neil Baldwin to clean their boots. That lot alone would fill the Victoria Stadium. Consequently, Gibraltar decided to play Germany at Faro in Portugal. It would have been even more interesting if Gibraltar drew Spain.

(Incidentally Gibraltar lost that game 7-0. I watched it on TV in Rio on the 15th of June. The Gibraltar boys didn't do too badly considering that Germany had beaten the mighty Brazil 7-1 only the year before. During the game the German manager, Joachim Löw, was filing his nails, the tart.)

My time in Gibraltar was coming to an end. It had been such a pleasure seeing Sharon. She was planning to meet me next in Sydney, but that was a lot of miles away. It was sad to say goodbye, but that's life.

I would hate to live the life of an ex-pat watching soaps and moaning about immigration, but if I had to live anywhere in the world outside of Britain, I think I would choose Gibraltar.

7 – Spain (Again)

Searching for adventure
With whatever comes your way

'Born to be Wild'
Steppenwolf

There I went, off into Spain again, heading for Ronda. I pedalled up and up, then more up, some down, more up, up, down, up. Eight bleeding hours of that. I was drenched in sweat, exhausted and demoralised. I cycled over a col higher than Snowdon (3560 ft), but I'm sure I climbed double that because the road was so up, up, up, down, up, down. I thought if the next van stops and offers to put my bike in the back and take me to the top of the next frigging hill, I'm going to accept. Unfortunately for my legs and bad mood no vans stopped. Fortunately for my pride and sense of achievement no vans stopped. The selfish bastards.

Knackered, I arrived. Ronda is a pretty groovy place, with its ancient, spectacular bridge across the gorge. You might have been there on a day trip if you've had a holiday on the Costa del Sol.

By this time I was sort of cultivating the Lee Marvin wild man look, ie week-old white stubble on a dark tanned face. That was doubly appropriate because most of the time I was 'Hank Marvin' ie starving.

Next stop would be Seville, where I'd arranged to meet my friend Marcos, a nurse from Southend. Thanks to all the climbing the day before the road from Ronda to Seville was mostly downhill so the cycling went pretty well. I was cycling fast down one hill, at about 35 mph (the fastest ever cyclist was Francois Gissy, who reached 163 mph) and before I could swerve I rode straight over a medium-sized lizard that was crossing the road. Splat. Sorry, man. Lo siento, hombre.

Some women say that men can't multi-task, but lizards are worse – they can't even breath and walk at the same time. Incidentally, that nonsense about men not being able to multi-task is a slanderous defamation. Any more talk on that subject and you'll be hearing from my lawyers in the morning. After I've finished what I'm doing. One thing at a time, naturally.

The countryside there in the south-west of Spain reminded me of Wiltshire. Huge rolling hills of wheat fields, although the temperature was 40 centigrade. I texted my friend Shaun, who lives in Trowbridge, Wiltshire and told him the similarities. It was Shaun, a keen cyclist, who had given my motivation a boost when I had doubts before I left home by saying cycling RTW was a "bold and brilliant" plan.

I've mentioned before the excellent conditions for cycling in Spain, with the one drawback that normal roads have a tendency to suddenly become *Autovias* (motorway) without warning. Well, surprise, surprise, twenty miles out from Seville the road I was on became *Autovia*. I had chosen my routes on the map very carefully to avoid them. Without meaning to lower the impeccably high tone of this book, I was fucking pissed-off. I had several hours of detours, service roads, dirt tracks, dead ends and asking people in my pidgin Spanish how to get to Seville twenty miles ahead of me. Eventually I asked a cyclist, who kindly led the way all through the suburbs and across the university to get me into the city centre. His name was Miguel. He worked in a bar. He was cycling during siesta time to keep fit, while his colleagues slept. Gracias amigo.

At last, I met Marcos in Seville, and he showed me around the city. It's a really lively, bustling place with fascinating historical buildings, including the Alcazar, where some of *Game of Thrones* was filmed. He took some pictures for Facebook. I still don't know what that is. I showed Marcos some of my photos, including Sharon in her Jamaican bikini in Gibraltar.

48

"She is very beautiful" said Marcos.

"Yes" said I, with a wink.

Next day, taking the little roads of course, I headed west towards Portugal. I was in what must be one of the most thinly populated and wildest parts of Western Europe. I pedalled for hours without seeing any people or buildings. The landscape reminded me of the prairies you see in old American cowboy films.

At the river Guadiana it is possible to go from Spain to Portugal by zip wire. This is the only International border in the world that can be crossed by zip wire. However, I would be taking the more conventional method of road tomorrow. So, thanks but no thanks!

8 – Portugal

My bags are packed
I'm ready to go...
Don't know when I'll be back again

'Leaving on a Jet Plane'
John Denver

A beautiful sunny morning, and over the border into Portugal I went. Straight away I noticed that the roads were in quite bad condition. More worrying was the bad driving. In truth, some of the drivers were total knobheads. It was like being back in England, where cycling can be a stiff test of character.

I was pleased that in France and Spain I had fairly quickly added to my knowledge of the languages and could converse quite well. But my knowledge of Portuguese could be written on a postcard. A small postcard. The stamp, in fact. This presented a bit of a concern because not only did I have to cope in Portugal, but I was flying to Portuguese-speaking Brazil the following Saturday and I would be there for several weeks. In the days of the British Empire the colonists would say "If they don't understand English, speak louder!" That sort of attitude these days would probably result in a punch in the mouth.

I was keen to cycle quickly across Portugal because Laura and Kevin had booked a city break to meet me in Lisbon before I jetted off to South America. I'd really missed them, and being a parent you worry about your kids even if they are 23 and 25. Like many fathers, I have a photo in my wallet of my kids where my money used to be.

While pedalling across Portugal I did something which I hadn't done since I'd left home – I overtook another cyclist! Admittedly he was about 100 years old, on an old shopping bike, laden down with vegetables. Normally racing cyclists flash past me. In fact, when I'm in first gear slogging up a hill pedestrians can flash past me. Anyway, I thought I would put on a little burst of speed as I overtook my first cyclist, so I could really savour the moment. I shouted a big "Ola!" as I went by. I think he was daydreaming, maybe thinking about his great-grandchildren, or the fig harvest, or something because as I called out he was so startled he wobbled and nearly fell off. "Christ" I thought, "I hope I don't have to do CPR." as he ate my dust.

Later, I was happily pedalling along through the pretty Portuguese countryside when an eagle swooped and flew along in front of me, only about ten metres ahead. Eagles, like owls, are predators so have forward facing eyes to hunt better, so I don't think that the eagle realised I was following it. Ducks, pigeons, etc. have eyes on the sides of their heads giving almost 360-degrees vision as protection to avoid predators (and cyclists).

*

On my first night in Portugal I stayed at a lovely hotel in Grândola. The receptionist told me a little about what happened in April,1974. Portugal had been ruled by the dictator Salazar since the 1920s. Salazar and his friends were extremely wealthy, whereas most of the people were desperately poor. There were no elections or democracy, of course. Anybody who voiced a protest was hunted down by the secret police (the PIDE). A few people managed to obtain radios and tried clandestinely to listen to the BBC. If your neighbours grassed you up you would be thrown into prison, tortured, or worse. Only rich people were given permission to leave the country. There had been bloody wars of independence going on in the Portuguese colonies of Angola and Mozambique since 1961. By 1974 Portuguese soldiers had had enough of the killing and started to disobey orders. It all came to a head on the

25th of April. There was massive social upheaval, symbolised by people putting flowers down the barrels of the soldiers' rifles. It became known as the Carnation Revolution.

Portugal has since developed into a modern, cosmopolitan, liberal democracy. It's a really nice country, apart from the shit drivers.

The next day was to be my last day cycling in Europe for at least six months. Lisbon beckoned, then Rio.

On the approaches to Lisbon I passed a gypsy family on a horse and cart. They were the first Travelers I'd seen since Essex. I wished them a cheery "Bom dia!" but got no reply. I wondered afterwards if maybe they didn't understand my beautifully pronounced Portuguese. Then I thought, maybe they only speak Romany. Or Irish, for all I knew.

*

I had to catch the little ferry across to Setúbal to get to Lisbon. A group of cyclists on a training run were waiting for it like me. They were diving off the pier, into the Atlantic, still in their Lycra cycling clothes, to keep cool. One of the older lads told me he had cycled 2000 km to Rome the year before on behalf of a cancer charity. He said he met and "shook hands with the Pope," which in London's East End has a different meaning!

Lisbon, at last. Noisy and bustling. Thousands of tourists. A lot of graffiti. Alcoholics sitting in doorways. People begging. Posh shops. Expensive cars. Three different people tried to sell me drugs within an hour. Broken, dirty pavements. Beautiful parks. The rough and ready nature of Lisbon reminded me of London. But I've always loved London, so I liked Lisbon too.

There was a huge, colourful patriotic demonstration through the city centre which was a very happy-clappy affair. The organisers described it as a March for Jesus. Most of the demonstrations I've been on usually ended up with everyone throwing bricks at the police, turning over cars, and doing a spot of looting. Each to their own I suppose.

Kevin and Laura joined me for a few days in Lisbon. I was so glad they had come to see me. It's a risky business this RTW cycling lark, so, I was extremely aware that maybe it would be the last time I'd see them. I had become so conscious of this fact that I determinedly posted home copies of my diary every week in case my family wanted to retrace my final days in the event of my death.

We had a lovely few days walking around, eating in restaurants, drinking in bars, visiting the Castelo de São Jorge, doing silly photo poses and mucking about as is our wont.

*

So, my last day on the continent of Europe. Several people said before I left England "How are you going to cross the sea?" implying that I would be cheating unless I somehow cycled or swam across the Atlantic and Pacific. When I explained, to one person in particular, that I had to catch a plane across the oceans he said "So basically you're flying around the world!" He thought this was hilariously witty. I was thinking "Well, eff you. If you tried cycling 14,000 miles across five continents, it's reasonable to say you've cycled around the world." Nobody says to a RTW sailor "How are you going to sail your boat over the Pyrenees, the Australian Outback, or the Argentinian Pampas?" But those were doable on my humble little bike. Well, I thought so. Well, I hoped so. I also comforted myself regarding taking my bike on a plane with the fact that Orville and Wilbur Wright were, first and foremost, bicycle engineers, so would undoubtedly have approved.

There were tears from Laura at the airport that Saturday. Kevin and me didn't cry because we're proper blokes. I took off the front wheel, handlebars, pedals and saddle, packed everything into a bike bag and whoosh, up into the sky and over the Atlantic I went, joining the other 500,000 people who, according to *QI*, are airborne at any one moment.

9 – Brazil

A baby wailing, a stray dog howling
The screech of brakes and lamplight blinking

'That's Entertainment'
The Jam

Rio proved to be quite a shock. I had really wanted to visit because somehow a world trip wouldn't have seemed complete otherwise. Rio has an exotic, sexy and fun image. The beach is Budgy Smuggler Central. Some of the ladies were jogging in bikinis. Clearly there were lots of 'Brazilians' there, and I'm not talking about the people. Barry Manilow said that "Music and passion were always in fashion at the Copa, Copacabana." What Bazza failed to mention were the injustices, the crazy people shouting at lamp posts, and the desperate struggle of thousands of poor sods trying to get a few crumbs to eat.

Rio de Janeiro translates to January River. It was named that accidentally – the city is not based on a river, but around a bay. The whole metropolis now has about 15 million residents. The stars on the beautiful flag of Brazil represent the sky over Rio on the night of independence, the 15th of November 1889.

Rio was hot and humid, with lots of beggars and there was graffiti on nearly every wall, some of it praising Jesus. I saw a man sleeping on a bed made of empty beer cans. That could have comedy potential, but it's not funny.

I joined a bus tour to see Rio's sights. When we stopped the tour guide told us not to wander too far from the bus in case we were robbed. Rio's iconic landmark, the statue of Christ the Redeemer, is huge and spectacular, although Karl Pilkington memorably described it as being a dead ringer for Jimmy Hill. It is the second tallest statue of Jesus in the world. (They're got a bigger one in Poland, so there). One of his fingers fell off in 2010. That could have comedy potential.

Apart from along the beach front almost no-one cycled in Rio, which worried me a bit. It might have been because the traffic was very fast, and the local people drive very aggressively. However, in the hostel where I was staying I met a Brazilian called Marcel who loved cycling. We had a long talk and he advised me to avoid certain areas because cyclists got attacked by junkies and crackheads, not especially to steal your wallet, but to steal your bike. He knew of about ten incidents like that in the past year, in three of which the cyclist had been stabbed. How I was supposed to know where these dodgy areas were Marcel couldn't explain.

Actually before I left England I had seen YouTube footage of bike-jacking in Brazil. There were clips of cyclists being held up with guns and other interesting weapons. I figured that the situation couldn't be that bad. Things are often exaggerated for TV. But if truth be told, now that I was there I was a tad nervous. Muggers, thieves, aggressive drivers, insects, poor roads, a difficult climate – and I hardly spoke any Portuguese. This leg of the trip was going to be a challenge alright!

*

I definitely felt vulnerable as one of the few people on a bike, and certainly the only one I'd seen with touring panniers. I stood out. I tried to reassure myself by thinking of Eisenhower's words "We have nothing to fear, but fear itself. And spiders." I wasn't bothered by spiders, but on a practical level I did carry a large heavy Maglite torch like security guards use as a nightstick. It could be a damn handy weapon for self-defence. I hoped I didn't have to use it.

In Dervla Murphy's 1965 epic and inspirational *Ireland To India With A Bicycle* for self-defence she didn't pussyfoot around with something as tame as a heavy-duty torch. She took a proper gun!

Not only that, she had to use it three times – once against wolves, once against a frisky policeman, and once against robbers.

Marcel said cycling out in the countryside should be less of a problem than in the city. He said you could see all sorts of unusual things from a bike. For example, he had seen a homeless man eating a roadkill dog, right there on the street.

It had been raining heavily for two days in Rio, but it was still very warm. The hostel I was staying in had broken showers, broken toilets, mosquitoes, snorers, no proper security, and no air con, so I'd decided to treat myself to a small hotel while I braced myself for the cycling. A sign on the reception desk said 'This hotel is opposed to sexual tourism'. That was another clue to Rio's sadness. I was leaving at 6 the next morning. It was shit or bust time.

Next day, cycling around the world for a laugh? I wasn't laughing now. Leaving Rio had been a nightmare. Cycle paths that lead straight into the ocean. Terrible roads. Terrible drivers. At one stage I had to carry my bike up stairs through a *favella*. A bus hit my panniers once, although it didn't knock me off, and I had countless near misses. I had to go through several tunnels, as there was no alternative route, and they were terrifying – narrow, poorly lit, fast aggressive drivers, very noisy, broken road surfaces, fumes. I genuinely thought this might be my last day on earth.

In the afternoon I pulled into a petrol station for a cold drink and they had two armed guards, with fingers on the triggers, looking extremely jumpy. Eventually I got about 70 miles out of Rio. I stopped in a small town called Mangaratiba and asked an old man for directions. The man said follow him which I did, and he waved to and greeted everyone he saw. He had to pop into a shop for ten seconds to see his friend and was adamant that I watch his bike for him. I thought "Jesus Christ, this man, who clearly knows everyone here, can't even trust any of them for ten seconds?" Brazilians with money live in gated compounds. Some banks are surrounded with rolls of barbed wire. Stealing stuff and a lack of trust seem normal in Brazil. I would hate to live there.

Compare that to rural Britain, where people leave vegetables, fruit or eggs by their front gate, and an honesty box to pay for them. It's easy to criticise Britain, and I'm guilty of that, but it's really not a bad place.

In Brazil the weather varied between hot and humid, so I was always soaked, or torrential rain, so I was always soaked. Me and my clothes smelled like a wet dog. It was impossible to camp there, mainly because so much of the country was thick mountainous jungle or swamp, but also because absolutely everything was dripping wet.

With camping out of the question I had to find a place to stay each night for a shower and a dry bed. I found a few little hotels, and a few *pousadas* (guest houses) that were cheap and cheerful. There were quite a few 'love hotels' in the suburbs too, although I'm not sure how much actual sleeping went on in those.

I had a plan C, now that plan B (camping) was not an option. If I couldn't get a room anywhere I would just shelter under a tree, or a bus stop, or in a petrol station and wait until morning, then carry on pedalling.

To be frank, I'd not found the Brazilians very friendly. Men didn't look me in the eye. I tried to say "Ola!" or "Bom dia!" but often got blanked. The only cheerful big "OLA!" I'd had in reply was from a Chinese man. Occasionally someone might give me a thumbs up, which I thought was a positive sign, unless they had the Australian usage of the gesture, which means "Up your bum," or so I've been told.

I passed a heron or crane type of bird on a fence about a yard away, and it had a large live lizard in its beak. The lizard looked pretty glum, which was not surprising, considering that it would soon be viewing the heron's stomach, from the inside. I wished I had taken a photo, but the heron would probably have flown off by the time I had gotten my camera out.

I'd succumbed to taking selfies, like everyone else. Didn't Cameron have one with Obama at Mandela's funeral? There is something weird about taking them. You see people puckering up and smiling at their phone. It's all a bit odd. I'm drawing the line at a selfie stick.

*

Towards the end of June I realised the days were merging into one long torment. Rain, rain and more rain. I had completely underestimated how cold and wet Brazil could be. Sometimes I didn't even mind the trucks roaring past and splashing me with water, because I couldn't get any wetter, and for a few seconds I got blasted with some warm air (and fumes) from their exhaust.

One day in particular the weather was really testing my willpower. I felt at the end of my tether. I had to find a hotel or *pousada* soon to get some shelter. Then, like Brad and Janet in *The Rocky Horror Show*, I saw a place set back off the main road. I rang the bell, and an extremely camp young man showed me to a lovely room. I was very grateful for his warm *pousada*.

The village was called Ubatuba, and a road sign said we were right on the Tropic of Capricorn. I tried to dry out all my stuff, but they didn't have heaters, so I knew I would have to put wet clothes on again the next day, as I had that morning.

The cycling, the wet, the heat, the cold and the long hours in the saddle had made my balls red raw. But you don't need to know that. Forget I said it.

The only hot food I could find that evening in Ubatuba was pizza, which I'm not too keen on. Pizza is the fast food with the most profit margin, because there's sod all there of any nutritional value. Commercial pizzas have that shine because they are sprayed with a kind of WD40. I used to work for Pizza Hut in Dagenham, delivering that shit on a moped. Obviously we got as much free pizza as we could eat, and within weeks my face and neck were covered in pus-filled zits. When the Blair government introduced the minimum wage in 1999 (Blair should try living on it) Pizza Hut actually reduced their wages to match the minimum wage. Do you want an insider tip? Never get the Meat Feast.

Pressing on the next day I realised that, away from the popular beach areas like Copacabana and Ipanema, I had only seen a couple of cyclists and a couple of joggers in the last 300 miles. Anyway, I found a quiet spot and was doing what bears do in woods, when surprise surprise, a jogger ran past. As I blushed I was too embarrassed to even say "Ola" to her.

I used the Indian method, because if I carried toilet paper it would only get soaked. So I employed a handful of grass and a bottle of water to wash my arse with my left hand. It's probably cleaner than using paper anyway. I once read about an Indian classical singer who was recognised as world class, but she could never relax and sing well in Europe. A journalist asked her why that was, and she said she couldn't get over the idea that most of the people in the audience had not washed their bottoms properly and only smeared some of the shit off with toilet paper. Actually, I discovered that when I poo in the woods I find it quite interesting, and strangely satisfying, to turn around afterwards and see what I've produced. (What's brown and lies under the piano? Beethoven's Last Movement.)

As I trundled along I'd pretty much hated Brazil since I got there, but I was slowly starting to get used to it. I'd not been murdered yet, and there were some nice places outside the big cities. In fact, the town I was in that day was quite lovely – It was called São Sebastião. I had a delicious meal of fish and chips, and then went to a bar where I watched Santos play Corinthians. The standard of football was really impressive. It's no wonder that Brazil has won the World Cup five times. The players are very religious though. When Santos scored the whole team got on their knees and prayed. At the start of the game, even the referee did wallet, watch, spectacles, testicles.

The whole of Brazil is a really religious place. Fuck knows why. The previous Pope was in the Hitler Youth. Catholicism has a worldwide reputation for priests rogering choirboys and the Vatican systematically trying to cover it up. In every town rich churches are surrounded by people who live in poverty. (Turn water into wine? Walk on water? Come on, get real, only Paul Daniels can do stuff like that.)

The following morning I passed some areas that were jaw-droppingly beautiful. Lush green jungle going down to long deserted white beaches. Wild pink and purple flowers, butterflies, gentle surf, perfect blue sky and a warm breeze. The only downside was I had my first dog chase – the vicious bastard tore down the road after me trying to eat my legs. I tried to kick him in the teeth as I was pedalling like mad with the other leg, but he kept dodging.

With ninty or so miles under my belt that day it was getting late so I started to look for somewhere to stay. I was in the rough end of Guarujá when I spotted Hotel Tulipas. It wasn't quite a normal hotel but I didn't think it was a *love hotel* either. I had to get somewhere to sleep so decided to check in. It was £25 per night, although I noticed you could hire a room by the hour. The corridors had numerous sculptures of ladies not wearing much. Gradually the penny dropped – I was staying in a brothel. The room was nice and clean, although the mattress was plastic with a sheet on it. The TV had all the usual channels, plus several *adulto* channels, but if you've seen one porno, you've seen them all, I think.

Refreshed and wiser I was back on the road at dawn as always, and after another series of close shaves I came to the conclusion that Brazilian drivers are not overloaded in the brains department. Some must fantasize that they are Ayrton Senna. They gave less consideration to cyclists than to the stray dogs which wandered across the highway. Frequently cars, buses or lorries swerved right in front of me, then sometimes stopped abruptly forcing me to brake hard.

The most futile waste of paint in Brazil was the sign written on the back of buses '*Mantenha Distância*'. Most Brazilians loved tailgating, the classic indication of poor driving. I'd seen three big smash-ups in a week – trucks upside down, ten tons of apples or tomatoes strewn across the road, people being carried into ambulances. In the world of motoring I don't actually believe that there is any such thing as an accident, only poor driving – too fast, too close, too reckless, too tired or too pissed.

*

Out in the countryside, the first time I saw a bunch of unshaven lads, dressed in rags, wearing knackered wellies, swinging two-foot-long machetes and coming towards me, it was a bit unnerving. I did a quick mental check for the Maglite. I was carrying about two thousand pounds on me in various currencies. Those lads were clearly desperately poor, and maybe had nothing to lose. Later, after I'd seen quite a few of them, I came to realise that the lads had probably just finished a hard day's work in the fields. They provided the food for Brazil. They fed us and I should have thanked them, providing they didn't take the easier and more attractive Option B, chopping me up and stealing my money!

I came through Santos one morning. It was a pretty place with a lovely beach, better than Copacabana. Pelé played for Santos for 19 years. After feeling like the only cyclist in Brazil for the past few weeks there are thousands in this city.

It had been a tough couple of days with long hours cycling in the rain and cold. I stayed in a hotel in Miracatu which was only £11 but I've been in cosier prison cells. I got bitten by things in the mattress, and got free hair with the breakfast. The cockroaches, I noticed, seemed to enjoy the breakfast too. I shouldn't complain though seeing as it was only £11.

That afternoon I had my first crash. I've mentioned before the uselessness of Brazilian drivers, but the truck drivers were the worst. I had noticed dozens of times that they swerved extra close to me on the hard shoulder, then once past, they returned to their normal lane. Even on deserted roads they would roar up right next to my left shoulder, even when I was as far over to the right as possible. Just for good measure some of them would blast their horn as they passed in an effort to intimidate me. The air would turn blue as I shouted some old-fashioned Anglo-Saxon language at them.

Anyway, on this particular occasion I was slogging up a steep hill in first gear, on the hard shoulder, which had a steep camber and a gravel surface. A truck roared up and it was so big, so fast and so close that the gust of air it created swept me off balance. It all happened so quickly I didn't have time to get my feet out of the toe grips, so I went down hard onto my left hip, elbow and hand. I got a few grazes and bruises but I was lucky the next truck didn't go over my head. My wrist was very swollen and painful. No, it wasn't writer's cramp. And no, it wasn't wanker's cramp either.

By the end of June I was near Joinville, which was settled by lots of German people and so had all sorts of Germanic things - shops, businesses, hotels, street names, etc. I had a double dog chase, but I pedalled too fast for the horrible bastards to bite me.

In hindsight I think the hard part of the trip was the poor drivers, dealing with motorways, missing meals, the uncertainty of getting somewhere to sleep, endless days of smelly wet clothes, dogs, mechanical problems, language barriers and missing home. Cycling 14,000 miles was the easy bit.

A few times I found an all-you-can-eat buffet, usually for about £5. However, I think the owners sometimes regretted my visit once they realised how much I can eat after cycling 100 miles in the cold and rain! The next day I would fart like a buffalo, which added some jet-propulsion to my speed!

*

Brazilian motorways (*autopistas*) are literally the only way from A to B for much of the country. There are no alternative minor roads.

Therefore, pedestrians, cyclists and everything else were all tolerated along the hard shoulder. At toll booths there was even a lane for cyclists. With the trucks roaring past just a few feet (or inches) away I could see all of human life there on the hard shoulder – children walking to school, farmers selling fruit and veg, cowboys on horses, men selling drugs and women selling their bodies. All this was fine and dandy until the motorway narrowed for a viaduct, tunnel or steep hill. Then the hard shoulder would run out, forcing everyone to squeeze onto the main carriageway. The trucks hammered along nose to tail, almost like a train, and wouldn't give way at all. They wouldn't slow down or give a little extra room, quite the opposite, they seemed to try to hit, or at least intimidate me off the road. I've done a solo parachute jump, been shot at (in Israel), and faced monsters on the Judo mat, but this was way more scary.

On one viaduct, where the barriers were just over knee height, I was nearly blown over the side by trucks doing at least 60 mph right next to me. The drop would have been about 100 feet. Another viaduct was so narrow, fast, uphill and long I thought the only way to stay alive was to go onto the *outside* of the barriers, so I carried my heavy, fully-laden bike with one hand, while clinging on with the other, and edged my way across trying not to look down at the rocks and river a long way below.

At other times I figured it was safer to try use the hard shoulder on the opposite carriage way, because it's better to be cycling the wrong way up a hard shoulder than going on the correct side where there's no hard shoulder. So then I had to somehow wait for a gap, sprint across the motorway, heave the loaded bike over the central reservation crash barrier then sprint again to the other side. One slip, or failure to heave the bike over the crash barriers at first attempt and I would have been killed.

As for the rest of Brazil, it was slowly growing on me. A few people had been friendly, not many, but a few. I'd never felt seriously threatened by any gun-toting, knife-wielding, drug-addled desperadoes, although when I was having a burger in one cafe the owner warned me to look out for "mucho vagabonds" in that area.

One sunny day I passed a full size replica of New York's Statue of Liberty. About ten miles later a full sized dinosaur, and about another ten miles later an aeroplane turned into a snack bar. I rode along with a Brazilian cyclist and we chatted in Spanish. He asked me if I liked Brazil. "Yes" I lied, so as not to hurt his feelings. We both agreed that the truck drivers showed no respect.

Further on, out in the countryside near Osorio, I rode next to half-a-dozen proud cowboys trotting along on their traditionally-liveried horses, and we greeted each other and smiled as I took a few rolling photos. Presumably they were on their way to work. They would look strange in Southend, but I was in their world now, so I suppose I was the strange one. My mum loved horses, despite having a busted nose from being kicked in the face by one, and used to say wryly that horses are "dangerous at both ends and unsafe in the middle."

Travelling down the coast of Brazil I'd mostly been on a road called BR-101. I could have taken a parallel road called BR-116. Then I would have gone through a town called Residência Fuck. I thought the F-word was known across the world, but perhaps not. (Someone later told me there have been documentaries on TV just about the BR-116, known as the Highway of Hell, because of all the kidnappings, robberies, child prostitution, and murders. So it was just as well that I'd taken the 101!)

I was in the south of Brazil now. It was wide open cattle country which I really liked. It was a bit like parts of Spain, with a reasonable standard of living and a few more cyclists around. Happy days.

*

I was doing well for time, so instead of my normal lunch of a litre of chocolate milk and a packet of crisps, I thought I'd treat myself to lunch at a roadside restaurant. There were no menus, and I didn't know how to ask for a meal properly, so I just said "Carne, por favour." After ten minutes the waitress brought two large plates of meat, a plate of spaghetti, a plate of rice, a plate of chips, a plate of beans and a large bowl of salad. I finished it all, of course, and it was only £7.

Back on the road I became aware that my athlete's foot had flared up again. This wasn't surprising really, seeing as I had worn the same trainers every day, wet and dry, since buying them in Lidl in France. Mind you, if you are going to have a recurring medical condition I think athlete's foot sounds preferable to, say, penile warts or an anal fistula.

So now my morning routine was sun cream on my ears (if it wasn't raining), petroleum jelly on my sore bollocks, and anti-fungal cream between my toes. Plus, an aspirin to prevent chest pain. Then I'd jump on the bike and away I'd go.

Pootling down through Brazil I reached Porto Alegre. I found a restaurant, had a big meal, and of course was still hungry. I spotted the word banana on the menu and pointed to that. After about fifteen minutes the waiter came back with what looked like a small pizza. In fact, I think it *was* a pizza base with a creamy, custardy, cheesy topping and sliced bananas and cinnamon powder sprinkled on top, which was then baked and served piping hot. It was delicious and the tastiest thing I'd had in weeks. The Brazilian food had not been bad, but it was very plain. They didn't like spices. I could have murdered for some Chinese or Indian.

Despite the difficulties I'd encountered cycling progress had been quite good as I was coming to the southern-most point in Brazil. I had mixed feelings about the country, which was an improvement to previously just hating it. Admittedly I'd just had a worm's eye view, or view from the gutter to be precise. David Attenborough would come to Brazil and find the wonderful flora

66

and fauna. Michael Palin went to Brazil and searched out all sorts of interesting people and places. My abiding memory was of almost being killed daily by cretinous truck drivers. They should send more stuff by rail anyway.

So goodbye Brazil. I didn't get killed, although the truck drivers tried. Martha Gelhorn said the only aspect of our travels that is interesting to others is disaster. Sorry to disappoint. I'm glad I went to Brazil, and I didn't have to use my Maglite torch except to see in the dark, but I never want to go back.

10 – Uruguay

From the dark end of the street
To the bright side of the road

'Bright Side of the Road'
Van Morrison

Over a crazy bridge, got the nod from a bloke with a big gun, and there I was in Uruguay. The first little town was called Rio Branco, and it looked like somebody has been through it that morning hitting everything with a hammer. Every vehicle and building seemed to be dented, cracked or smashed. If you looked closely there were patches of road between the potholes. It must have been the law to have a mangy dog asleep on the doorstep of every shop. Having said that, most people were well dressed, and chatted away happily as they tiptoed around the detritus. Rio Branco was a duty-free zone so you'd think it'd be posh. Not so. Litter was everywhere. The town should have changed its name to something more appropriate, like Landfill or Shithole.

On the subject of litter, I remember that when I lived in the London Borough of Hammersmith and Fulham in 1978 the council decided to get rid of all the rubbish bins. The reason? – "Bins attract litter."

I'd really been looking forward to Uruguay, partly because it was an achievement to have cycled across Brazil, but also because they speak Spanish there, which I was much more confident in. In England I had read that Punta del Este, a small town on the coast near Montevideo, was the St. Tropez of South America, and that Uruguay was in general very European. I'm not too sure which part of Europe they were referring to, but Rio Branco is like the arse end of Canning Town before it got yuppiefied.

On the road next day I had terrible wind. Perhaps that needs a little explanation. I was cycling against a terrible headwind. Head down, low gears, relentlessly exposed and battered about, I even had to pedal hard to go downhill! The road was as straight as an arrow for 85 miles, making it very hard work on the bike. On the map there were towns marked on the way but in my humble opinion a crossroads with a bus shelter on an open windswept prairie does not really qualify as a conurbation.

For 85 miles I saw virtually no-one, apart from the odd car. To pass the time I sometimes sang, or abused rain clouds in a selection of languages, or saw how loud I could burp, or how far I could spit, or played car bingo, or examined my bogies, or made V-signs at the circling vultures, or watched the eagles trying to catch those guinea-pig type animals, or did anything else I could think of to distract my attention away from my painful arse and sore balls.

Anyway, to pass the time that particular day as I was going by a field of cows (steers and heifers, to get technical - this was beef country) I started shouting at them. I mean really shouting. I'm surprised you didn't hear me in England. Just at that moment two proper cyclists on racing bikes, wearing Lycra, came cruising up quietly behind me then rode alongside and we started chatting. They must have thought I was a right nutcase. Maybe I am. Their names were Juan and Eric, and they were really nice lads, and quite impressed that I'd just cycled there from Rio de Janeiro, unless they thought I'd just escaped from a secure psychiatric unit.

The other thing I did to pass the time was continually calculate distances in km and miles and work out how long it would take to get to the next landmark / crossroads / town. I've always liked maths. Did you know there are three types of mathematician? Those who can count, and those who can't.

Eventually I arrived at an actual town called Trienta y Tres, and after asking directions a man and his family kindly led me zig-zag about two miles to a lovely hotel. After a tough day I rewarded myself with a massive steak in the restaurant.

69

I'd found more nice people, who had been friendly and helpful, there in Uruguay in my first 24 hours than I had in Brazil in 3 weeks. Rio Branco was a bit rough and ready, being a frontier town, but overall I really liked Uruguay so far.

Until very recently the President of Uruguay had been José Mujica, a man who talked the talk and walked the walk. In his youth he had been a lefty guerrilla. As president he lived modestly and gave away 90% of his salary to worthy causes. He accepted prisoners from Guantanamo to give them a new life, describing America's incarceration of these men, some for up to twelve years without trial or charges, as an "atrocious kidnapping." Which, of course, it was.

Anybody who has ever done a pub quiz knows that Uruguay hosted and won the first World Cup in 1930. India sent a team who were familiar with playing barefoot. That was not unreasonable, seeing as football was the poor man's game, and many people then and now play barefoot (especially in Brazil). When the Indian team found out all the other national teams were wearing boots they figured that was an unfair advantage, and refused to play.

This area of Uruguay was like you see in Wild West films. Big wide prairies with a few cattle grazing, and occasionally a little homestead with wood smoke drifting out of the chimney. Sometimes I saw gauchos (cowboys) riding across the land, often with a couple of Border Collies trotting along behind. I always waved and shout "Hola!" and they always waved back and gave a cheery greeting. Sometimes, in the middle of nowhere, there was a massive industrial factory or warehouse belching smoke, which somewhat spoiled the old-time Wild West image.

*

I had a problem one day with my debit card, which gave me a bit of a panic, because I couldn't get any local money from the cashpoint. (Did you know the whirring sound in an ATM is added

70

to give you confidence that your money is being counted?) Laura solved the problem, texting instructions to help her technologically-incompetent Dad. I am frequently baffled by the modern world and I often rely on her for back-up. I didn't get my first mobile phone until I was 50, or my own email address until I was 54. In my head I call her *Team Laura*. (On the other hand, if you want some shelves putting up, a motorbike fixing or your garden to bloom, then I'm your man!)

If you've cycled a bit in Europe, and fancy something a bit more exotic, then you might find Uruguay would be ideal for a two-week biking holiday. The standard of living is the best in South America. Most of the roads are good. The countryside and the coast are very pretty. You could visit the town of Fray Bentos to sample their famous meat pies! Uruguay is one of the most liberal countries in the world regarding personal, sexual and religious freedoms. Marijuana is legal. The Uruguayan people are friendly, the hotels are cheap, the steaks are fantastic and the beer is cold. Have I sold it to you yet?

The men in Uruguay often wear a large beret, like the old boys in Spain, and they look proud and damn cool – not at all like Frank Spencer. The men also often wear riding boots, which is not surprising really, considering that the horse is still a commonly used form of transport to cross the prairies. Tradition seems to sit comfortably with modernity in Uruguay. I've seen people texting while riding horses.

One morning I woke up and it was bitterly cold. I never expected that in Uruguay. There was thick frost on the grass and after ten minutes cycling there was thick frost on me too. I was wearing all my clothes, like in Andorra, with my socks on my hands again. My fingers were really painful from the cold, but on the bright side, that meant my blistered arse didn't seem so bad. Riding past the fields I thought I shouldn't complain because the cows had got iced grass for breakfast!

It must be so disappointing to be a young calf. In the morning you say "What's for breakfast Mum? Ooh yummy, grass, my favourite!" Then at midday "What's for lunch? Grass! But we had that for breakfast!" By evening "What's for supper Mum? It's not bleeding grass again is it?"

On a deserted road that morning I came across a small van. The front and cab had been completely stoved in. I couldn't imagine the driver survived in there. A policeman was sort of standing guard. Thirty yards along the road was a large dead horse in a ditch, covered in fresh blood. Que sera sera.

The sun came out, the sky was blue, and after a pleasant day's riding I arrived in Minas, a cute little town. It was Sunday afternoon and about 500 men, women and children were in the main square for a 5 km race. Half the people were running, half were cheering and everyone was happy. Loud feel-good music was pumping out for a Zumba warm up and the atmosphere was buzzing with excitement. I'm a big fan of mass sporting events. They combine the best things about being alive – exercise, fresh air, common purpose and friendship. In his London Olympics opening ceremony speech Seb Coe said "There is a truth in Sport." I don't really know what that means, but it brings a lump to my throat each time I hear him say it.

I was nearly at the capital, Montevideo. The harbour was the scene of the only action in South America during WW2. The Royal Navy fooled Captain Langsdorff of the Nazi battleship *Graf Spee* that they were going to attack and sink his ship. So what did the captain of the *Graf Spee* do? Sank his own ship! Hitler was furious. Oh, bless, never mind. Apart from the deadly submarine fleet, the German Navy, the Kriegsmarine, was, fortunately, really a waste of space. They sunk a load of their own ships at Scapa Flow in WW1, and in WW2 they had the biggest warship in Europe, the *Tirpitz*, but they didn't let it venture out of a Norwegian fjord because it was too valuable to lose. The RAF sunk it anyway, in its fjord, in 1944.

72

It was another beautiful sunny day, and downhill all the way, as I rode into Montevideo. It's a really big, bustling city very like Madrid. I jumped on the ferry to cross the River Plate, and off to Argentina. Everyone on the ferry was given blue plastic disposable overshoes, I think as a preventative measure against Dengue Fever, or maybe smelly feet.

11 – Argentina

if you ever plan to motor West
Take my way … the highway that's the best

'Route 66'
The Rolling Stones

My nephew Jon and his father-in-law Daniel met me at the ferry port in Buenos Aires. I was so happy meeting them and unwinding after the stress of Brazil. It was nearly midnight so we put the bike in the boot of the car and drove to their home in the suburbs.

We are a close family and Jon and his brothers would often stay with us for weekends when they were small, visits which regularly tied in with a trip to Loftus Road to watch QPR. I remember telling them not to brush their teeth – only brush the gaps between their teeth.

Argentina is a massive country, the eighth biggest in the world. It is longer than from London to the North Pole. The population is 42 million, 13 million of whom live in Buenos Aires, and fifty percent have some Italian connection. Argentina also has the 8th biggest Jewish population in the world. A lot of German people went to live in the Barioloche area. (When the Nazi war criminal Josef Mengele fled to Argentina after WW2 he went through customs with several suitcases full of human body parts). About 25,000 Welsh speaking people live in Chubut. Their Patagonian-Welsh dialect is maintained by a Welsh school, Welsh TV channel and Welsh cultural activities sponsored by the Welsh Assembly in Cardiff.

I'd been to Buenos Aires before. Seventeen of us had gone there for Jon and Meli's wedding the previous year. First we had an absolute belter of a New Year Party. We had hot weather, huge

74

steaks on an all-night barbeque, long arm drinking (drinking bottles of beer without bending your elbow - messy, but a great laugh!), music, dancing, and afterwards everyone ended up in the pool fully clothed. Awesome.

Two days after our Buenos Aires' New Year we played the much-anticipated England vs. Argentina football match. We had been training hard for it (sorry, I'm lying, we had only been talking about training hard for it!) and were determined to win, as were they. We all had the red 1966 England kit on and Melisa's brother Mauro led the Argentinian team out in their famous blue and white stripes. It was a tough game, but naturally we let them win 11-7. We finished with a penalty shoot-out, just for the craic, and they bloody won that as well. Then it was off to the pub for another barbecue, more liquid refreshment and some animated discussions about 'The Hand of God'. The winner's trophy now proudly sits on Daniels' mantelpiece, in between the Boca Juniors memorabilia.

Then came Jon and Melissa's wedding, way out in the countryside on an *estancia* (ranch). There was beautiful scenery, horses, music, drink, crazy dancing and wild antics. The barbecue was about twenty feet long, and meat was cooked all night. It was an epic night. We got indoors about 8am.

However, Buenos Aires does have some rough areas, maybe worse than Rio de Janeiro. Melisa's Mum, Nancy, had been held up at gunpoint. Mauro had been held up at gunpoint twice. When Jon and the family were on their way home in the car one evening they were ambushed. A brick came smashing through a side window (Jon thought a bomb had gone off) but instead of stopping Daniel had the good sense to step on the gas and escape. When we came for the wedding my brother-in-law Andy was mugged and injured on the first day, and when Sharon and I went on the sightseeing tour of Buenos Aires a gang of kids attacked the bus with bottles. Coming from Essex we felt right at home.

The rough side of Argentina is counterbalanced by their fantastic dancing. The Argentinian Tango has got to be the sexiest dance ever. Sex on legs. It originated in the brothels and slums of Buenos Aires in the 1890's. Similarly, the split skirt and sexy heels were inspired by prostitutes.

Back to 2015 and it was Melisa's birthday, July 6th, and her family made me feel at home straight away and we had a lovely few days in Buenos Aires. Nancy offered to wash my clothes, but I said I would do it because, to be honest, after wearing my pants for two months I didn't want anyone else to see the state of them! We had big steaks, of course, went to some lovely restaurants and pubs and visited some nice places. Jon downloaded WhatsApp onto my phone, which was a revelation and began slowly dragging me out of the dark ages. I could even connect to the internet and look for somewhere to stay in the next town. Gradually I was joining the twenty-first century.

It was great using the Wi-Fi. Spanish speakers pronounce it "whiffy" which sounds funny to English ears. WhatsApp was a good start but I'd no desire yet to get on the Book of Faces.

After a lovely time in Buenos Aires, and a couple of days' rest, I said goodbye and started pedalling west. Quite a few towns I passed had English-sounding names – Wheelwright, Benjamin Gould, Reynolds, Hereford, Drysdale and even a Beasley. Council rubbish collections do not seem a top priority in Argentina. In fact, people just drive to the edge of town and dump all their stinking garbage by the road. It's disgusting, and a rat magnet.

The roads are mostly narrow, fast, straight and flat. From where I was starting out to Mendoza, my destination on the other side of Argentina, was one straight road for 800 miles, and hardly a hill. The majority of drivers were quite considerate, sometimes giving a friendly Toot! Toot! like Thomas the Tank Engine, although there were always a few jerks who tried to intimidate cyclists, usually in BMW's for some reason. I'm not sure if BMW stands for Bayerische Motoren Werke or Being a Monumental Wanker.

*

Sometimes the roads had a hard shoulder, but far from being a safe zone for cyclists, they were just a free-for-all. Cars, motorbikes, lorries, tractors and packs of stray dogs went in every direction, sometimes straight at me.

I don't recall seeing a single church across Argentina, but every few miles there was often a large flamboyant red shrine to Gaucho Gil. He was a Robin Hood-type character in Argentinian folklore who is treated like a Catholic saint. Other shrines seemed to be honouring the Virgin Mary. Lots of stuff is left there – flags, candles, wine bottles (empty), and food. One even had a copy of *Playboy*, god knows why.

Anyway, back to the cycling. I was about halfway across Argentina in a small town called La Carlotta, in a cheap and cheerful hotel which cost less than £10 per night including breakfast. The bathroom was very small, not much bigger than a phone box, and there wasn't a shower curtain. In fact, you could multitask and have a shower while sitting on the toilet having a tom tit.

I was getting used to dog chases. I spotted the buggers earlier and pedalled faster. There were thousands of strays in South America, especially in Argentina. I considered getting a water pistol, but when the bastards are in the process of chasing me, hoping to have my ankles for lunch, I'd actually prefer a 12-bore shotgun. Also, imagine the reaction I would have got, using sign language and my broken Spanish, going into an Argentinian shop and asking to buy a gun! I like dogs, as do most English people. (Someone I know, who, as she is putting the lead on her Border Terrier to go out for a walk, cheerfully says she is going dogging! I'm never too sure how to respond to that). But I'll be honest with you, when I saw a dog run over in the road, which was every day, in various states of mangledness, I gave a little cheer. I hope they were chasing another poor cyclist when they got splattered by a juggernaut.

I'd started to build up a roadkill photo collection, to keep myself amused and pass the time. I didn't take pictures of dead dogs, because there were too many of them, but there were hundreds of other dead exotic animals and birds which I didn't know the name of. Am I sick in the head? Don't answer that.

14th July 2015 was Bastille Day and my sister Juliet's birthday. I slogged my usual 80-90 miles. I'd only had two days off the bike in over a month and I was so tired. Three more days to Mendoza. Then I could rest. Worse than the tiredness was my sore arse. It was blistered and bruised and agony all day, every day. Worse, there were big problems at home, so I had to decide in the next few days whether I should fly back to Blighty.

One evening I had chest pain for the first time that year. I took four aspirin, a bunch of painkillers and had two puffs of GTN spray, and that cocktail cured it. It also cured, for a few hours, the nagging toothache that I'd had for weeks.

Thinking of health issues, I'm reminded that Ernesto 'Che' Guevara was an Argentinian doctor, although he is always associated with Cuba. Like me, he also made a tour of South America on two wheels, but he had an engine. The film about it, *The Motorcycle Diaries* is a bit boring, unlike Che Guevara, who had a thrilling life until the Bolivian police finished him off, the bastards.

On the subject of politics, I discussed The Falklands/Las Malvinas with a few people. All the Argentinians I met believed they should own the islands because although they are over 400 miles from Argentina, they are over 8000 miles from Britain. One man, Carlos, an engineer based in the UK, said it's the colonial-style arrogance of the British which upsets them.

Nobody lived on the Falklands until Europeans arrived there. Initially, the British, French and Spanish resorted to handbags at dawn over them, and much later the Argentinians claimed the islands. The German Navy failed in their attempt to occupy the Falklands in WW1. Consequently, though they're a very difficult place to live – cold, wet, windy and isolated, which suits only the most hardy people, and penguins – they've been a British colony for nearly 200 years. I'm not quite sure why the Argentinians get so excited about the matter – I bet most of them would hate to live there. It's not like they need the room - they have loads of unused space on the mainland.

On the approaches to many towns there was often a big sign saying 'Las Malvinas Son Argentinas' (The Falklands are Argentinian). This slogan was also on buses, police cars, bank notes and lots of other places. In fact, since 2014 it is not just jingoism that the slogan is on all public transport, but a legal requirement! There was a Malvinas museum, a large memorial/exhibition at Buenos Aires airport, and patriotic programmes on the subject on TV. National maps simply marked Las Malvinas as Argentinian, with Port Stanley as Puerto Argentino, and made no mention that the Brits were there at all. One man I spoke to, who was nine during the Falklands War, said all the schoolkids had to write letters and send chocolate to the soldiers at the time (which he said they never received).

All this Argentinian sabre-rattling seemed like pissing in the wind. They could never win possession of the islands through the democratic process. The last vote was to stay British, by 1513 to 3. The military attempt to wrestle the Falklands from Britain in 1982 ended in humiliating surrender. Admittedly half their army was waiting in Patagonia because they thought Chile was going to exploit the situation and invade Tierra Del Fuego. That rumour was no doubt encouraged, or perhaps even started, by the British, because as any journalist knows "The first casualty of war is truth."

So will the Argentinian army try to occupy the Falklands again? Unlikely, because the British military is very experienced at fighting abroad. Of the 200-plus countries in the world there are only 22 that Britain hasn't at some time invaded. The British military also have all the Big Guns. "Take the toys from the boys" my mum used to say, being a peace campaigner, and also an ex-Royal Navy radio operator.

The war resulted in 649 Argentinian dead (323 just from when *HMS Conqueror* sank *The Belgrano*), 255 British dead, and three Falkland Island women were killed by British shelling. Any death is a tragedy, but you must admit it was a small affair compared to, say, the London Blitz, where 40,000 died.

The capitulation and embarrassment of the Argentinian army caused the collapse of the military dictatorship, which led to the modern democracy Argentina now is. You would normally wait a long time before you hear me say anything complimentary about Margaret Thatcher, but I must say two good things now. Firstly, she helped invent Mr Whippy ice cream, which is delicious, especially with a chocolate flake in it. Secondly, she was instrumental in getting rid of the Argentinian dictator Galtieri. Of course, Thatcher had no qualms about being friends with plenty of other murderous dictators such as Pinochet, Pol Pot, Saddam Hussein and other charmers. She even supported Apartheid in South Africa, for God's sake. But getting rid of Galtieri was definitely a good thing.

Under Galtieri, during Argentina's Dirty War, 1976-83, the police and military initially arrested, tortured and killed political opponents. Then they abducted and killed trade unionists and student activists. Eventually, completely out of control, they just grabbed pretty girls, and knowing human nature, pretty boys, off the street. They bundled them into cars, raped them and killed them. The bodies were thrown out of aeroplanes over the Atlantic. Some of the worst torture imaginable took place at the innocuous sounding Navy Mechanics Institute in Buenos Aires.

Argentina does have a long history of brutal politics. In 1955 their own Air Force bombed a political demonstration in the main square in Buenos Aires, La Plaza de Mayo, killing 308 civilians.

So looking at things like that, you might think that the Argentinian people would be grateful to Britain concerning the

80

Falklands War, because it helped to get rid of their military dictatorship. Not a bit of it. Argentinians are extremely patriotic, and they express this partly through their national football team and partly through the rallying-cry of 'Las Malvinas Son Argentinas'. The people I spoke to are not stupid, far from it, and they realise the government uses 'Las Malvinas' and the jingoism associated with it to divert attention away from their own economic mismanagement and corruption. But I don't think the national psyche will be changing any time soon. (Alternative answer to pub quiz question: "What do the Argentinians call The Falklands?" Answer: "la nuestra" – "ours!")

You sometimes hear that, for example, more Falklands veterans have committed suicide since the war than were killed in action. The same is said of Vietnam, Iraq, Afghanistan and some other wars. It's true that 255 British troops died in the Falklands, and more than that have committed suicide since. But overall there were nearly 30,000 troops involved, so a suicide level of about 250 in that number of people over a period of 30 years is normal. In fact, more people die on British construction sites every year than from being a soldier – but there is not much Help For those unsung Heroes.

Besly, get back on with the story! By this time I was in San Luis, progressing steadily across Argentina. It looked like Spain. There were even proper cycle lanes. I found a nice little hotel on Avenida Heroes de Malvinas (they just won't let it rest!) But best of all San Luis had a Chinese restaurant! Wahey! I was waiting until eight o'clock when it opened then I was going to eat myself stupid. I thought they might need to fly in extra food from China!

Next day I had bad wind again. Yes, you know, a strong headwind, which made the whole day hard work. The only interesting thing that happened was when I nearly ran over a large pink dildo (see photo). Why it was in the road we'll never know. I texted my brother and he thought maybe it was being used as a speed hump. Afterwards I thought it could make an attention-grabbing first line in a detective novel. For example, "Only one person alive knew why a large pink dildo was lying on that road in Argentina, and Miss Marple was determined to find out who that person was..."

*

At long last I'd arrived in Mendoza, having cycled right across Argentina. My original plan had been to cycle the hundred miles or so from there over the Andes to Santiago, but it was winter now and the road was closed because of snow. Privately, between you and me, I was glad it was closed, not because of the 10,000 feet climb, nor because of the cold, but because at the top is a 3.2 km long tunnel. If you google images of the Tunel del Cristo Redentor you will see a narrow black hole disappearing into the rock with trucks roaring in and out. To pedal into that would be cycle suicide. Cyclicide you could say. I wonder if cyclicide should be in the OUD?

So I decided the next day I was going to hop on a short flight over the Andes from Mendoza to Santiago. That is the exact same route as the plane carrying the Uruguayan rugby team took in 1972 when they crashed in the mountains due to pilot error. 29 people died and 16 survived. After they'd eaten everything possible including the leather seats they ate the dead bodies. It was made into a gripping film called *Alive*. (Where does a South American General keep his armies? On the end of his Andes.)

In Spanish they call the Andes, *La Cordillera,* which translates as the rope or cord, because it's the longest mountain range in the world. In the Andes is the peak of Chimborazo, which is only 20,564 feet above sea level, but due to the bulge of the equator it is the furthest point on the earth's surface away from the centre of the earth. Also consider Mauna Kea in Hawaii, which rises from the ocean floor 33,465 feet, although only 13,796 feet of it is above sea level. Then remember that Everest is 29,029 feet. So what is

82

the tallest mountain in the World? There is a choice of three. You decide. They would make a world-class Three Peaks Challenge.

Anyway, regarding Argentina, I believe it has tremendous tourism potential, including winter sun and summer skiing. There are spectacular mountains and lovely beaches. At one of the coastal nature reserves you can see elephant seals, penguins, sea lions and whales. Experiencing the gaucho lifestyle on a ranch would be a great holiday. The population density is only about 15 people per square kilometre. Compare that to England – 395; Monaco – 19,000; Macau – 21,000, and Australia – 3. Restaurants and hotels are quite cheap in Argentina. The hotels invariably have a buffet breakfast and seeing as I almost ate my own weight each morning, I virtually got the hotel room for free!

I was leaving Argentina with pretty good feelings about it. Nancy's cousin, Adriana, had texted me every single day since I left Buenos Aires to make sure I was alright, which was sweet. All the Argentinians I'd spoken to had been friendly, even when I said I'm English, although that sometimes raised a few eyebrows. I suspect it would have been a red rag to a bull to fly a Union Jack from my bike though. I'd come across more hostility directed at Chileans and Bolivians, but that was just familiar, lazy, prejudice in the style of the *Daily Mail*. So I said "goodbye, *adios, ciao, hasta Iluego* and Don't Cry for Me Argentina."

12 – Chile

The panorama around Santiago, the capital city of Chile, was like a cross between Switzerland and the USA. In the distance were huge, spectacular snowy mountains – the Andes. Half an hour from town is, apparently, the best skiing in South America. I wouldn't know, I've never tried skiing.

The standard of living was good. It seemed very safe to walk about. The climate was Californian. The flag could have been mistaken for that of Texas. The money was plastic, like Australian money. The streets were crowded but swept so clean you could almost eat your dinner off them.

The historical heroes of Chilean independence were McKenna and O'Higgins, both of Irish descent. Like the rest of South America there were some stray dogs running about, but the dogs were so civilised they even waited for the green man before crossing the road.

For a few days I didn't know what the police looked like because I never saw any. Later I saw some female *carabineros*. They wore funny hats, but there was nothing funny about the guns they were packing.

The towering glass skyscrapers of the financial district were like New York, so the locals call it Sanhatten. Chile had the world's biggest earthquake in 1960. Thousands died. It sent a tsunami over 80 feet tall across the Pacific, hitting Alaska, Japan, New Zealand

84

and devastating Hawaii. That Santiago now had so many skyscrapers seemed mad.

Sometimes it appeared that on every advertising hoarding in Santiago was a picture of Alexis Sánchez. Arsenal and Chile have the benefit of his footballing talents. Sanchez and Chile won the Copa America just a few weeks before I was there, which was a big, big deal for them. I saw Sánchez advertising razors and stroking his chin. I saw Sánchez advertising hair products and stroking his hair. I was expecting to see Sánchez advertising condoms and stroking his ... well, you get the idea.

Chile hosted the World Cup in 1962, and came third. The South American nations had threatened to boycott the competition unless one of their own got to host the tournament that year, because they felt Europe was getting all the fun. Now, now, children. Play nicely.

I went on the city sight-seeing bus tour. The English man next to me on the bus asked what job I did. I said "Nurse."

"Oh, you mean *male* nurse," he said.

The President of Chile is Michelle Bachelet (who incidentally has an honorary degree from the University of Essex, where I went for a year). She and her mother were tortured, and her father tortured to death, under the orders of General Pinochet following the military coup in 1973. The left-wing Salvador Allende had been democratically elected as President, then Pinochet and the CIA destabilised the country financially, and militarily took over. The photo of Allende, gun in hand, wearing a GI helmet, defending himself and democracy at the Moneda Palace, just before they both died, is awe inspiring and won the News Photograph of the Year Award in 1974. Google it. When Pinochet took power he rounded up an estimated 30,000 people, dragging many of them into the National Sports Stadium. He had them tortured, then shot. Jack Lemon, normally a comedy actor, made an Oscar-winning film about these events called *Missing*, about losing his son. Powerful Stuff.

In 1986 my then fiancée, Latha, and I were caught fly-posting anti-Pinochet posters in London. We got a £50 fine each and were bound over to keep the peace for a year. The smarmy clerk of the court asked us, though it was none of his business, "So don't you like General Pinochet then?" What a wanker.

My anarchist mates had a whip-round and paid our fines, but it was all a bit dicey for Latha at the time, because she was only in England on a nursing work permit. Actually, soon afterwards the plod sent one of their finest all the way from Scotland Yard to interview me in our 15th floor council flat in Dagenham. For two hours he asked loaded questions, which I evaded. I made tea and drank several cups in front him, but I wouldn't offer him one. His mouth must have been as dry as sandpaper. Eventually he cleared off, maybe to get a drink.

Pinochet came to London in 1999 for medical treatment and to see his "good friend" (her words) Margaret Thatcher. Can you imagine Hitler or Mussolini popping over to use our NHS? The Spanish government wanted Pinochet extradited from England to Spain and tried for genocide, in particular for murdering Spanish citizens. The Labour Home Secretary, Jack Straw, with Tony Blair's permission, dithered for a few months while Pinochet relaxed under house arrest in a luxury mansion in Surrey. Eventually the spineless Straw permitted Pinochet to return home to Chile, no doubt with the stern words "You naughty boy" ringing in his ears.

In 2014 some of Pinochet's favourite murderers were brought to court, some 41 years late. They were given the ludicrously lenient sentences of two years each. This produced the remarkable spectacle of the President of a country, Michelle Bachelet, plus her mother and other families of "the disappeared", waving placards in a protest outside the court in Santiago.

So there I was in Santiago and eating and eating. They've got democracy now and it's a vibrant, modern and friendly city. You can buy T-shirts with pictures of Allende on them, who remains a popular and well-respected hero.

Sixty miles down the road from Santiago was the Pacific. I could cycle that in a morning. For the sake of completion, coast to coast, I knew I should pedal down there, but my blistered bum was screaming "No! No!" Therefore, I decided not to go, on humanitarian grounds.

One evening I repaired to the bar (that's a funny phrase, normally after I've been to the bar I need a few repairs) to watch the football on TV. Footballers in England have restrictions on how much of their kit they can cover with sponsorship logos, but in Chile the players were head-to-foot walking billboards. The next stage must be signs on their shirts that light up. (In the USA, baseball games actually stop every ten minutes or so and the players just stand around while TV companies broadcasting the game show adverts to their viewers at home). The game on TV was Wanderers vs San Marcos. The standard of league football in Chile was wonderfully crap. QPR would massacre them. The purpose of every pass seemed to be to give the ball to the other team. The game finished 1-1. The celebrations when a goal was scored looked decidedly homoerotic. When San Marcos equalised things got so emotional I thought the players were going to pull down each other's shorts and start bumming each other in a daisy chain. Even more alarming was the commentator, who was so ecstatic I think he actually orgasmed.

Of course football is the true religion of South America. The football stadiums are packed with worshippers week in and week out. In the 19th Century Karl Marx said "Religion is the opiate of the people", but you're out of touch mate, now it's football.

Pondering these things, I supped my beer. You can order a small *cerveza chica* (trans: girls beer) or a *litra*, which is more my style. After several happy hours of watching football, and several *litras*, I left, frankly, pissed as a fart, with a touch of double vision. Back at the hotel, when I went to the toilet I thought I had two willies.

In 2010 Chile received daily worldwide media coverage when 33 miners were trapped 700 metres underground. A slab of rock the size of a 45-storey tower block had shifted down and trapped them. They had a little food, and drank radiator cooling fluids from the machinery. After a few weeks they were reduced to one biscuit every 3 days. Someone found a slice of peach, so they used a sharp knife to cut it into 33 slivers – the miners knew that the next stage of survival was cannibalism. 32 miners were Chilean, and one was Bolivian who, they joked, would be the first to be eaten.

It took 17 exploratory drills by the rescuers and a fortuitous stroke of luck to locate them, and a truly wonderful and heart-warming achievement to get them all out after ten weeks. Many have suffered psychological problems since, such as nightmares. A film about it, starring Antonio Banderas, called *Las 33*, was being made as I wrote this book.

*

I had a week in Chile before my flight to New Zealand, so I thought I'd spend a few days on the fabled Easter Island. It cost me over £500, but YOLO.

Within half an hour of landing I'd found a nice hotel, been given a garland of flowers, and met the local alcoholic. Next to the hotel there was a little wooden restaurant, which had no menu, but a sign on the door saying 'Chefs choice tonight'. I would have loved the adventure of eating there, but it was closed, so I presumed the chef's choice that night was not to bother. Instead, I went for an exploratory walk and rapidly fell in love with Easter Island.

It really seemed like paradise, until I got back to the hotel and read the Welcome Book, which had four pages of safety procedures to follow in case of Earthquake, Volcano, Tsunami or Landslide. *Ay Carumba!* The place was a death trap! I might as well have phoned all my family and friends and said goodbye!

Big stone heads are what Easter Island is famous for, and they are very dramatic and extraordinary. The islanders had no metal, so carved the heads using harder stones. Many mysteries remain about them. You can rent a bicycle to explore the island and I considered this for a millisecond, before realising that I'd prefer to stick needles in my eyes. My arse was just starting to heal. Instead I went on the minibus tour with three cheerful girls from Ireland, all teachers, who took one look at the place and decided it needed an Irish bar.

They being teachers, I told them about my father, who taught biology. To make the science more interesting, and as a bit of showmanship, Dad would drink dilute hydrochloric acid in front of the kids to demonstrate that the stomach works by acid. I don't think teachers do that kind of thing any more in classrooms.

The islanders put on a very entertaining Polynesian show in the evening. Pretty girls did an energetic dance wearing only grass skirts and two coconut half-shells on their boobies. I thought there was going to be a wardrobe malfunction any moment, but it wasn't to be. The lady tourists were entertained by island men with big muscles and small loincloths dancing a fierce *haka*, a traditional war dance.

Only a few thousand people live on Easter Island, so the next day I was very surprised to see the *carabineros* driving around in a riot van. If you discounted the children, pensioners, expectant mums and my alcoholic friend, that only left about four lads capable of holding a riot, and they were all wearing flip-flops instead of the *de rigeur* Doc Martens. Perhaps the *carabineros* were expecting West Ham's ICF to land on the next plane or, more likely, prison ship.

The locals were passionate about their traditional culture. A lot of their historical knowledge of art, astronomy, literature etc was lost when 90% of the islanders were abducted by Peruvian slave traders. Later Catholic missionaries tried to finish the job and eradicate any remaining aspects of the local culture. In response, the local people didn't like to call their home Easter Island or Isla de Pascua (the Spanish name), but Rapa Nui. They had their own language, flag, national football team and parliament, which was in a shed. The standard of living was good and there were no taxes. The islanders received subsidies from Chile, but no Chileans or anyone apart from the local people of Rapa Nui were allowed to own land there – which was perhaps a tad unfair on the Chileans.

Try to imagine the most idyllic place on earth. I bet Easter Island ticks all the boxes. Obviously there would be some disadvantages living there like ... erm... hang on, I'll think of something in a minute.

Ok, I've got one. Places like Easter Island attract Glastonbury-types who wear headbands and insist on playing the guitar even when Chuck Berry or Jimmy Cliff are on the radio. I think they went there to 'connect' with the local culture, but in reality they would have benefited more if my boot had connected with their arses. (Sometimes I can be an intolerant bastard!)

Easter Island is so calm and safe. There's no crime. It's so relaxed. Unfortunately for you it gave me the time to compose a poem.

It's got the palm trees
It's got the warm breeze
It gets some earthquakes
Not now for fucks sake!

You have the time
To chat and sit
Which is just as well
'cos the TV's shit.

I think the Poet Laureate's job is safe.

*

Being an Accident & Emergency nurse, I was keen to look around the hospital. I love working in A&E because, apart from the drama and tragedies, there are always slightly comical or strange cases of people with household gadgets lodged in a selection of orifices, men with skateboard wheels stuck on their cocks, pregnant nuns, people claiming to be constipated because they know the doctor must investigate by putting his finger up where the sun don't shine, and other toe-curling situations to make the workday interesting.

The hospital on Easter Island was new and spacious and spick and span. It appeared calm, but I suspect A&E nurses the world over need the same dress code – thick skin. Seeing some staff in theatre scrubs reminded me of the old surgeon's joke.

"Scalpel, Nurse!"
"Sister, Doctor!"
"Mister, Sister!"

Easter Island is the second most remote inhabited place in the world. (The British island of Tristan da Cunha in the Atlantic is the most remote). The Chilean Mainland is 2182 miles away. In fact, their nearest neighbours are 1289 miles away – the British Overseas Territory of Pitcairn Island, of HMS *Bounty* and child abuse infamy.

On my last evening on Easter Island I chose a beachside restaurant for supper as the sun went down. Fish curry, mmm... my favourite. The waiter warned me that it was spicy, but that's how I like it. Actually the fish curry was about as spicy as a Cornish Pasty, but was still very tasty. Being English, naturally I had a few beers with my meal, sitting there on my ownsome. By about my seventh Heineken I noticed the bar staff looking at me like I was some sort of freak (don't say a fucking word) instead of a normal English bloke. I imagined a few ideas were crossing their minds such as:

91

(a) he's a raving alcoholic.
(b) he's very thirsty
(c) he's a raving alcoholic

Obviously the answer is (b). Having sufficiently quenched my thirst, I paid the bill, left a fat tip, and staggered back to the hotel.

In the morning I returned to Santiago to wait for my flight to New Zealand on the following Monday. My arse seemed to have improved and I was keen to get cycling, but there were problems at home again, so I was torn as to whether to return. Dilemmas like that were proving to be the hard part about the trip.

On arrival in Santiago again I needed some 'comfort food' so went to Burger King. A transvestite with broad shoulders, slim hips and bright red lipstick served me. He or she seemed alright but some teenagers were laughing at him or her. As I mentioned before, we all just want to love and be loved. The only burger they seemed to have available was an 'Italian', which was about as Italian as Michael Caine. As usual, junk food was a disappointment.

After that I went out onto the main street, Avenida Liberatador Bernado O'Higgins, and was a little surprised at all the gays and straights snogging like there's no tomorrow. Forget Paris, Santiago is the City of Lurve.

Next day, I was up, up and away flying over the Pacific. It was named that when early sailors realised it was generally such a calm ocean. The flight cost £501 which works out at about 8p per mile. Prices on the London Underground are currently £4 minimum cash fare for one stop, which is usually about half a mile. Therefore, at London Underground rates crossing the Pacific would cost £80,000. Consequently £501 seemed very good value to me. (I told you I like maths!)

Halfway over the Pacific we crossed the International Date Line, which sounds like a phone service for ordering a Russian bride. There was a dispute originally about the IDL. To be situated on the corresponding prime meridian was considered quite a status symbol. Berlin, Paris, New York and Jerusalem all wanted the honour, but Greenwich, London got it probably because we were the biggest bullies. Between 10.00am and 11.59am GMT every day there are three different calendar days ticking along somewhere in the world. This presents all sorts of problems for religious people, as if they don't have enough problems, because the idea that the Sabbath is a day set in stone is nonsense. It is clearly flexible.

Crossing the IDL is as good a place as any to reflect on this whole round-the-world concept. No sensible, educated person has believed the earth is flat for thousands of years (although a Flat Earth Society still exists in London). You can tell the world is curved at the seaside. If you hold something straight, like a piece of wood, at eye level with the horizon you can see the sea dipping down at both ends. Also, ships sailing away from land dip downwards over the horizon. The ancient Greeks surmised that the earth is round and travels around the sun, although Copernicus, 1800 years later, is normally credited with proving it. Nevertheless, for hundreds of years the Catholic church severely punished people at the stake for saying just that. In fact, not until 1992 did the Catholic Church officially acknowledge that Galileo's views on the solar system were correct, 23 years after Neil and Buzz had walked on the moon!

The wonderful thing about crossing the IDL and the Pacific was that I felt like I was turning a corner. From that point on I was not going away from home but towards it. I had been really missing Sharon, Kevin Laura, Judo, QPR, The Plough and *The Jeremy Vine Show*. Perhaps I could have asked the pilot to fly faster, though actually I'd have been wasting my breath, because to save fuel commercial jet planes fly 10% slower now than in the 1960s. Dammit.

Photo Album #1

Rude French cycling lane

Long brown gloves and brown stockings

Hold on tight to your dreams…
and your sandwiches

The author and Jimmy Hill

Rain, pizza, and more rain

Miss Marple was determined to find out why the dildo was in that Argentinian road

The Falklands are Argentinian, apparently

Ay carumba!

No wucking furries Charles

Cute… but stinky

Shayne
Jacks
suggests
I buy the
next
round

We hugged and hugged...

13 – New Zealand

To get from Santiago to New Zealand the easiest way was to go via Sydney. On the plane was a whole bunch of Wallabies, which is to say the Australian rugby team, on their way back from thrashing Argentina. They all sported the same uniform: dark blazer, white shirt, beige trousers, broken nose, cauliflower ear. At the Sydney arrivals terminal film crews and crowds awaited. As I came through I thought they all must have come to see Yours Truly, the great world traveller, so I quickly prepared a humble speech. For some reason nobody gave a shit about me, only about the rugby boys.

To be truthful, I was absolutely delighted to have got so far. I felt I'd done the hard part of the trip (though also realised I was probably deluding myself) and that from now on it was going to be all downhill home. When no-one was looking I did a little jump for joy and a "*Whoop, Whoop!*"

Transferring from Sydney to Auckland, the Qantas lady asked where I was going. I told her. She calmly said "Okay, only New Zealand." I smiled and thought "*Only* New Zealand?" To an English person, who lives 12,000 miles away, those three words would never be in the same sentence.

My cousin Charles was waiting at Auckland airport. I'd not seen him for 17 years, but he looked just the same, not even any grey hair, the bastard. With family, no matter how long the gap since last seeing each other, you straight away slip into the comfort and

100

reassurance of their company as if you'd last met the previous week.

That evening Charles' wife Barbara cooked a delicious beef stroganoff. I polished off three bowlfuls and we talked about the old times when Charles lived in England. As a kid I would stay at Charles' house for a week every Christmas, and we had summer holidays together. I think it's fair to say that, as a team, Charles and I caused a tidal wave of mayhem in their otherwise quiet corner of Twickenham. We would swing from trees, throw snowballs at traffic, break anything we could, put fireworks through people's letterboxes, knock on doors and run away. We even sank a small boat on the Thames. In short, we had a blast.

Charles emigrated to New Zealand aged 20, and by all accounts continued his wild ways. In his typically frank Kiwi way he described those years as "Young, dumb and full of cum." I suppose I was no angel either. Mum used to tell my sisters to "Go and find out what Adrian is doing and tell him to stop it."

I'd never been there before, but the people were so welcoming that straight away New Zealand felt like home. It was such a pleasure to speak English again. Just going into a shop and being able to communicate fully sent a little shiver of joy down my spine, and made me smile. I was reminded of an episode of *The Simpsons*, when, during a flashback to his schooldays, Homer was late for English class. "It doesn't matter" he said, "I'll probably never go there."

A glance at the map of New Zealand and you could be forgiven for thinking it was a colony of Scotland, and in a sense it was. Place names such as Hamilton, Clyde, Invercargill and Dunedin (the Gaelic name for Edinburgh) abound. For over 150 years they've even had a Scottish Highland Games in New Zealand. The Maoris can look fierce, but when the first Scotsmen got off the boat with their wild ginger beards, sporrans swinging in the wind, playing their bagpipes, the Maoris must have thought they'd met their match!

101

It's curious that New Zealand is a similar size and shape to Italy, almost like left and right legs. If they were next to each other they would look like a pair of riding boots in a shoebox.

My anarchist mate, Jamie, visited the country about ten years ago, bought a lottery ticket, and won! The top prize then was $38,000 and the New Zealand newspapers moaned that a tourist had won it.

New Zealand is bigger than the UK but smaller than Japan. The population is only four-and-a-half million, nearly two million of whom live around Auckland, although the capital is the windy little city of Wellington. There are six million cows in the country, thirty million sheep, and no litter. In 1982 New Zealand had over seventy million sheep, but the US insistence on a Western trade blockade of Iran devastated the lamb export industry.

New Zealand drifted away from the other land masses 84 million years ago, even before *Coronation Street* started, resulting in the majority of their animals and plants being unique. There is a lizard called a Tuatara which has three eyes. There was also a huge bird, called a Moa, which was hunted to extinction, and now resides, stuffed, in the Auckland War Memorial Museum. From the neck down it had the powerful thighs and huge killer claws, just like a T-Rex. From the neck up it looks like the Funky Chicken. Now the people of New Zealand have no dangerous creatures to worry about. The spiders are harmless. Like Ireland, there are no snakes. In fact, snakes are illegal in New Zealand.

*

Charles and Barbara showed me around town. We saw the First World War memorial with Barbara's great uncle's name on it. He was killed at Ypres, Belgium. In WW2 Montgomery took the credit for winning the North African war at El Alamein, but it was mainly the Kiwis who did it. We saw Sir Edmund Hilary's ice axe in the museum. Charles had met him. It's no surprise that a Kiwi

102

conquered Everest because their whole culture is athletic and adventurous, the two main requirements for mountaineering. We also tried the Earthquake Experience in the museum, and the earth moved, darling.

Next they took me to the Sky Tower, the tallest building in the Southern Hemisphere, and I jumped off. They have a bungy jump thing, 600 feet up, so I leapt off attached to something that looked like knicker elastic.

If you talk to anybody who has ever been to New Zealand they will rave about how good it is there. After my first few days in Auckland, and I was raving about it too. It was clean, efficient, friendly, prosperous, but not flashy. Efforts were made to preserve and celebrate Maori culture. For example, while I was there they had Maori Language Week and all the place names on the TV weather map were in Maori. All New Zealand children learn the language at school. The word Maori translates as "normal" or "we are normal", because when Europeans first arrived they looked sort of "abnormal". The orange squash drink we have in the UK called Kia Ora is the Maori phrase for 'good health'. Funnily enough, although the word 'papa' means father in many languages, and 'the Pope' in Italian, it means 'arse' in Maori. My papa was still very sore.

*

The New Zealand attitude to life is encapsulated in the phrase 'no worries' which they use at all possible occasions. It sums up their laid-back, tolerant, happy outlook. When Charles was in an exceptionally good mood he might even say "No wucking furries."

Charles told me about his job. He said "I don't mind going in to work, but the eight-hour wait to go home really gets on my nerves."

After three days it was time to hit the road, so with a sad goodbye to Charles and Barbara I set off. The forecast was for increasing rain, wind and snow, the further south I go.

I pedalled through the rough end of Auckland, which was like the posh end of Basildon. I only saw one man begging. He was a Maori with tribal tattoos all over his face. He was shaking a small coffee cup asking for spare change while he was smoking and chatting on his mobile. Actually, he was a bit overweight, and could have done with losing a few pounds. My American sister-in-law deployed some devastating one-liners when people in the street asked her for spare change. Either she would say "I don't know, I haven't finished living my life yet" or "I gave at the office."

I stopped to chat to some Kiwi cyclists and they warned me how terrible New Zealand drivers were. It's funny how often people think the drivers in their own country are the worst in the world. To be honest, I had thought that about England. But now that I'd pedalled across a dozen countries I felt qualified to comment on the subject. I can confidently say that most New Zealand drivers are quite good. (I suppose everywhere compares favourably to the daily near-death experiences I endured in Brazil and to a lesser extent Argentina). Also, roads in New Zealand were good, usually with a nice hard shoulder for cyclists.

I was pushing my bike up a steep hill, not so much to save my legs as to give my blistered bum a rest, when the driver of a pickup truck offered me a lift. Nothing like that had happened in the last 4500 cycling miles, but it was a typically generous Kiwi thing to do. (It happened again a few days later). I had to decline because I was supposed to be cycling around the world, not hitch-hiking.

New Zealand is so sweet and old school that they still have proper hitch-hikers. I saw plenty of men and women hitching. I have had some great adventures hitch-hiking all over Britain and the Continent. Stupid Hollywood horror films destroyed the hitch-hiking culture in Europe and North America thirty years ago — famously, there are signs outside an Arizona prison advising motorists not to pick up hitch-hikers – but it survives in New Zealand, and good for them.

In the 1980's I shared a house with a New Zealander called John. He was hitch-hiking near Southampton when a man in a Hillman Imp stopped to give him a lift. After a few miles the car broke down. The driver said "I'm sick of this bloody car. You can have it if you want." He left the keys in the ignition, slammed the door, and stamped off down the road. John knew enough about cars to get it going, and drove around in it for the next six months until he returned to New Zealand.

In New Zealand, nearly everyone has a detached house on a decent sized plot of land called a section. You might think that sounds perfect, but ironically, according to a nurse I spoke to, it is the cause of about 20 small children dying every year. The children are usually Pacific Islanders. The reason is that Pacific Islanders have a communal attitude to raising children. All adult family members and friends collectively raise the kids. This is very good in many respects, except that no particular adult looks out for any particular kid. Therefore, the children sort of play unsupervised, and hence they get run over and killed on the driveways of those lovely detached New Zealand homes.

The same nurse told me that New Zealand has a very high suicide rate and a high rate of child abuse. These things seemed baffling in such a lovely country. Possibly different standards of reporting make the figures look high. The Kiwi nurse told me that Pacific Island parents discipline their children very severely, to the point of death. On average, a small child is beaten to death every five weeks in New Zealand.

I was still plodding along, pedalling south. You could say I'm ploddaling. The area looked very like Devon in England, apart from the occasional fields of llamas and alpacas. Peter Jackson filmed *The Hobbit* and some of *The Lord of the Rings* in the area and you can tour the film sets. (I'd only been back on the bike for two days and my ring was agony). During the filming of *The Lord of the*

Rings, some of the New Zealand army was used as extras, the soldiers dressed up as orcs. I thought it's a funny coincidence that the biggest city in New Zealand, Auckland, was pronounced the same as orc-land. I have heard people say that *The Lord of the Rings* is the greatest film ever made. That's nonsense of course. Obviously it's *The Blues Brothers*.

*

The Maori place names all had a story behind them, and one of the towns I passed, Urewera, meant 'hot penis'. One legend says Urewera was named so because a warrior fell asleep beside the fire, rolled over, and burnt his meat and two veg. An alternative legend says the name refers to a case of infidelity, when a warrior cut off his love rival's male reproductive appendage and threw it in the fire.

There seemed to be hardly any pubs in New Zealand, at least compared to Southend. After three days, in a village called Cambridge, I found one called the Prince Albert. That's a slightly unfortunate name because, in their innocence, I don't think the Kiwis realised that a Prince Albert is a piercing through your knob.

I arrived in Rotorua and the land looked like it was on fire with steam jets emerging from hundreds of holes around the town. It was strange to see small children playing normally on the swings in the local park while a few feet away was a primeval scene of steam and hot, bubbling, grey mud emerging from deep within the earth.

I went to the Polynesian Spa in Rotorua which overlooked the lake of the same name and had soothing thermal hot pools said to be good for your health. The steaming, milky-coloured water smelled of sulphur, like egg farts, which was just as well because I had baked beans twice the day before and could let rip today without anybody noticing anything different. Couples, such as honeymooners, could book a private pool. I have a naughty mind, so I presume private pools are for having sex in, which would be fun. On the subject of romance, sort of, one of Kevin's best friends went on a blind date with a young lady earlier this year and before they met she texted him a photo of her vagina. That's not yer average selfie. Or is it? Ahh, the youth of today, such rascals!

Later that evening there was a pub quiz at Hennessey's Irish Bar, so I joined some other lads and we made a team. Quizzes are always fun, but this was quite a genteel affair compared to the raucous pub quizzes run by Terry at The Plough in Southend. For example, in The Plough there is a prize every week for the rudest team name. One Christmas 'Santa and his Merry Fisters' won. On Hollywood theme night, the winners were the 'Red Carpet Munchers'. Another time, a group of ladies called their team 'Quiz On My Tits'.

As always I was on the road at dawn the next morning. In the middle of New Zealand's North Island was a large barren area, bisected by the ominously named Desert Road. This road had a fearsome reputation in winter, and the owner of the motel in Taupo advised me not to cross it on a bike. The New Zealanders have a reputation for being tough, but I'm English, and we're bleeding tougher, therefore, I had to have a go.

Before crossing, I went into a petrol station to get some hot coffee and load up with bars of chocolate. Another customer said I should get to the top of the moorland, chain up my bike, and go hiking (tramping, they called it) to admire the mountains. I considered this, then thought "No way, José!" Firstly, it's hard enough cycling 14,000 miles, without making it harder by adding hiking tours. Secondly, If I'd stopped at every interesting place on the way I would still be in France. Thirdly, after travelling halfway around the world my senses had become dulled to pretty scenery – actually I didn't give a damn about seeing a few mountains. I'd seen the Andes for chrissakes, and scenery doesn't get any better than that. I realise this makes me sound like a heathen, but it's the truth. I felt that I was doing a cycling challenge, not on a sightseeing jolly. It's like when someone runs the London Marathon, they don't stop on the way to visit Madame Tussauds or to feed the pigeons in Trafalgar Square. Anyway, it's the people that make a place interesting, not the scenery.

The dictionary definition of desert is an absence of rain. New Zealand's Desert Road does not have that handicap. In fact, it lashed down all day, like Dartmoor. It was also cold and windy, like Dartmoor. There was a prison there, like Dartmoor. The army blew stuff up there, like Dartmoor. It would be a good setting for *The Hounds of the Baskervilles*, like Dartmoor. So you thought cycling around the world would be all sunny beaches and palm trees? Wrong. (I saw on the news two days later that the traffic on the Desert Road was all stranded by thick blizzards!)

Anyway, I made it across, because I'm English, and on down to the more regular wooded and agricultural areas below. I stopped to water the horses. I was happily standing there, looked down, and realised I was pissing on a Silver Fern the national symbol of New Zealand and the All Blacks. Sorry about that. No offence meant. Please don't hurt me.

*

Barbara arranged for me to stay over with her son John and his wife Ruth in Ashhurst. I arrived and we had a lovely meal and some liquid refreshment down the pub and they told me all sorts of interesting things about rural New Zealand. For starters, there were the earthquakes. Small ones were very frequent, and a recent one had shaken their TV off its stand.

We also talked about farming. A top class Merino sheep could sell for $25,000 (£12,000), whereas I'd heard previously that English farmers only get about £50 per lamb. John said the only mammals native to New Zealand were bats and seals. All the rest – rabbits, possums, wild boar, deer, etc – were introduced and had become a real nuisance because they had no natural predators and so upset the ecosystem.

Conversely, venison became very popular for a while and farmers wanted to catch the wild deer for breeding purposes. So how did those crazy Kiwi daredevils do it? They jumped out of helicopters and wrestled the deer to the ground. Yes, you did read that correctly. Later they developed a kind of home-made gun that fired a net, then the farmer would jump on the deer and tie its legs up. Next day I passed a small museum which celebrated these Live Capture Techniques. There was one of the little helicopters outside.

John, Ruth and I discussed the debate then dominating the TV and newspapers concerning whether to modernise the New Zealand flag, as Canada did in 1965. (Before their maple leaf flag, which, incidentally, was designed by a Chinese schoolboy, Canada had a red flag with the Union Jack in the corner). In New Zealand $26 million had been spent designing forty possible alternatives, all of which were quite forgettable, in order to get rid of the Union Jack in the corner. They were going to vote in a referendum, and – update – in March 2016 decided not to change it anyway.

Pub quiz question: What is the only country that does not have a rectangular flag?
Answer: Nepal.

Next day I passed through Feilding, voted New Zealand's most beautiful town. Everything was immaculate and pristine. To be honest it was just a bit too bloody twee for my liking and reminded me of *The Stepford Wives*.

On I went. However, my backside was so sore I thought I'd seek help. My first thought was to find a surgeon to get a total arse transplant, but before that I thought I had better try a bike shop for suggestions. There was a big bike shop in Paraparaumu with expert staff. After I had explained the problem the salesman fixed me with his gaze and said gravely "What you need to avoid is numbness."

"Numb Nuts?" I wondered.

He said he had been a racing cyclist for ten years, and had the wrong saddle, and now was paying for it. I was too embarrassed to ask, but my mind was whirring around wondering whether he had urinary incontinence, urinary retention, had gone sterile, had prolapsed 'Rockford Files', or something else very personal and unpleasant. He frightened the life out of me so I immediately took his advice and bought the best fitting, most expensive saddle in the shop, and the most expensive shorts. He also advised me to go "commando" which seemed strange at first, but helped a bit. There is a Naked Bike Ride through London every summer, but I'm not going that far.

After a few days there was a definite improvement in the bum department. In fact, some mornings, after I slapped on a load of petroleum jelly around my goolies, pulled on my gel-lined Lycra shorts, commando-style, and got into a nice rhythm pedalling on my comfy new saddle it could be a pretty nice feeling, if you know what I mean. There could be a market for something like it in some of the more specialist Amsterdam sex shops.

*

You probably know that New Zealanders are sport mad. They work hard to be the best, and often succeed. Their top sports are rugby, cricket, netball, hockey and rowing, which sounds like the P.E. curriculum at an English public school. They just need Eton Fives to complete the set. However, my favourite New Zealand sporting fact is that the national basketball team are called the Tall Blacks.

I cycled through a small town (I can't remember its name) and saw they were playing the next town the following Sunday afternoon. At 1.30 there was netball (for the girls) and at three o'clock rugby (for the boys). I thought what an excellent idea – a double sport challenge which would bring the whole town together.

My Kiwi nurse friend said that because New Zealanders are very sporty and outdoorsy that they tend to have fewer health problems, such as diabetes and heart and lung disease. Instead they get lost in woods, swept away in rivers, fall off cliffs, and get frozen in the snow. They are also keen on healthy, nutritious food. I saw drinks that claimed to have anti-oxidant properties but I always avoided them because I like oxygen.

New Zealand gets a lot of rain, so I arrived wet through but relieved in Wellington at the foot of the North Island. The ferry goes from there to Picton in the South Island. Waiting for the ferry were plenty of the backpacker crowd on organised tours. They were all young and good looking, had all the right equipment, laughed loudly all the time, and sported beards. Silence fell abruptly, and I looked around and every single one of them was on their mobile Facebooking, perhaps posting profound messages such as 'I'm on the ferry', 'I'm laughing' or 'I've got a beard'.

An irritating habit of backpackers is to say they've 'done' Paris, or 'done' India, or 'done' New Zealand, or wherever. In reality they've just visited the normal tourist hotspots surrounded by people of the same age (twenties) and social class (middle). To say you have 'done' a city or country is impossible, because there is always something new to learn, discover or experience. I suppose I was just jealous of their youthfulness and safe, carefree lives, but still they really got on my tits. Bah, humbug!

The ship going from the North Island to the South Island has the reputation of being the most scenic ferry ride in the world. Google images of Marlborough Sounds will show you better photos than I could ever take. The ship went between forested mountains under blue skies through crystal-clear water. There were seals nearby ("within a coo-ee" the captain announced) and dolphins leapt out of the water doing tricks, presumably just for the love of life.

Picton was gorgeous and, in my opinion, the second best town in the world (after Southend, of course). The air is wonderfully fresh, the setting magnificent, and the people are nice. Picton is not bad either. It's claim to fame was having the *Edwin Fox* in the harbour, which is the ninth oldest wooden ship in the world. I suppose if the fine residents there really wanted to put Picton on the map they could go around the world and burn the other eight, but I suspect they're happy enough as they are.

*

I'd arranged to stay nearby at Anakiwa with Shayne Jacks and his wife Tanya, who were judo friends of Larry Ralph. Shayne and Tanya own a guesthouse overlooking their own idyllic bay. Sometimes they collect guests, or shopping, from Picton by speedboat. Their little bay is visited by orcas, dolphins, penguins and leopard seals. Shayne and Tanya are not so keen on the regular fur seals because they bark, are smelly and aggressive. Sometimes they get onto your boat and you can't get them off.

Shayne was a British judo champion. His brother Brian was British champion, twice European champion, went to the Olympics three times, and won the *Superstars* competition on TV. I've won a dozen or so regional competitions, but my best results at the Nationals have been bronze, twice, and silver, once. I've had the broken bones -- fingers, toes, ribs, clavicles and leg – to prove it. Judo, 'The Gentle Way' – my arse. Still, I would dearly love to be British judo champion. In summary, Brian Jacks is a legend of British judo, and I am a leg end of British judo. My son Kevin is now a black belt too. He has great potential and has already been ranked 18th in Britain. Shayne had started two judo clubs in New Zealand, but the population is so low that they had proved difficult to sustain. We spent a couple of happy hours chatting about judo, and Shayne's new sporting love – barefoot water skiing.

112

Shayne and Tanya talked about the rural life and made it seem like a right good laugh. New Zealanders are extremely careful to try to preserve the environment. Consequently, keeping a domestic cat is severely discouraged because they kill so much local wildlife. Also, however, this means New Zealanders take every possible opportunity to kill introduced species such as deer, wild pigs, rabbits and possums. They had a Country Fair nearby where the men did a kind of triathlon which involved carrying a boar on their shoulders over an obstacle course, pulling the fur off a possum, and shearing a sheep. For the kids, there's Toss a Possum.

Watching TV that evening I noticed they refer to chasing the Kiwi Dream, akin to the American Dream. Presumably they meant a big house, 2.4 children, big car, etc. It's strange that we never discuss the British Dream. Perhaps it would be a nightmare? One quirky thing they had on TV was a show called *Low Gear* (the opposite of *Top Gear*) which was two slow old boys talking slowly about slow old cars. Riveting.

After breakfast I said goodbye to Shayne and Tanya and, just outside Picton, promptly had my second crash. My own fault. My shoe laces got wrapped around the pedal and got tighter and tighter. When I realised I couldn't get my foot out I just fell sideways. I must have looked like a right plonker. Don't answer that.

I sorted myself out, cycled on then spent the night in a motel in the little town of Ward. New Zealanders are so used to global travelling that when I said to the lady there which countries I had cycled through she replied, completely non-plussed, "Oh yeah, you're doing that round the world thing."

In the morning, after telling the same lady I was cycling from Ward to Kaikoura she said "You'll have a nice ride today". OMG how wrong she was. Maybe a nice ride by car, but on my bike it was torture, pedalling all day against a strong, freezing wind. My eyes and nose were streaming. My hands were so cold I couldn't operate the gears properly. I was hungry, shivering and exhausted.

The road was along the coast, and at one stage I thought "At least it's not raining." Then a crashing wave soaked me.

However, it was interesting passing a huge fur seal colony. Thousands of them were snoozing on the rocks between the ocean and the road. But man, do they stink! You can smell the colony long before you see any seals.

Eventually, utterly knackered, I made it to Kaikoura, and found a room above a pub. I asked if they had Wi-Fi. They didn't but said if I hung about outside the library I could get it there. I'm glad they didn't say hang about outside the primary school.

Kaikoura is a centre for whale-watching, and all the tours in the boats, planes and helicopters are run by the local Maori tribe. The setting of the small town was spectacular, with the sparkling Pacific on one side and huge snowy mountains behind. Kaikoura prided itself on being a zero-waste town. Very commendable, although the view was totally wasted on me because I was too tired to give a damn.

I had some hot tea and a hot shower and felt revitalised enough to venture out to the supermarket. Cards on the noticeboard there were interesting – 'Free puppies', 'Free horse poo', 'Free goat'.

A few days later I finally made it to Christchurch, the biggest city on, and capital of, the South Island. New Zealand's South Island alone is bigger than England, but only one million people live there. Christchurch has a population slightly larger than Barking in Essex, which incidentally was briefly, before 1066, the royal capital of England. Now Barking is the teenage pregnancy capital of England.

Christchurch was still rebuilding from the devastating earthquake of 2011. A total of 185 people died. 115 just in the CTV Building. The building was shared between a TV company, a health centre and an English language school. 19 doctors and nurses died. 70 students died, mostly Japanese and Chinese who were there to learn English. Some of the Japanese, while trapped, managed to phone their parents. Those students subsequently

114

died. The seven-storey building collapsed in seconds. Only a few people on the top floor survived. Everyone on floors ground to six died. The earthquake struck at 12.51 pm so some lucky people had popped out for lunch. Most who died were crushed, but some perished in the subsequent fire, and some are believed to have drowned as the fire brigade tried to put out the flames. Surviving a quake, surviving a fire, then drowning has got to be the epitome of bad luck.

I talked to one couple about the disaster and they said their friend was in an office in another building, on the sixth floor, actually receiving counselling about the traumatic events of a previous earthquake, when this one struck. She survived.

*

This was my last night in New Zealand, and I was left with just enough time to send one final text – 'No wucking furries' – to my cousin Charles. It had been a delight to catch up with family and friends, and New Zealand is a wonderful country which I highly recommend. My flight to Melbourne, Australia, 'across the ditch' as they said, was at 06.15 the next morning. I was getting up at 3 o'clock, so I turned in early. Goodnight and Kia Ora.

14 – Australia

I said "Do you speak-a my language?"
He just smiled and gave me a vegemite sandwich

'Down Under'
Men At Work

When I was struggling across Europe and South America I was really looking forward to Australia. It was English-speaking, modern, sunny and halfway home. But when I actually arrived in Melbourne I lost my mojo for some reason. I found it difficult to get motivated or interested. I suppose I was just so tired, and homesick. I was bored of eating alone like Billy No Mates (or as they said Down Under, Nigel No Mates). It didn't help that the bike had been smashed up in the plane over from Christchurch, and I'd spent all day sourcing spare parts and doing repairs. Clearly Melbourne was a world-class city. They had free trams and free Wi-Fi for all in the city centre. It was lively, cosmopolitan, clean and welcoming, so the fault must have been with me. I needed something to cheer me up.

While having a mooch around town I spotted a comedy night at one of the pubs overlooking the Yarra River. That was just what I needed. There were only about fifteen people inside. The comedians were just doing short turns of about 10 minutes each. I gradually worked out that I was the only person in the bar not there to have a go, and momentarily I considered standing up and telling my favourite doctor jokes. At first I thought the comedians were all diabolically crap, apart from the MC, but as time went by I got into the zone (read: got pissed) and realised what a great evening it was. Anybody and anything was lampooned – Christians, Jews, Muslims, the blind, wheelchair users. No subject was out of bounds for piss-taking. Anybody of a sensitive disposition would have been offended, but that's not the Australian Way. One comedian even managed to have a dig at New Zealanders, which I had previously thought not possible because they are all so nice – "How do you know when a New Zealand woman is having her period? She's only wearing one sock."

Towards midnight I went back to the hotel, had a good night's sleep, felt better in the morning, and got started on the little matter of cycling 2500 miles to Cairns. Australia is such a huge country, 370 times bigger than Wales. One of the farms, Anna Creek Station, is larger than Israel.

Before leaving Melbourne I had to get some road maps. I went to newsagents, bookshops, car shops and department stores. It was proving very difficult to get a simple map, because everybody now seems to use Sat Nav. Eventually I asked in a petrol station. The cashier rummaged through a cupboard under the counter and, with a flourish, brought out a dusty road atlas, maybe the last one in Australia! Let's rock 'n' roll!

From my trusty dusty map I obviously had to avoid the motorways, so I chose what I thought would be one of the quieter minor roads out of Melbourne – St.Kilda Road. When I got there it was actually twelve lanes wide and went on for miles and miles through suburbia and vast construction sites. I kept thinking of the Joni Mitchell lyrics…

They paved paradise
And put up a parking lot

…I shouldn't criticize though. People have got to live somewhere.

By the afternoon I was happily pootling along across the State of Victoria thinking that *The Lucky Country* is such a pleasant place. Blue sky, warm sun, beautiful countryside, then, BANG! Fucking birds started attacking me! Black and white bastards about the size

117

of a crow. They always attack from behind, which is quite unnerving. Australians call them magpies, but they are much bigger than our English ones. I suspect that their full Latin name is *Bastardii Effingo Magpiemus*. They are usually silent until the last moment when they smash into the back of your head. Other times they just swooped close and brushed the top of my head as they let out a nerve-jangling screech.

Two days later I heard a professor on the radio say that quite a few Australians, especially children, get blinded by those damn magpies every year. They swoop down from behind, people instinctively turn around, then get a claw or beak in their eye. I was very glad I'm wearing a cycle helmet and sunglasses. It felt like I'd landed in the Hitchcock film *The Birds*. (To digress, my favourite Hitchcock story was when he was directing a film starring Tallulah Bankhead. The cameraman whispered that it was obvious the leading lady was not wearing any underwear, to which Hitchcock replied "I'm not sure if that is a case for wardrobe or hairdressing!")

The bird attacks were a persistent daily problem and made cycling quite stressful. They obviously had a particular dislike of people on bikes. My cycling pace of 10-12 mph made for an easy target. Apparently it was nesting season so they were extra aggressive. Eventually when they swooped down, doing their best to cause me damage, I took to greeting them with my loudest shout of "FUCK OFF, YOU FUCKING FUCKFACED FUCKERS!" (the breadth of my vocabulary still needed a bit of work). There were cockatoos, budgies and other birds in massive noisy swarms as well, but at least they didn't attack.

Still, I persevered across Australia. That night I was staying in a motel in a village called Stratford. I really wanted to stay there because I was a member of Stratford Judo Club in East London for twelve years. New Zealand were playing Australia on the TV in the pub, and I was under strict instructions from my Kiwi cousin

Charles to cheer for the All Blacks. The Aussies lost 13-41 but I kept a bit quiet!

Most Australian TV channels were saturated with adverts, including some intended to entice people to move to Darwin in the Northern Territory. There were channels in lots of languages – Russian, French, Spanish, Arabic, Chinese, and other languages which I could not recognise, possibly Double Dutch or Geordie. Australian sports coverage often included the Premier League, which they call the *English* Premier League, which no doubt upsets Swansea fans. They also covered Aussie-rules football (AFL) a lot. It's a bit of a strange game halfway between soccer and rugby that is not really played anywhere else. I think many Australians view AFL as part of their national identity in the same way as Americans view baseball. I was hoping to catch an AFL game in Sydney the following week.

Before that, I had to *get* to Sydney. Pedalling along I met a French man coming the other way on a recumbent tricycle. Often I thought it could be dangerous riding a normal, narrow bike on some of those roads, but riding a wide recumbent trike seemed like a suicide wish – cyclicide! We got chatting in a mixture of French and English. He was a lovely bloke, apart from being a maniac. He had cycled across Canada and was now doing a circuit of Australia. I asked his name, and I thought he said "Heidi". I asked again, and this time it sounded like "Aidee." Then he said "You know, like zee cicliste Belgique, Merckx."

"Oh, Eddy Merckx!" says I. "Pleased to meet you Eddy!"

It was really heart-warming to meet another touring cyclist, even if he was barking. I wonder if he thought that about me? After trading stories for half an hour we wished each other "Bonne chance" and went our opposite ways through the jungle.

Vast areas of south and east Australia are covered in forest. I didn't expect that. You can see from the burnt tree trunks that many areas have had bush fires, but the plants all adapt, and grow back the following spring as if nothing had happened. I read in the

Darwin Awards book that a scuba diver was found dead in a Californian forest after a bushfire. Police were baffled. They eventually worked out that one of the helicopters that scooped up seawater from the nearby ocean to douse the flames must have picked up the diver as well and chucked him on the fire.

The Australian forests were sometimes very noisy with birds and insects and other mysterious creatures rustling about in the undergrowth. Deep in the jungle was a tiny village called Cann River. I checked into the motel. A sign above the door said 'Stay for the *rest* of your life'. It was so pleasant, I was quite tempted.

On the 18th of August the news reported that a woman bitten by a snake in a park in Perth had died. A bomb had gone off in Bangkok killing twenty people. I'd be there in two months. On a lighter note, I crossed the border from Victoria into New South Wales. Only 285 miles to Sydney. I was really looking forward to that because Sharon was coming to see me for two weeks. She texted me that day, knowing that my favourite food is a cheese sandwich, offering to bring over some Hovis and cheddar. She is so sweet, but I declined. Secretly, I was very much missing my own invention, the inside-out toasted cheese sandwich.

*

Can we digress for a little and talk about Australian animals, starting with the kangaroo? Early Europeans thought it was a species of giant rat because of the long fat tail. Female kangaroos have three vaginas, which, let's be honest, is just plain greedy. I started taking pictures of dead kangaroos for my roadkill photo collection, but stopped because there were just too many beside the road. I saw one that had its head knocked off. Perhaps the head was dangling on the roo-bar on the front of one of those massive Kenworth or Mack trucks that ply up and down Australia's spectacularly long roads.

There were also hundreds of dead wombats along the road. In my ignorance I previously thought they were small, like a little rabbit, but they were actually quite big, about the size of a bulldog, with short powerful legs and strong claws for digging. Apparently they can run faster that Usain Bolt which, unfortunately, was still not fast enough to dodge the Australian traffic. Wombats have a pouch for their babies (joeys) like a kangaroo, but a wombat's pouch is upside-down so it doesn't fill up with mud when mum is digging tunnels. Wombats have an incredibly tough rear end, and when being chased they run down a tunnel and block it bum outwards. No indigenous Australian predator is able to get past that virtually bulletproof arse. Wombats have cubic poo, well almost. Due to their anatomy, the faeces comes out like large Oxo cubes. One dead wombat I passed, with its four legs up in the air, had actually been shitting at the moment of death. There were cubic turds halfway out of its bum. That is not what you could call a dignified death.

Descriptions of the quirky wildlife in Australia could easily fill numerous books on its own, but I'll briefly mention a few more now. There is the duck-billed platypus, which is a mammal like you and me, though the female lays eggs. The male can shoot poison out of its feet, which is reminiscent of a creature in *Doctor Who*.

Koala bears are another strange bunch. The babies are weaned on poo direct from mum's anus. (Imagine – "Mum, this food tastes like shit.") Also worth noting, 50% of Koalas have chlamydia, so always use protection.

Camels were brought to Australia two hundred years ago for transport purposes, but when motor vehicles became widespread from the 1930s the camels were released into the wild. They bred like crazy and now Australia has the largest wild camel population in the world. Thousands are culled each year and some are sent to Saudi Arabia where the disease free meat is highly valued.

Australia has some unusual sharks in Queensland waters. The baby sharks are sometimes caught by fishermen, but no human has ever seen one of the adult sharks of this particular species. It's a mystery.

Apart from sharks and other weird wildlife Australia is also famous for boomerangs. The Aborigines have been using them for 14,000 years sometimes to hunt kangaroos but also to imitate hawks and drive game birds into nets that are strung between trees. The Aborigines became expert boomerang throwers but never developed the bow and arrow. Maybe there was no springy wood suitable for a bow. In fact, boomerangs have been found inside Tutankhamun's tomb in Egypt, and others 18,000 years old have been found in Polish and Spanish caves.

Anyway, I carried on pushing those pedals. One afternoon, straining my calves, puffing and panting, soaked in sweat, in first gear, I eventually crested the top of a big hill near Narooma. I was so pleased. Ahead, and to the right, was the Pacific Ocean, sparkling in the sunshine. With relief I shouted out a big Austin Powers-style "YEAH, BABY!" What I didn't notice, until too late, was a young teenage girl in school uniform standing about three yards away on the left in the shade of a tree. I think she thought I was shouting at her. Besly embarrasses himself again.

In Australia, as there seem to be in every country, there were a few idiotic drivers. Why do people change behind the wheel? I even had a gang of motorcyclists ride straight at me, trying to intimidate. You would think they would know better, also being on two wheels. On the plus side, I saw a funny sun visor on a van windscreen. It didn't say 'Gary and Tracy' or 'Ali G and M'Julie Innit', but 'Caution. Blind man driving'. Less amusingly, I noticed that some Australian truck drivers had the disgusting habit, as they did in Spain, of pissing into a plastic bottle and throwing it out of the window.

On the subject of piss, one day I nearly ran over a urinary catheter. It was amazing what I found on the road, and made me wonder how it got there, and why. As a nurse we obviously have to drain urine catheter bags regularly. If I thought the patient liked

122

a joke I might say "Don't mind me, I'm just taking the piss." (Funnily enough, the machine used in hospital to test urine for pregnancy is made by Siemens). I have seen two bra's beside the road (did two women suddenly discover radical feminism?) but more usually it was coins, spanners, car exhausts, hats and porn mags.

Near Eden I settled into a motel and relaxed. The advertising board for the motel said 'Sleep with someone experienced'. After a tough day's cycling I liked to go out for a few beers in the local pub. I've noticed that if I have one beer then I need to get up in the night once for a pee. Two beers equal two pees. Three equal three, etc. This seems clear evidence that you don't buy beer, you rent it.

A few years ago I went to an ANZAC Day party on a hot sunny afternoon in the garden of a pub in Acton, West London. It seemed strangely appropriate that on the sombre occasion of commemorating their war dead the Aussies celebrated life by having a wild party. They had lots of whacky drinking games. One involved half-a-dozen blokes lined up, hands behind their backs, in a race to eat a whole Mars bar, which basically meant the compere just rammed it into their mouths. Round two of the game was a similar race to eat a whole Mars Bar, but this time they left the wrapper on!

As I pedalled across Australia I was looking for a friend of mine. When I worked as a postman in Romford I had a mate there called… well, I won't tell you his name because his hobby was armed robbery. You might think that armed robbery is an unusual hobby, but you need to consider that in our part of Essex the best qualification that some people got was an ASBO. He was actually a really nice bloke, and as he lived down my road so I knew him quite well.

I think he worked at the Royal Mail mainly as a cover. The rozzers must have picked up his trail because he suddenly decided to move to Australia. About six years later I bumped into him, all suntanned, in ASDA in Dagenham. He had come back to visit his mum. He had done well for himself in Australia, joined the cops in his small town, and told me he was now the Chief of Police! I was buggered if I could remember the name of the town otherwise I would definitely have gone and seen him. I wondered if he still pursued his hobby, and in the meantime I just kept looking.

Further on I went through the town of Douin, where they had a joint car and dog wash. I thought that was such a great business idea. It could be expanded so you got your laundry cleaned, and maybe even customers could have a hot shower or a swim while they waited.

That evening I managed to get through to Laura on the phone and was having a nice chat, when all of a sudden she screamed and dropped the phone. My mind raced – what was happening? Eventually, her boyfriend Lee picked up the phone. He explained that while Laura was talking she absent-mindedly opened a cupboard, and screamed because Kevin had left a half-eaten Kentucky Fried Chicken in there, which was crawling with maggots. Laura wouldn't even return to the room until Lee had hoovered them all up!

Still chuckling, I wandered down to the local pub for some liquid refreshment and then thumbed my way through the *Sydney Morning Herald*. According to the paper obesity in Australia was at a similar level to the USA, possibly because as in the USA most people drive everywhere. As an example, when I was staying in High Hill I asked a young man where the fish and chip shop was. He gave directions and said I would "definitely need to drive to get there." Being carless, obviously I walked. It was only 100 yards away! Incidentally, the month before I left home a very obese man presented at Southend A&E. He told the assessing doctor that he had decided to lose weight, so for the past three days he had been doing a lot of walking. The doctor, puzzled, said "Okay, that all sounds good. But why have you come to A&E today?"

The man replied "My feet hurt."

*

Yippee! Sydney at last. A wonderful city of four-and-half million, about the same number of people as the whole of New Zealand. It was named after Lord Sydney, but who remembers him?

Sharon didn't arrive in Sydney for a few days, which gave me time to find a nice apartment for us to rent in the suburb of Parramatta. That sorted, I thought I would go for a swim. After four months on the road I was very cycle-fit but unfit for anything else. While I was doing a few gentle lengths of breast stroke I pulled a muscle in my groin, after which I was hobbling about like Quasimodo. When Sharon arrived I'd probably try some more breast stroke. Settle down at the back there!

5am, August 30th, 2015, Sydney Airport. I was waiting in the arrivals lounge with butterflies in my stomach. Hugh Grant in *Love Actually* said whenever he wanted to cheer himself up he went to the arrivals lounge at Heathrow Airport to see all the delighted and happy people meeting their friends and family. That is how I felt too. Eventually Sharon came through, pulling possibly the world's largest suitcase, and I jumped for joy and we hugged and hugged.

It was a Sunday morning, over 24 hours since she had left England on the Friday, but in typical selfless Sharon style she was more worried that I'd not had any breakfast yet! It's nice to be loved. Sharon and I have always got on really well and rarely disagree. The curious thing is that when we do have the occasional little argument, funnily enough I am always right. Amazing.

Back at the apartment in Parramatta Sharon examined me from head to toe. My legs were bigger but my arms were smaller. Thanks to regular judo I used to have biceps, pecs and a six-pack, but now I had thin arms, a flat chest and thanks to regular junk food, a little pot belly. I had a large zit on my chest, like the *Bond* villain Scaramanga's third nipple, probably because I'd been eating a lot of chocolate. There were cuts on my face because at home I used an electric razor, but now had to use a disposable blade, and I usually made a bollocks of it. The varicose veins on my left leg were much more pronounced now and went all the way down to my ankle. My arse was still sore, but not as bad as it was. I still had the kooky suntan, as if I was wearing long brown gloves and brown stockings. I'd got calluses on my palms from the handlebars. Cycling takes its toll!

Once satisfied that overall I am medically-fit, Sharon virtually raped me. I am such a lucky boy. We spent that night and every night as spoons.

Many people have asked why Sharon and me were not doing this cycle trip together. The three main reasons were, first, that Sharon is not very confident on a bike. We did hire a tandem for the day the year before, to see if that would be an option, but Sharon's lady bits got so bruised she could hardly walk for three days afterwards. Second, Sharon likes her own cooking and not much else. If the only thing available was pig's trotters in Spain, or camel burger in Australia, or grilled dragonflies in Indonesia, then I had to eat it, otherwise I would literally not have enough energy to cycle. And third, we would have needed a big trailer for that massive suitcase!

Sharon and I visited the Opera House, the Olympic Park, the Sky Tower and the Zoo. I texted a photo of a kangaroo to my judo mate Ian, and he replied

"Those squirrels are big out there!"

I texted back "You should see their nuts!"

We caught the ferry to the idyllic Watsons Bay, which became my favourite place in Australia so far, and had fish and chips at Doyles restaurant. Doyles, with the waves lapping at the terrace, is a Sydney institution. Mel Gibson and Prince Charles had eaten here, and Richard Branson occasionally zoomed over by speedboat from his nearby waterfront mansion. But I didn't give a toss about those three. I wanted to go there because Billy Connolly did in his

126

World Tour of Australia. After some superb fish and chips, which was nearly as good as you can get at Oldhams in Southend, Sharon and I caught the bus to Bondi Beach and had a chilly paddle. It was winter after all. (The following week I saw on TV that a 90-year old lady fell off the pier at Watsons Bay. She was rescued and I think she was okay.)

We went on a memorable minibus tour to the Blue Mountains. Rod, the driver, took us to an isolated beauty spot with no fences where he said he used to come to smoke weed. I peered gingerly over the cliff, several hundred feet high, but the Germans in our group walked right up to the edge, like cats, with no fear.

Rod, in typical Aussie fashion, but with a twinkle in his eye, was blunt with his words. An Israeli man with a beard on our tour he called Bin Laden. A thin Dutch lad wearing a bobble hat he called 'Where's Wally'. Sharon he called 'The Aborigine'. Being thin-skinned is not a trait admired by Australians.

Rod mentioned an interesting comparison between Australians and the English, "Australians think one hundred years is a long time, whereas the English think one hundred miles is a long way." (He was paraphrasing Bill Bryson.) By the time we got back to Sydney that evening we were all best buddies.

In Parramatta the next day I went to the pharmacy to get some anti-malaria tablets in preparation for going to Asia. They would only dispense them with a prescription, so I paid $75 and got to see a doctor within ten minutes. I told him where I was going and he listed all the things I should get protection against – polio, hepatitis A, hepatitis B, rabies, diphtheria, influenza, cholera, bird flu, typhoid, Japanese encephalitis, measles, oh, and nearly forgot, malaria. While the doctor was rattling off all the potentially fatal diseases my mind wandered to something my best mate John once said while describing someone who he knew who is always ill "He's got every disease known to man, except hypochondria!" Anyway, in the end I just settled for injections and pills against hepatitis A, cholera, typhoid, oh, and nearly forgot, malaria.

Malaria was named that because the Victorians thought the disease derived from bad air, not the devilish little female mosquito. Literally billions of people have had malaria over the past 10,000 years. Animals and birds can catch malaria too. Oliver Cromwell died of malaria and millions more have been extremely ill with it – Michael Caine, Cheryl Cole, Ross Kemp, Didier Drogba and David Attenborough, to name a few. Malaria is not totally bad news, however, because mild doses have been given to people to cure syphilis.

While on the subject of health, it seems weird that CT scans done in Southend Hospital are emailed over to Australia. A doctor in Australia looks at the images, then emails back a report. What a strange world we live in.

My sister Juliet emigrated to Sydney about thirty years ago as a 'Ten Pound Pom', although she has moved back to Blighty now. In those days the Australian Government encouraged immigration by subsidising the fare so that you only had to pay £10 to get there. She trained as a nurse at the Royal North Shore Hospital. Australians are big tea drinkers, like us, and I thought it was pretty cute and symbolic that during their Citizenship Ceremony the new immigrants, such as Juliet, were presented with a little fancy teaspoon.

Obviously Juliet still knew lots of people in Australia and she arranged for us to meet one of her old friends ("Less of the old!") Linda in Chatswood, and we spent a lovely morning with her. Juliet had arranged for Linda to buy some specialist drugs, unavailable in England, to give Sharon to bring home. That may sound worse than it actually was, Your Honour.

Another day Sharon and I went on a walking tour of the historical part of Sydney. The guide, Gay, told us that Australian history is not like ours, with castles, royalty, wars, poverty and rebellion in crowded cities. Instead, their long-term history is about the Aboriginal culture. She said many more Australians are now realising how proud they are of that, and celebrate it. Previous generations had shot the Aborigines like dogs, and poisoned their waterholes. But now I had noticed that the Aborigine flag flies alongside the Australian flag outside most public buildings in Victoria and New South Wales.

As we walked Gay also told us about the early European settlers, who were a colourful crowd. After the American Revolution in 1776 the British initially had nowhere to send their convicts. So two years later they started to send them to Australia. Eventually 168,000 would make the journey. One of their number was Ned Kelly.

"He liked to shoot,
And he liked to loot,
In his home-made
Cast-iron, bullet-proof suit."

His stoical last words, just before being shot dead, were "That's life!"

Another early Aussie, Francis Greenway, was a convict sent to the country for forgery. He served his time, then used his knowledge of architecture to design some of Sydney's most prominent buildings. His hard work was honoured by having his picture on the Australian ten-dollar bill, the only known case of a forger having his face on a banknote!

Our walking tour took us in the shadow of Sydney Harbour Bridge. It was enormous. (I once asked my Dad how you spell enormous. He thought for a few moments then spelt out "B.I.G."). So, as I was saying, to build this *big* bridge over 400 homes were demolished, and there was no compensation for the poor buggers who lived there. Sixteen men died during its construction. That was the human cost, brushed under the carpet, for us to cross Sydney Harbour quickly now.

The bridge-opening ceremony in 1932 was quite an occasion. All the great and the good, plus 300,000 spectators, came to

129

witness the event. The NSW Premier, James Laing, was about to cut the ribbon when an Irish fascist called Francis de Groot rode up on his horse and cut the ribbon with his sabre. The crowd swarmed across, and Sydney's top knobs lost their moment of glory. De Groot was arrested, taken for psychiatric assessment, and pronounced sane! The authorities appealed and got him pronounced insane, whereupon de Groot successfully sued the police for wrongful arrest! Truth can be stranger than fiction.

We said goodbye to our guide. We had really enjoyed our Gay Walk. Christ, I bet she was as sick of hearing lame jokes like that about her name as I am of people spelling mine Adrain!

While Sharon and I enjoyed the delights of Sydney I got my bike serviced. During the trip so far I'd replaced the saddle, pedals, seat post, brakes, bearings, cables, chain sets, wheels and tyres. By the time I got to England the bike would be like Trigger's broom in *Only Fools and Horses* ("This old broom has had seventeen new heads and fourteen new handles....") Some people give a name to their bike. I call my bike 'The Rack'.

Sorry to be such a nerd, but I must tell you about my tyres. I'd done about 5000 miles since I got them in Castello, Spain. They were *Schwalbe* tyres made with Kevlar and I'd not had a single puncture with them. I met a New Zealand couple cycling on regular tyres, on the same roads as me, and they had had eight punctures in a single day. I was so happy with those tyres I could have kissed them. I wouldn't get too romantic with my bike though, unlike Robert Stewart of Ayr, Scotland who was put on the Sex Offenders Register for having sex with his bicycle in 2007. Even worse was Karl Watkins of Redditch, near Birmingham, who went to prison in 1993 for having sex with the pavement. Presumably that date didn't require chocolates and flowers.

With my bike fighting fit again the next thing was to get the relevant visas for Asia. The British passport is one of the best in the world for travelling visa-free. However, everybody needs to get a visa if they want to go to Burma (Myanmar) or India. I couldn't get an Indian visa in London because they are only valid for six months, and it would have expired by the time I got there, so I knew I would have to get it in Sydney.

I found a good travel agent and asked them to help me to get a visa for Burma. Burma had been under an oppressive military dictatorship until recently, and had on-going armed conflicts with various ethnic groups in its border areas. After a long telephone conversation with the Burmese Consulate in Canberra they said I would only be permitted to travel overland there if I had a government guide with me. That would have been totally impractical on a bike even if I had had the money to pay for it, which I didn't because I was running low. Therefore, I had to resign myself to skirting around Burma by sea or air.

This was a great disappointment to me because I had wanted to go to the village of Kin-U where my Dad fought the Japanese in WW2, got shot through the leg and earned the Military Cross. He wrote an epic account of the action in a letter home to his sister Mary which I did consider shoehorning into this diary. It's such a classic of war reporting that it is a waste for it just to sit in the drawer at home.

Nevertheless, I went back to the travel agent for their help in getting an Indian visa. They got all my paperwork in order and I trotted off to the Indian Consulate bright and early the following morning. I presented all the correct documents and the woman I spoke to calmly said it would take between two and nine weeks! I couldn't believe my ears. This was the 21ˢᵗ Century and they could get all the information they need at the speed of light if they wanted to. Frigging bureaucrats.

To get an Indian visa in London is normally a same day service, I know because I've done it several times, and it would have been in Australia too if I had been an Australian citizen. I didn't have the time or money to wait in Sydney, which is an expensive place, for up to nine weeks. Consequently, I needed a new plan.

After discussing the options with Sharon I decided to cycle north, make my way to China, then fly over India and Myanmar to the Middle East. I had been to India, Pakistan, Afghanistan and Iran before anyway, I hitch-hiked to India when I was 17 years old, and had no special desire to go again. The new plan solved the problem of travelling across Syria. I had previously wondered how I was going to cross the war zone in Syria where those Islamic State lunatics were beheading infidels and non-believers like me. Now I would go through Thailand, Laos, Vietnam, China and Macau to Hong Kong, then fly from there to Tel Aviv in Israel. The new plan meant I'd go to lots of countries I've never been to before – so every cloud had a silver lining. For some strange female reason Sharon thought the girls would be throwing themselves at me in Vietnam and China – I thought "Not with my feet!"

That evening we found a big pub in town called Scruffy Murphy's. It was buzzing. They had three drag queens doing a show, which was bound to be a laugh. One of them was called Dawn Service. After buying some drinks we got chatting to a construction worker from Yorkshire who had emigrated the year before. He said that Scruffy Murphy's had the reputation for being one of the toughest pubs in Sydney, but compared to the pubs he knew in Leeds it was like a vicars' tea party. As the alcohol began to flow more freely and the evening progressed Sharon and I ended up on stage with the drag queens. They were, as expected, filthy-minded and outrageous, so a good time was had by all.

We blinked and two weeks was gone. On Sharon's last evening we watched a film and Sharon cooked up two huge steaks, each the size of a Frisbee. We spent the rest of the evening sitting in the bath together, giggling, polishing off half a bottle of vodka.

Next day, sadness at the Airport. Not at all like the arrivals lounge.

*

Off I went again. I gritted my teeth and got back on the bike heading out of Sydney. The bird attacks started within half an hour. Going through the suburbs I passed Burwood Professional Dentists. It would be fun to open a store next door and call it Burwood Amateur Dentists. Also along the way was a scrap metal recycling firm called Aus Crap. The Australians are famous for talking straight.

Pedalling up to the top of the hills that surround Sydney, near Berowra, I found the Pie In The Sky café. In my opinion Australia and New Zealand have the best pies in the world, and the Pie in the Sky, I had been told previously, was supposed to be the best of the best, so I stopped for lunch and filled my face.   There were about fifty motorcyclists tucking into pies. Eating is most bikers' favourite activity, after which they like getting together and discussing their Big Ends, or maybe giving their helmets a quick rub down.

At least half a dozen times in Australia I had a motorbike overtake me only to see the rider was wearing a Nazi-style WW2 helmet. Presumably they thought they were bad-ass rebels. In actual fact they are stupid wankers who need to learn a bit about history. They are *Rebels Without A Clue*.

I saw some Japanese and German bikes in Australia, but the most popular weapon of choice is the Harley Davidson. I'm a qualified motorcycle mechanic and our teacher used to contemptuously describe Harley's as "A bag of bits." I didn't heed his advice and in 2010 I bought a brand new Harley Davidson as part of my mid-life crisis (my menopause, as Sharon called it!), and realised within a few weeks how poorly designed they are. It reminded me of a Soviet tractor. Harley Davidson have cleverly cultivated a prestigious iconic brand with the result that many of us aspire to own one. It wouldn't surprise me if Harley Davidson sell discounted bikes to the Hells Angels in order to boost the brand's bad boy image, thus enabling them to charge a fortune for their other bikes to gullible buggers like me, for a machine that is basically agricultural. I've learnt my lesson. The next motorbike I buy will be Japanese.

HD did try to break into the sports bike market with the Harley Davidson Buell range but their technology was so clunky and out of date they never won a race. In 2009 the Buell division was closed down. Now they aim all their sales strictly at silly middle-aged old gits like me, and Australian lesbians, who lead Sydney's Gay Pride parade every year on their Harley's. (The lesbians lead the parade, not the old gits.)

Enough about bikes with engines. I used my legs to pedal on and found a room above a pub in Wyong. Standard Aussie fare is beer with a steak. They call it Swill & Grill. The Six O'clock Swill is an Australian tradition. Previously, the government said all pubs must stop serving at 6pm. Therefore, all the blokes would get rat-arsed by drinking as much as they could, as fast as they could, until six o'clock every evening. The breweries made a fortune and the pubs were happy because they didn't have to pay staff to work late into the night. Consequently, when the government decided to relax the licencing laws slightly it was, ironically, the pubs and the breweries who opposed it. Bowing to people pressure the government relaxed the drinking laws until seven o'clock, so long as the customer bought a meal with their drink. This resulted in pubs giving a miniscule pot of curry or stew with every beer whether the drinker wanted it or not (usually not). Nowadays it's normal for city pubs to be open until 4am, although rural pubs often close by 9pm.

I mentioned to the barman in Wyong that I would like to see some AFL. He explained that in New South Wales the main sport is Rugby League (as played in t'North of England), and AFL is mostly played in Perth and Melbourne. The barman was extremely partisan towards Rugby League and didn't even like Rugby Union, which he said just involved "A load of blokes lying around on top of each other." (Whenever I watch Rugby Union now I smile – he had a point!) But he saved his biggest contempt for AFL which, among other things, he described as "Gay FL." No doubt he thought soccer was completely beyond the pale, not even worth talking about, only played by effeminate drama queens. To be truthful, some of them are.

On the road next morning, between Swansea and Newcastle, streams of Ferraris overtook me. I didn't realise there were that many in the world. They must have been on their way to a rally of some sort. That there were so many Ferraris was symbolic of Australia's wealth. They had had twenty-five years of continuous economic growth there, unlike Britain, Europe and the USA which all seemed to stagger from one financial crisis to the next.

The further north I went the warmer it became, and there seemed to be more insects. They tended to go in my mouth as I puffed and panted up a steep hill. It has been estimated that there are 1.4 billion insects in the world for every human being, and Australia certainly has their fair share. Sometimes it could be a little amusing to see the insects crawl around on the inside of my sunglasses. I went cross-eyed like Mowgli with a butterfly on his nose in *The Jungle Book*.

I stayed the night at a motel in Karuah. The owner, Brendan, and I gelled straight away and we had a good laugh trading jokes. He had his own CDs for sale at the reception desk. I asked what sort of music he played. He said "Australian." I nodded knowingly, but actually had no clue what Australian music is. Brendan was about 70 so I guessed it wasn't thrash metal. Having said that, when I did *Britain's Got Talent* one of the other acts consisted of five old boys, all well over 60, who did a sensational breakdance routine, so you shouldn't judge a book by its cover.

Before I turned in for the evening Brendan told me about his friend who had won the lottery. Brendan asked him "Are you worried about the begging letters?"

His friend replied "No, I'll still keep sending them!"

My latest wheeze to pass the time on the long stretches between towns involved peanuts. I bought a family packet then rammed as

135

many as I could into my mouth, jumped on the bike and pedalled. I was incapable of speech and my cheeks were huge like J.Lo's butt, though not as pretty. It took ages to work the peanuts around my mouth and chew them all up. Eventually my mouth was clear and I repeated the process. The miles flew by!

Since I had got the new saddle and padded shorts in New Zealand my bum only hurt about half as much, which was a great improvement to my life. My latest ache though was in my little toes. Pedalling squashed the toes into my trainers until it became really painful. When I got off the bike I really hobbled about. However, I solved the problem by cutting a hole in my shoe so my toes could poke out.

You know what they say about big feet? Yes, that's right, big socks.

15th September 2015: I woke to hear the news that the Prime Minister, Tony Abbott, has been manoeuvred out and replaced by his erstwhile friend Malcolm Turnbull. Former PM Paul Keating, commenting on the backstabbing, said "If you want a friend in politics, get a dog."

Malcolm Turnbull had a poor childhood but was now one of the richest men in Australia. He owned an $18 million house overlooking Sydney Harbour. One of his political opponents said on the TV "It's like putting Dracula in charge of the National Blood Transfusion Service."

He was the fifth prime minister Australia had had in five years. It never occurred to any of them to ask the people, in the form of a vote, who they would like to run the country. Voting, incidentally, is compulsory in Australia, or you face a $200 fine. (Australia's grooviest Prime Minister must have been Bob Hawke, who was in *The Guinness Book of Records* for drinking two-and-a-half pints of ale in 11 seconds.)

To his credit, in his first speech as Prime Minister Malcolm Turnbull promised action to help reduce the high incidence of domestic violence, which he described as Australia's Shame. One third of Australian women have experienced domestic violence. 63 had already been killed in 2015 by their boyfriend or husband. The feminist slogan comes to mind "It starts when you sink into his arms, and finishes with your arms in his sink."

Later in the afternoon I started looking for a place to stay. I was passing through the village of Grafton when I spotted the España Motel. "Muy bueno" thinks I.

I went into the reception office and said "Hola. Tiene una habitaccion por mio solo para una noche, por favor?"

The owner said "G'day mate. Do you need a room?"

Next morning on the way out of Grafton I passed a pet boarding business called Cat Utopia. I texted Laura to tell Wilson (our cat) to pack a suitcase.

Australia is normally sunny but by the afternoon it was hammering down with rain so much that I could hardly see where I was going. Stair rods, I think people call it. It was too warm to put on my coat, which would have been ineffective anyway, so I just got drenched. I cycled 150 km and the only place to stay was a fancy guesthouse in Bangalow which cost £90 per night, the most expensive place I'd stayed all trip. But sod it, I just wanted to get dry. In the morning I tried to get value for money by eating about £30 worth of breakfast.

The next town along was Byron Bay, which was featured in the hilarious *The Inbetweeners 2* movie. That schoolboy humour is about my level, as you probably noticed. Also just nearby is Murwillumbah, where they film *I'm A Celebrity… Get Me Out Of Here!* I kept my eyes peeled in case my *Britain's Got Talent* ex-mates, Ant and Dec, popped out of the woods to offer me some dingo scrotum or emu anus, or whatever it is they eat on that show.

Speaking of deceased animals, I'd given up with my roadkill photo collection. It was a bit morbid after all, and I'd gotten bored with it. It was quite depressing seeing all the dead kangaroos, wallabies, kookaburras, wombats, deer, snakes, echidnas and koala bears. The only creatures I'd not seen splattered on the roads were

137

any of those effing magpies. They still attacked me most days as I cycled along and I would have been happy to see them all run over. Some of the persistent bastards smashed into my head three or four times each.

Meanwhile, I went across the border and into Queensland. The first sign I saw said there was a $44,000 fine for keeping a pet rabbit. Ann Summers in Southend High Street sell a lot of rabbits.

I found a cheap motel in Surfers Paradise. It wasn't a cyclist's paradise because it was pouring with rain again. It was a novel sight for me seeing all the racks and racks of second-hand surf boards for sale in Cash Converters, which is not something you would see in my local Essex branch of Cash Converters.

There was a 'domestic' in the motel corridor that evening. I heard screaming so went out to see if help was necessary. A man and a woman were raging at each other nose-to-nose. The woman was shouting that the man had hit their toddler. Someone else had phoned the police, who arrived a few minutes later.

Next morning the sun was out and I realised why the place was called Surfers Paradise. It was like California, but without all the homeless people living under the freeways pushing shopping carts.

I carried on to Brisbane and went through a suburb where a road sign proclaimed 'Welcome to Deception Bay, where lifestyle really counts'. It was one of those meaningless bland statements no doubt invented by the local estate agent. It would be more fun if the road sign said 'Welcome to Deception Bay, where deception really counts'. (I wished I had a big black marker pen on me!)

After a few more hours my left hamstring started to hurt, as did my right knee. I normally ignored aches and pains in one leg, compensating by making the other leg do more work. But pain in both legs was a problem, so I found a motel near Dicky Beach and rested up for the afternoon.

The motel had a trendy restaurant alongside called Fusion, which I thought I would investigate. They didn't really seem to have a theme or plan and served everything – fish, steak, pasta,

138

pizza, sushi, kebabs, salad, and curry. It might have been more appropriate to call the restaurant ConFusion.

Both legs improved after a good night's sleep, so it was back on the road for me. Near the town of Childers a truck zoomed past loaded with cars clearly destined for the scrapheap. However, not everything was going to the scrapheap – part of a car's bodywork fell off and hit me on the arm. I got a bruise, and a shock, but it could have been much worse if a whole car had fallen off.

I was going native there in Australia. The Aussies, in the countryside at least, get up very early. It was normal for people to go to work, and for shops and cafes to be open, at 5 or 6 in the morning. So I got into the habit of setting my alarm for 4.30. I had a *shit, shave and shampoo*, then got cycling as soon as the sun came up at 5.30.

Naturally I was picking up the lingo too. Dawn was 'sparrow's fart'. I greeted the friendly locals as they do with a "G'day mate." Anything good was 'ripper', but if I wasn't feeling well then I'm 'crook'. Cycling was hot work so I liked to go for a 'schooner' of 'amber nectar' in the 'arvo' at a local 'hotel'.

Australia had such wonderful place names too. The nation's capital, Canberra, means, appropriately enough, 'meeting place' in the local Aboriginal language. Around where I was in Queensland there was Moocoorooba, Sharon, Bens Knob, Seventeen Seventy and Goodnight Scrub.

I spent the night in the town of Gin Gin. The landlord of the pub where I was staying came from Glasgow, had been a semi-pro footballer and trained with Celtic as a kid. They had their own restaurant attached to the pub. As usual the food was outstanding. I had the best lasagne I'd ever had in my life, followed by a homemade Mars bar, which was nothing like a normal Mars bar, but because this was ten times better.

I used to think Italian food was the best in the world, apart from what my mother made, but I'd changed my mind. Now I had come to think Australian was the best, no doubt because they had taken the best culinary influences from all the different immigrants who had settled there.

Strolling around Gin Gin, and other Aussie towns, I noticed that they like to make their own entertainment (please excuse the cliché). For example, there was camel racing, a dump truck pull, frog racing, ride-on mower racing, a woodchop, sheep racing, drag racing, a tractor bash, a dingo trap throwing competition, and funniest of all, a leg waxing competition for men. Country living seemed like a riot.

Onwards north towards Rockhampton. Just before that came Mount Morgan, where, for a century, until 1981, there was a gold mine that produced 225 tonnes of gold. That seemed like a lot to me, an equivalent weight to one hundred Indian elephants, until I found out that 2700 tonnes are mined annually worldwide.

Amazingly, one ton of gold ore dug up in South Africa contains the same amount of gold as thirty-five old mobile phones, yet it is uneconomical to recover the gold from the phones.

In a spare moment I texted Sharon with some good news and some bad news. The good news was that I was not going to grow a moustache. I grew one for Movember two years before – Kevin thought I'd been slurping a cappuccino, Laura thought my nasal hair had grown out of control, the Sister at work said I looked like a paedophile, and Sharon simply hated it. All of that I found baffling, because when I looked in the mirror I saw a dashing RAF Squadron Leader.

Instead, I decided I was going to grow sideburns. Unfortunately Sharon would also consider that bad news because she liked me clean shaven. Hirsute does not suit her. I think sideburns can look good on a bloke, take Elvis, Jack Nicholson or Bradley Wiggins, as a for instance. However, I admit care is needed to keep them tidy. There was a supervisor at the post office in Romford who had massive sideburns. We often thought he was on the phone.

Enough of my waffle, let's get back to the biking. About once a week in Australia I bumped into another cyclist. There was Mad

French Eddy, then Brian from Wisconsin, Dave from Melbourne (Dave said camping was good for your back, but I figured that having a comfy bed is good for your sanity), Valentin from Switzerland, and, most interestingly, a couple of Aussie hippies left over from the 1960s. I found them in the shade of a tree eating seeds. They said they only cycled about 10 km per day, which I could do in half an hour. They had learnt to live on bush tucker and got odd jobs on farms as they travelled along. They seemed happy enough. Flower power lives, man! I also met Martin and Marian, a Dutch couple. Their friend Joanne had been killed two weeks before while cycling in Brazil. It was a tragedy, but I was not surprised – having experienced cycling in that country, I realised I was lucky to be alive.

Speaking of lucky, or unlucky maybe, as I approached Rockhampton someone threw a bottle out of their car window at me. It missed, but it could have caused a head injury, knocked me into the path of another vehicle, or gone into my front spokes causing me to fly over the handlebars. You would rightly surmise that I was not best pleased.

I had already noticed that the level of abuse shouted out at cyclists was greater in Queensland than anywhere else in the world that I have biked through. Some people even went to the trouble of winding down their window and making the wanker gesture. That was dedication to the cause, of being a twat.

I arrived in Rockhampton, or as the locals call it, Rocky. I've got a lot to tell you about this place, so strap yourself in, scream if you want to go faster, you could be in for a *rocky* ride.

Rocky was on the Tropic of Capricorn, which reminded me that the last time I crossed it was at Ubatuba in Brazil. This was cattle country and there was a real Wild West or Texan feel to the place. They had proper rodeos, like in the USA, where they pulled a tight painful strap around the bull's knackers to make them jump, then the cowboy had to hang on for eight seconds.

141

Rocky was quite a rough old place, by Australian standards, although even the unemployed get a detached council house. This was the Beef Capital of Australia. The main breed of cows there, chosen because they can survive the heat, are Indian Brahmans, you know, with the high shoulder blades and droopy ears. It's ironic that in India those cows are venerated as potential demi-gods, while in Australia they are venerated as potential meat pies.

I checked into a motel, then went off to explore. I went past the gun shops, cowboy clothing stores, and A Man's Toyshop (no it's not a Gay Love Emporium, oh, no, no, no, not here. Mind you, that would make the place more interesting), and soon I came to the Allenstown Hotel, ie the pub. Time for a nice cold beer. There was a band due to play at seven o'clock, so I thought I'd have a meal and hang about.

In the meantime, a local biker called Laurie introduced himself and we had a good old chinwag. During the evening Laurie introduced me to all the regular drinkers, bikers and cowboys. I was fascinated to learn that Laurie had met Billy Connolly in Rocky when Billy was filming his *World Tour of Australia*.

One of Laurie's mates was Paul, who had the brightest ginger hair I'd ever seen, basically Hi-Vis. Paul said Aussies like ironic humour, so many ginger people are known as Blue, although Paul hated being called that.

Paul was a Meteorologist and the government had sent him to Rocky five months before. Australia gets such devastating floods, droughts, cyclones and storms that weather forecasting can literally be a matter of life or death. It's much more serious than deciding whether to hang your smalls on the line or not.

As the evening progressed, and the band belted out some good standards, people naturally drank more and started loosening up. Laurie and I moved onto double whiskies and coke, something I wasn't used to, but 'When in Rome do as the Romans do'. Most of the people in there were a good bunch and we had a right old laugh.

142

Later in the evening one of the bikers pointed to his belt buckle – there was a white Southern Cross, which I got the impression meant something like the Aussie version of the KKK. After some more drinks he said their entertainment years ago had been beating up gays. He also told me "We fucking hate Muslims and niggers up here". It's strange that the people with the most obnoxious things to say always feel the need to say them the loudest. He 'qualified' his prejudices, as bigots often do, by saying "Don't get me wrong, I'm not a racist. I've got some good mates who are black fellas, although I wouldn't invite them round my house." Morons like him seem to think it's some sort of achievement to be born 'white', as if we get a choice.

Another man chipped in "We used to have a black fella at work, but he got the sack. He didn't get the sack because he was black, he got the sack because he was a cunt." If he was just a c*nt you may wonder why there was any need to mention his skin colour.

So, apart from a few idiots, which you can get anywhere, even in Southend, it was a good night in the Allenstown Hotel. Pubs in Australia often provide a free minibus home for the punters. About 9 o'clock the minibus came to collect one of our drinking buddies, Theresa, who was almost paralytic. As she walked outside she keeled over backwards like a sack of spuds, hitting her head on the road. As the back of her skull hit the tarmac it made a noise like hitting a melon with a mallet. The driver's medical assessment simply involved checking that her eyes were open. Then he picked her up, seemingly very familiar with this situation, bundled her into the van and drove her home. I took that as my cue to go home too, so said goodbye to Laurie, Paul and the sensible lads and took a zig-zag route along the pavement to my motel.

The alarm went off at 4.30 next morning, and unsurprisingly I was feeling a bit groggy. However, I couldn't let a little hangover get in the way of me conquering the world, so I got my act together and hit the road. The bird attacks started immediately – they

143

seemed to become more frequent and more vicious the further north I went.

On the way out of Rocky I stopped to get a sandwich for later in a petrol station. Petrol stations there sold an ethanol spray to help you get your car going on cold mornings – in typical Aussie style it was called *Start Ya Bastard*.

After about four hours cycling I pulled into a picnic area to eat my sandwich. There was a strong smell and I looked behind the benches and there was a large, steaming human turd. About 100 flies were knee-deep in it, chowing down and really enjoying themselves. That was enough of a prompt for me to jump on the bike and have my sandwich elsewhere.

Half an hour later I found a nice shady tree, with no shit under it, so I pulled over to eat my sandwich. I took off my cycle helmet and for the first time noticed the damage on it. The magpies had generally aimed to attack the highest point, where my helmet had tough plastic on top which was difficult for them to penetrate, but sometimes they attacked the side of my head. The sides of my cycle helmet were just coated polystyrene and there were about forty puncture holes and scratches caused by beaks and claws. I was so glad the damage was to the helmet and not my scalp.

Depending where the sun was shining from I could sometimes see the shadow of a magpie just before it dive-bombed into my head. If I tried to punch it with a free arm that seemed to rile it more, and it would become even more aggressive. The solution seemed to be to just pedal faster to get out of their territory. Unfortunately, as I left one territory I often entered another, so the next magpie would start to attack straight away, almost like they were running a tag-team. I was looking forward to getting to Townsville, partly because Juliet had arranged for me to stay with a friend of hers, Sandra, but also because another cyclist told me that the bird attacks cease north of that point because the climate becomes wetter.

144

If I remember rightly Steven Fry said "Everybody who comes to Australia loves it, none more so than the Australians themselves," and I agree with him, but for a variety of reasons I'd come to realise that Queensland was not my favourite state. I'd noticed that, unlike New South Wales and Victoria, they did not fly the Aborigine flag alongside the Australian flag outside public buildings. There had been domestics in motels, things falling off or being thrown from vehicles, shit in picnic areas, worse bird attacks, and some racist people with brains smaller than those of the birds. Maybe the hot temperatures in Queensland sent people a bit doolally.

Whatever.

I was off bright and early one morning when I saw my first live snake in the grass next to me. It was about a yard long and moving as fast as I could run. I didn't try to get a closer look because, as my mate Duncan recently reminded me, the top ten most deadly snakes in the world are all native to Australia. I also saw my first big spider, waiting for its breakfast in a large web. Even better, I saw my first live kangaroo. I was so happy. It made my day.

Kangaroos are my favourite wild animal, and probably have been since watching *Skippy* on TV as a kid. This one hopped across the road in front of me. It's funny how they bounce like Zebedee or Tigger. A truck was coming the other way. It blasted its horn, so the kangaroo turned around and hopped back in front of me again. I wanted to get my camera out, but it was all over in a few seconds and soon the kangaroo disappeared into the long dry grass which was the same colour as its fur.

That stretch of road going north from Rocky had hundreds and hundreds of kangaroos splattered on it, from great big ones down to little joeys. However, as the days went by I started to see one or two live ones each day.

In Australia there are more kangaroos (30 million) than people (24 million) and the kangaroos are treated as pests, but I was still sad when I saw a dead one. I also saw an injured eagle flapping about helplessly on the ground. That would be lunch for a dingo.

I stayed in a room attached to a traditional rural pub in Marlborough. It was very basic, mainly used by migrant farm workers, and only cost $18 (about £9) including breakfast. The locals were very friendly. The walls in the bar were covered with people's names and witty comments. I asked the landlord for a marker pen and wrote my name and date and the only proper poem I know, Spike Milligan's ode that begins... *"There was a young man called Ghandi, Who went to the pub for a shandy..."*

*

The Australian Roads Authority had some great ideas. Motorists falling asleep was an issue they took seriously, and at regular intervals they provided 'Driver Reviver' cafes with free tea, coffee, squash and biscuits, day and night. They also had trivia questions on road signs, which gave a few kilometres to think about it, then provided the answer. Other road signs can be quite hard-hitting, for example, one read *Rest or RIP*.

Christine Sexton from the *Southend Echo* phoned me. She asked dozens of questions and said she would put an article in the paper. I hoped she did, because I knew Sharon, Kevin and Laura were struggling at home, and a positive article in the newspaper might help them cope.

I was staying in the Rover Motel in Mackay that night. I mentioned to the owner that somebody had thrown a bottle at me the previous week. She said she felt ashamed, and apologised on behalf of the whole of Australia. She said "Help yourself to a free drink from the fridge." I thanked her, and I was "not backwards in coming forwards" as the Aussies say.

This whole area around Mackay, which was I guestimate about the size of Ireland, was dominated by sugar cane production. Criss-crossing the region were hundreds of miles of private narrow-gauge railways. Small railways in England only really exist

146

as a hobby for steam railway buffs, or for day-trippers to take a sedate tour around the grounds of stately homes, such as Audley End House in Essex. In Australia narrow-gauge railways were used for the very twenty-first century practical reason of moving thousands of tons of sugar cane to the factories. Australians are sensible like that, investing in rail transport. When I grow up I want to be a train driver.

After another hot day's cycling I felt I'd earned a few cold drinks. I checked my watch and it was beer o'clock, so I strolled down to O'Dunns Irish bar in Proserpine and listened to IRA rebel songs until they closed at 9pm. Later, as I was walking down the middle of the deserted Main Street, I found the Central Hotel bar was still serving. The only other customers in there were three generations of a large Aboriginal family playing pool. We took turns to put songs on the jukebox. They put on reggae and I put on punk, and everybody was happy. The pub had a raffle every Saturday evening. The prize was 1kg of prawns.

Townsville, thank goodness. I called in to stay with Juliet's friend, Sandra. She used to be a model, then a nurse, in Sydney, which is where Juliet met her. She kindly gave me a tour of Townsville and pointed out Magnetic Island off the coast, where Captain Cook's compass went haywire, hence the name.

Sandra told me she had previously stood as a candidate for the Liberal Party (equivalent to the British Conservative Party) and she had been told by HQ to bluff, blag or evade any questions to do with policy, because they didn't have any, except to get into power. It seemed very reminiscent of when Groucho Marx said "Those are my principles, and if you don't like them ... well, I have others." In the evening we went to an expensive restaurant and ate crocodile which was delicious and tasted halfway between chicken and squid.

After breakfast at Sandra's house I hit the road. North of Townsville Australia changed from dry scrubland to a wet and tropical environment. The magpies didn't like the wetter climate

147

so I didn't get a bird attack all day, which was a relief. I was hit by a stone as a truck roared past though. Luckily it only caused a scratch on my face.

In the late morning Robinson Crusoe came cycling up towards me. Well, he looked like a castaway. Actually his name was Frederick and he was a 70-year old Belgian vegetarian who was cycling all over Australia. He normally chose the most remote tracks in the Outback and once he didn't see another human being for eleven days. Fred said that three times motorists had thrown things at him while cycling in Australia. When I met him he was heading towards some sort of hippy commune near Byron Bay. He was a very cheerful fellow, probably due to all that Free Love, although he really did look like Robinson Crusoe on a bike.

Only 150 miles remained to Cairns, which was two nice easy days' riding. I pulled into one of the Driver Reviver cafes in Ingham for free tea and got talking to Darren. He said crocodiles lurked in the nearby creeks, and strongly advised not to go into any water or camp near a river. Every few years they had big floods and the crocodiles swam right up the High Street in Ingham and would try to eat your dog, or you. (My Dad's friend was eaten by a crocodile in Burma during the war).

There was hardly any traffic that day because the new Prime Minister had just declared it a public holiday for the AFL Cup Final. Australia also has a public holiday for the Melbourne Cup horse race. Do you think we should have a public holiday in Britain for the FA Cup Final? What about a day off for the Welsh Bog-Snorkelling Championships?

Most of Australia had been bone-dry scrubland but when I arrived in Cairns it is tropical rainforest, like Brazil. There were thousands of backpackers there, mostly English and German. I would like to have gone sub-aqua diving on the Great Barrier Reef, but the weather was too stormy.

I needed to get a few jobs done on my bike so I took it to a nearby cycle shop. The manager spent the first ten minutes lecturing me where I'd gone wrong, and that I'd got the wrong equipment, self-righteously missing the obvious fact that I was the one who had already successfully cycled two-thirds of the way around the world, not him.

My time in Australia was coming to an end. The forests, mountains, coast and countryside had filled my lungs with lovely fresh air and made me happy to be alive. The Aussies were nearly all friendly, polite and enjoyed having a laugh. As Barbara from the TV show *The Royle Family* said "Well, I don't care what anybody is - I don't care whether they're gay, straight or Australian. It's what they're like as a person that matters." Fair dinkum, cobber.

15 – Indonesia

Hot town, summer in the city
Back of my neck getting dirty and gritty

'Summer in the City'
The Lovin' Spoonfull

Cairns to Bali was one small step for a plane and one giant leap into the Third World. The airport at Denpasar, Bali was stylish and clean, but when I got outside there was rubbish and dirt everywhere. You can't drink the tap water, of course, unless you fancy an exotic disease. I'd been told to avoid the dogs at all costs because they have rabies. The rivers, I noticed, apart from being full of garbage, had that fine aroma of human faeces. I passed graveyards where people just fly-tip their piles of stinking trash. That is wrong on every level. I have no idea why anyone would want to come to Indonesia for a holiday, although changing £200 and getting four million rupiah was a pretty nice feeling. I'd never been a millionaire before.

Tall buildings were constructed using rickety bamboo scaffolding with swarms of blokes climbing up wearing flip-flops in clouds of concrete dust. Bricks and wood kept falling off. Hard hats? Don't be silly. Jeremy Clarkson likes to rant and rave against Health and Safety from the comfort of his luxury home in Chipping Norton, but he would consider it more important if he had to live and die like those poor buggers.

Indonesia is the fourth most populous country in the world (after China, India and the USA) and has more Muslims than any other nation. The Indonesian flag is the same as the Polish flag, but one of them is upside down. Barack Obama's mum married an Indonesian man, so Barack went to school there for four years.

He went back to visit in 2010 as President of the United States of America. Now that is what I call a High Achiever! And he's one year younger than me, the bastard.

My friend Alberto had gone to Indonesia the month before and texted me a list of things to do – go to the Bromo Volcano, visit Borobudur Temple and go snorkelling with turtles. However, it was a big country and I had my work cut out just cycling across it. I had left some emergency money with Kevin and Laura before I left home and they had decided to use it to meet me in Singapore in two weeks. I couldn't be late for that.

It was extremely hot and sweaty. I forced myself to drink gallons, but hardly ever peed. The sweat rolled down my arms, onto the handlebars, then left drips all along the road, a bit like a wet version of the *Hansel and Gretel* story.

Hardly anyone spoke English, and for a while I only knew one word of Indonesian - "Selamat", which I thought meant "thank you." It took me a week to discover that I should have been saying "Terima Kasih."

People shouted "Hello Mister!" at least one hundred times a day. I smiled and shouted back "Hello", but that could get a bit wearisome by the ninety-ninth time. In fact, some days it got wearisome after the first time.

I went into a shop for a cold drink and said "Selamat." The man replied "Gracias," which I thought was cute. Someone else shouted out "Have a nice day, Papa!" I realised my grey hair was unusual in Indonesia. The locals all had black hair, which must either have been due to good hair-genes or because they didn't live long enough to go grey. (It occurred to me later that maybe that man called me Papa because he spoke Maori and thought I was an arse.)

Sometimes men came up and asked me for cigarettes, which seemed to be a euphemism for money. Other times adults pointed me out to their children or stood in front of me to take my photo, like I was some sort of freak. I suppose to them I was just Johnny Foreigner.

151

The traffic was mind-boggling. I'd seen on Wikipedia that they drive on the left in Indonesia. What I didn't realise was that meant they go in both directions on the left as well as both directions on the right. It would be perfectly feasible, and an interesting *Top Gear*-style challenge, to cycle from one end of Indonesia to the other on the wrong side of the road. Nobody would mind, or even notice.

There were literally millions of mopeds zooming all over the place, as if the riders had a death wish. They carried loads which were suspension-crushing and gravity-defying. I saw people riding with live chickens in their coats, a live sheep riding pillion, several people with sniper rifles, but most startling was a man riding his moped while balancing a double bed. Whole families squeezed onto a single moped - Mum bottle-feeding baby while Dad weaved at top speed, like a boy racer, between cars, trucks and buses over the bumpy carriageway. Small children hung on as best they could, and if they were lucky they would be wearing one of those pretend crash helmets that you can buy at Toys R Us.

I got forced off the road several times every day. Overtaking, oncoming cars or trucks drive straight at me and I just had to get onto the grass on the left quick. I didn't take it personally, because I saw it happen to plenty of other people too.

After studying the traffic for eight or more hours every day I concluded that there were no rules of the road. Zero. Nada. Zilch. Anybody of any age drives anything. Number plates are only decorative. The mosques set up their own roadblocks, stopping the traffic to get donations. We worry about emissions in the West, but what is the point if all the vehicles in Indonesia are pumping out thick black smoke? Some vehicles were homemade out of angle-iron with an old engine strapped on. It seemed like absolute mayhem, but strangely they got by, and I only saw two crashes. Nobody gave way, or obeyed any road sign. Because nobody obeyed traffic lights men or boys stood in the road to stop the traffic so cars from side roads could join the main carriageway. For this death-defying service they expected a modest tip. What a desperate job.

They used the horn a lot in Indonesia. That got on my nerves at first, but after a while I didn't mind getting a little *beep beep* warning that a moped, car or truck was approaching. That, in fact, is the correct use of the horn as defined in *The Highway Code*, ie to warn other road-users of your presence. In England, using the horn is usually the same as asking "Do you want a fight?"

After a few days I was dodging and weaving with the best of them. One day I was up and out at five o'clock in the morning to get the car ferry from Bali to Java. It was about ten miles across and cost about 20p. I noticed another ferry, carrying trucks, crossing parallel to us, with its bow doors open. That was how the *Herald of Free Enterprise* capsized in 1987 on its way to Dover, drowning 193 people.

Anyway, after leaving the car ferry I passed through some towns and farming areas then the road went through a national park jungle for about ten miles, where two effing arseholes tried to mug me. Being a national park there were no houses and hardly any traffic. A moped rider came from the other direction, passed me, did a U-turn and started following me. As I was cycling along he came up by my right shoulder and started jabbering away and making hand signals saying he wanted food, cigarettes and money. I made a quick mental reminder where my Maglite was which I kept ready for rapid use. He made a big show of reaching into his pocket for something such as a weapon, but I didn't actually see what he had because he was riding slightly behind my right shoulder. Then he dropped back about ten feet and kept shouting "One dollar – No problem" and a lot of stuff in Indonesian which of course I couldn't understand.

After about five minutes of this a mate of his arrived from the other direction and also did a U-turn, so now both were following me while they conferred with each other. Then his mate overtook me, so I had one of the bastards in front and one behind. Arsehole

153

Number One started shouting at me again from behind. I think they hoped I would wimp out and give them some money. That is not my style. I'm quite a big bloke by Indonesian standards which went in my favour, but two against one could have been dicey, depending whether they had knives or guns.

I was acutely conscious of the fact that I was a long way from home alone in the jungle with two malcontents. I said to myself "Besly, you could be in shit here". My plan was simple. Any sign that they were going to try to kick me off the bike, or to draw a weapon, and I would not wait to defend myself. I would drop my bike in the middle of the road (so if any traffic passed I might hopefully get some assistance) whip out the Maglite and attack them both as hard and fast as I could. I would aim for their kneecaps. One blow from that Maglite might cripple them for life, but that would be their problem. If they played with fire they risked getting burnt. After a few more minutes Number One, who was behind me, overtook to join matey-boy ahead, and then the two of them sped up and pulled into a layby about a hundred metres further on. They both got off.

I thought "Here we go, get ready." It crossed my mind to turn around and go back to the previous town, but I thought I would front it out. As luck would have it, as I approached them a bit of traffic also appeared, which, I presume, put them off apart from shouting at me as I passed. Another half mile further on there were some park rangers, as well as some motorists who had stopped to feed the wild monkeys. Soon after that was a town where I found somewhere to stay and I breathed a sigh of relief.

In the morning I was up and off at dawn. In the next village I passed through a man pointed at me then drew his finger across his throat. Charming. Perhaps he was a buddy of those two I had come across in the jungle the day before. Alberto came to Indonesia and saw all the highlights. I'd come and met all the lowlifes.

I pressed on and had a good day's cycling, then in the evening found a hotel at Besuki. A sign in reception said no unmarried couples were allowed to stay. It seemed like a religious place and had its own mosque attached. The mosque had a big grand entrance in the front for the men and a poky little second-class door down the side for the women. The hotel was quite new but I still had to share my room with lizards, mosquitos and cockroaches. On the ceiling, in the bedroom, was a green arrow pointing towards Mecca (not the bingo hall, the other one).

The hotels were cheap, usually about £10 per night including breakfast. No toilet paper of course, I had to use my left hand to wipe. Sometimes there was long hair in the beds, which led me to think they didn't always change the sheets. I did laugh in one hotel where the bed looked smart and fresh though the blanket on top was a bit grubby. "Never mind" I thought "the top-sheet will protect me from the blanket." However, when I went to turn back the covers the top-sheet was only about a foot wide, folded over the edge of the blanket near the pillow to give the appearance of being a full sheet!

As usual the *muezzin* woke me up at 4am blasting out his favourite Top Ten album hits. This could be where the Church of England, with its declining attendances, is going wrong. The C of E should wake everybody up at four in the morning for a jihad, or at least for a stoning of somebody the Vicar of Dibley has had a tiff with.

Apart from "Hello Mister!" the only English the citizens of Indonesia seemed to know was "Where are you from?" For the first few days I replied "England" but nobody seemed to understand, they just smiled. To amuse myself I started saying Canada or Ireland, then I jazzed it up a bit, saying I was from Vladivostok or Jerusalem or Milton Keynes or Jamaica. It made no difference, the people just smiled back. I decided that the next person who shouted "Where are you from?" was going to be told

"The Hamburg Red Light District!" (porn is illegal in Indonesia) and smile.

Another little bit of fun I liked to have as I cycled along was to give a big flamboyant wave and shout "Hello Ladies!" to the groups of shy girls waiting for the bus in their headscarfs and immaculate school uniforms. Sometimes they giggled, sometimes they look petrified. I had a little scoring system – two points for giggles, one point for petrified, and *nul point* for being blanked.

Indonesia has a big population and a high birth rate, but I was still surprised to see large lorries carrying *Semen*. There are even big *Semen* factories, which I guessed must be massive sperm banks. I guessed wrong, of course. It turned out that *Semen* was the Indonesian word for cement. There were quite a few Indonesian words vaguely recognisable in English. For example, if you suddenly felt the need to say "Successful English karaoke export business" in Indonesian, it would be "Sukses Inggris Singgalang ekspor bisnis."

Enough of this tittle-tattle. Back to the story. One day I rode 160 km in the lovely company of two cyclists called Mahmood and Johani. It was interesting and fun to chat about football, music, and bikes, and to try to find Johani a wife. Among other questions they asked if I was Christian or Jewish and were slightly baffled but thought it was hilarious when I said I had "Zero religion." (We can joke about it but there are severe punishments, up to and including the death penalty, for being an atheist in 13 countries - Afghanistan, Iran, Malaysia, Maldives, Mauritania, Nigeria, Pakistan, Qatar, Saudi Arabia, Somalia, Sudan, United Arab Emirates and Yemen.)

We stopped at a restaurant for lunch and had chicken soup. I was wondering what bit of the chicken I had until I realised it was the face, complete with eye socket. Suitably refuelled, the three of us got back on the road. As the trip went on, recognising that life is short, I began losing some of my inhibitions. (Kevin said to me afterwards "Oh no, you didn't get your cock out did you?")

156

Anyway, after lunch as we pedalled through a village we were talking about The Rolling Stones and I just burst into song as loud as I could, waving my arms while cycling no-handed, doing my best Mick Jagger impersonation.

"I can't get no satisfaction
I can't get no good reaction

...
Oh, no, no, no."

It was quite a showstopper, even if I say so myself. All the village folk were staring, and Mahmood and Johani laughed their heads off. 160 km flashed by in their company.

Next day as I rode out of Kudus the road ran parallel to a water channel which was about twelve feet wide. The water was absolutely putrid and stinking with a dirty scum on the surface and rotting trash fly-tipped all along the banks, or just thrown in. A factory was discharging some black greasy gunk into the water channel further along. There was nothing surprising so far because this was Indonesia. What shocked me was a man standing in the middle of the revolting water channel, nearly up to his chest, fishing. He was using a system of nets trying to catch fish or eels, but I think he was more likely to catch cholera or typhus. Can you imagine eating the creatures he caught from that water? I bet Robson Green hadn't got the balls to do that type of *Extreme Fishing*, but if he did whatever was in that water would have destroyed his balls anyway.

The next town was Kendal, which made me wish I was in the English Lake District. Alongside the road, with its fumes, heat and honking horns was a construction site. In front of the site, just near the road, was a pile of builders' sand about five feet high. Reclining gracefully on the top of the sand was an elderly lady, completely naked apart from a headband, who reminded me of *Hiawatha*. Perhaps in her mind she thought she was relaxing on one

157

of the upmarket nudist beaches in the South of France, rather than beside a deafening, smoky, dirty, sweaty road in Java. I can't say I enjoyed Indonesia, but there were some unusual sights.

I was averaging well over 120 km every day and hoped to be in Jakarta a day or two early to relax. I've already mentioned the hot, sweaty cycling conditions. That morning I'd been pedalling for about four hours and the sweat was rolling off me as per usual. The sun was beating down at 37 degrees. Noisy trucks, buses and mopeds were roaring past belching out thick black smoke. The road surfaces were bone shaking. People were shouting "Hello Mister!" as always. My hands and the handlebars were hot and soaking from the sweat so it was difficult to keep grip. I had one lapse of concentration over the bumpy road and my left hand slipped off. My weight went forward on my right hand, the front wheel went sideways, and BANG, I was down.

Crash number three.

Immediately I had to get myself and my bike off to the side before we were both run over. Normally I carried plenty of water with me, but Sod's Law now applied, and I only had a few drops to wash the grazes. Therefore I decided to check into the next hotel I saw to clean the cuts properly. Fortunately, there was a hotel just a few kilometres further on.

The grazes were not too bad, but the swellings on my right elbow and right hip were spectacular. My elbow had developed a swollen lump the size of an orange and the end of the ulna didn't feel the correct shape. My hip had a bruise like I'd got a soup bowl down the side of my pants. These dramatic swellings might have been because I take a daily aspirin, and bleed easily. In the afternoon I felt really dizzy (known in the trade as a vasovagal episode) when I stood up and I had to hold on to something before I fainted. There were a few more war wounds on the bike too, and my shorts needed some sewing repairs. I began thinking I wouldn't be in Jakarta as soon as I'd planned.

That evening I forced myself to drink several litres of fluids, had a good night's sleep, and in the morning felt just fit enough to tackle the last 150 km to Jakarta. Jakarta has over ten million people, and when Indonesia was a Dutch colony was known as Batavia, which I think is a much nicer name. New York's nickname is the Big Apple, and the nickname of Jakarta is the Big Durian. Durian is also known as Heaven and Hell fruit, because it tastes like heaven, but smells like hell. I was tempted to make a smartass comment about Jakarta being hell, but actually it was the cleanest and nicest place I'd been in all of Indonesia (these things are relative). I suppose I was so happy to have arrived, with that leg of the cycling trip over, that it put me in a good mood. In reality, I hated almost every minute I was in Indonesia. The only enjoyable time was the day I spent cycling with Mahmood and Johani. I thought that if the rest of South East Asia was as unpleasant as this country then the only Orient I would want to visit in future would be in Leyton.

It was as cheap as chips to fly across the Straits of Malacca from Jakarta to Singapore. Kevin and Laura had already arrived there, and I couldn't wait to meet them. Singapore was not a Muslim country, so the first items on the agenda would be a ham sandwich and a cold beer. Line 'em up Kev!

16 – Singapore

...I no longer shop happily
I came in for a special offer
A guaranteed personality

'Lost in the Supermarket'
The Clash

OMG – what a leap from Third World Indonesia to First World Singapore. Kevin and Laura met me at the airport and they'd booked a five-star hotel. The streets were knee deep in Lamborghinis and Ferraris. We went window shopping at Rolex, Cartier, Hugo Boss (who made uniforms for the Nazis), Prada and Herpes (sorry, Hermes). At home we are not restricted to going window shopping at Primark and Aldi, because we can walk in and buy anything.

All the people in Singapore were good looking and immaculately dressed. As we strolled around I thought out loud "It seems to be the law that only beautiful people can live in Singapore".

Kevin looked me up and down and remarked "Well, you're fucked then."

I thought I'd better try and smarten myself up so I went for a Ten Minute Haircut. That is how they do it – not nine minutes or eleven, but ten.

Over the next few days we toured all the usual sights and were dazzled by the high standard of living and displays of wealth. Singapore has the third highest standard of living in the world (1st – Qatar, 2nd – Luxembourg, 27th – UK). However, the highlight for us was spotting the Meow Cat Café. Laura loves cats so she was in heaven as we spent an afternoon feeding and playing with them.

Singapore's food was world class. They had anything and everything. We saw pig organ soup, but gave that a miss. I had Mac & Cheeks one evening which was macaroni with beef cheeks (presumably from the face, not the butt).

Since 1845 the main newspaper in Singapore had been *The Straits Times*, which was not the sister paper of *Gay Times*. The story dominating the news was about the 'pastor' of the Singaporean City Harvest Church, who had embezzled $50 million from church funds. Thou Shalt Not Steal? Yeah, when it suits. Anyway, the true God of Singapore was consumerism, and lots of it.

Singapore was British from 1819 until 1963, apart from the Japanese occupation between 1942-45. Then 85,000 British troops surrendered to 36,000 Japanese, which Churchill described as the "Worst disaster and largest capitulation" in British military history.

A New Zealander, Patrick Heenan, was shot for radioing information about British troop movements to the Japanese. During the first month of the occupation the Japanese employed the British army to keep order and prevent looting. Then they chucked them into Changi POW camp and starved or beat them to death. In-between times, the Japanese army got on with their main business of slaughtering as many Chinese people as they could.

Singapore was part of Malaysia for two years, but the religious loonies in Kuala Lumpur said the Muslim Malays should get preferential treatment. The local governor of Singapore, Lee Kuan Yew, disagreed, saying all people should be treated equally. Good on yer, geezer! Consequently, Singapore was expelled from Malaysia, and became an independent nation in 1965.

Since Independence the People's Action Party had continuously ruled Singapore, almost like a benevolent dictatorship. The current Prime Minister was the son of the previous Prime Minister. There was negligible unemployment or homelessness. The country is very prosperous and everybody was happy so long as you agreed with the government. Otherwise they kill you (a slight exaggeration).

Actually, Singapore does have one of the highest rates of capital punishment in the world, for all sorts of things including rape, murder, treason, mutiny, piracy, gun crime, drug trafficking and assisting suicide. One third of those executed are foreigners. They use 'long drop' hanging, which has been the favoured method since British colonial days. Darshan Singh, the Chief Executioner, has hung over 850 people. Executions always take place on a Friday at dawn (that would definitely ruin your weekend), once totalling 18 on one single day. That must have seemed like a proper production line. Broadly speaking with legal systems around the world, it is generally recognised that about ten per cent of those convicted are not guilty, so Darshan has hung about 85 innocent people.

In Singapore there are fines of thousands of dollars for lesser crimes such as vandalism, littering, spitting, or not flushing the toilet. That was kind of ironic because in my part of Essex those are some of the ingredients for a good night out.

On a more cheerful note, Kevin, Laura and myself made the most of our time in Singapore. We were the only ones in the swimming pool, so broke all the normal rules. We sampled the electric soup (beer) at various hostelries, and, of course, had Singapore Slings in the Raffles Hotel. Kevin and Laura ripped the piss out of my sideburns, so clearly they had a lot to learn about fashion. They were quite stunned by the bruises from my last bike crash, and took photos.

Time goes quickly when you are having fun. After four days in Singapore Kevin and Laura had to fly home. I think they were extra pleased to visit because their mum was born there. It had been great seeing them. Short but sweet.

162

17 – Malaysia

This is the time
The time for action
... The time to be seen

'Time for Action'
Secret Affair

Warm, clean and modern. No, I'm not talking about me, I'm talking about Malaysia. Excellent roads with a nice hard shoulder. Clean water in the taps and rivers. Hardly any litter. Well-maintained towns and villages. The standard of living seemed about the same as England. Friendly people, many of whom spoke English, and not a single bastard shouted "Hello Mister!" I couldn't help think that Malaysia was what Indonesia would be like if the Indonesians respected each other a bit more and didn't throw their trash everywhere.

Malaysia had the death penalty by hanging, the same as Singapore. I read in *The Darwin Awards* that one of the assistant executioners wanted a photo of himself with his head in the noose. Unfortunately, the trap-door fell open, and the noose did what it was designed to do.

Malaysian Airlines has had a lot of bad news recently. In 2014 one of their planes mysteriously vanished while heading north to China and wreckage was found south in the Indian Ocean. There were no survivors. In the same year another Malaysian Airlines plane was shot down over the Ukraine by Russian separatists. Again there were no survivors. A few years ago Malaysian Airlines was in trouble for persistently jumping the landing queue at

163

Heathrow by having the pilot claim to be low on fuel. Everyone survived, but it was a classic case of 'crying wolf'.

The bruise on my right hip from the crash in Indonesia was still about the size of half a grapefruit. It looked like my hip was pregnant. It was very tender and I couldn't sleep on that side. Wearing my tight Lycra cycling shorts looked a bit weird, like I'd got a sort of sideways hard-on. My swollen elbow was now down to about the size of a plum, but was still painful and bruised. The bone did not feel the same shape as my good elbow, so I wondered if maybe I'd chipped something.

In New Zealand road signs warned of seals; in Australia they warned of kangaroos; in Malaysia the road signs warned me about elephants. I knew there were wild tigers in the Malay jungle as well. (Although there are more privately-owned tigers in Texas than there are wild in the entire world). Cycling is almost silent so I could hear all sorts of mysterious animal, bird and insect noises coming from the thick forest. Sometimes there were the crashing sounds of breaking branches, which was probably the monkeys swinging about, but for all I knew might have been elephants or tigers, or maybe the last Japanese soldiers from WW2. (I'd seen some of the WW2 British pillboxes beside the roads, some shell-damaged).

For the previous month there had been a haze over Malaysia due to Indonesian pollution which has drifted over. Singapore was also under the haze, but we hadn't really noticed because we were in air conditioned rooms for much of the time. The haze meant I couldn't see the sun, but the heat became even more sweltering, and it caused breathing difficulties to vulnerable people. The government was drawing up plans to evacuate children to less polluted areas. However, I had to pedal on, haze or no haze.

That morning the sweat was pouring off me like a river. I was near the equator, after all. I'd done some serious sweating in Spain, Brazil and Australia but this was in another league. I was drenched and salt was caked on me from my forehead to my foreskin. This foreshadowed a forbidding feeling of foreboding and a future forecast of further ferment. (OK Besly, that's enough f's). I had always, until that moment, worn sunglasses as protection against branches, gravel and insects, but I couldn't wear them now because the air was so hot and humid that they steamed up and I couldn't see eff-all (I knew I'd missed one).

For the first 100 km or so that day I couldn't find an ATM that would accept my card, so I had no food and my water was running low. To make matters worse, Malaysia was proving to be a very hilly country. From space it must have looked like corrugated iron or egg cartons, which made cycling very hard work. So there I was – hot, hungry, exhausted, dehydrated and the haze seemed to make breathing more difficult.

Previously I have played down how tough cycling RTW can be, describing the actual cycling as the easy bit. Of course that was not the whole truth, because cycling 80-100 miles every day was bloody hard work. Now, as I was pedalling through the Malaysian jungle, worn out, I started to get cramps in my legs and hands. I felt wobbly, dizzy and nauseous. I got off the bike, before I fell off, and realised I couldn't stand up. I sat on the grass next to the road, but even then I felt I had to lie down.

Lying down, ants immediately stated swarming all over me and biting, but I didn't have the energy to do much about that. Just by chance I had stopped near a logging/timber yard, and one of the workers came out to help me. His name was Murti and he phoned for an ambulance, but they wouldn't come, I don't know why. So Murti phoned for a taxi, which soon arrived.

There was a hospital in the next town, Mersing, twenty kilometres further on. I just took my passport and money and asked Murti to look after my bike. The taxi driver bundled me into the front seat and off we roared. I was in quite a bad way, on the brink of collapse.

With a screech of brakes, we arrived at Mersing Hospital. The A&E department only had five beds, and I was the only patient.

After a saline drip, some drugs and a couple of hours' rest on the trolley I felt much better. The doctor said I was suffering from the heat and exhaustion. I had to pay 65 ringgit (about £10), and she said I could go home (England? I wondered).

I wouldn't criticise the hospital in Mersing because it clearly operated on a very modest budget (well, 65 ringgit, to be precise!) in a small town in the middle of the jungle. But seeing it made me realise how superb our NHS was.

There was a hotel opposite Mersing Hospital so I spent the night there, making sure I had a good meal in a nearby restaurant before bed. It was kind of funny that, in such a conservative Muslim country, the restaurant waiter was a full-on transvestite. Nobody seemed to mind, least of all me.

In the morning I got a taxi back to the logging yard. The driver picked his nose continuously all the way. The wonderful Murti was there and he had kept my bike safe, as well as possibly saving my life. He wouldn't accept any money for his phone calls or the inconvenience, so I just hoped one day somebody else would do him the kindness that he deserved.

I decided to have a rest day in a cheap hotel (with cheap food exposed to the flies). The day after, I was off pedalling at dawn as usual. Within half an hour my tummy started to feel a bit dodgy. I told myself "Besly, don't fart!" just in case. A few more miles further on and I could hold it no longer, and I had to dash into the jungle where the world fell out of my arse. There was a mini-mountain of poo looking like yellow porridge, and immediately a dozen flies jumped in for a paddle thinking all their birthdays had come at once, although that is probably more information than you need. Over the next hour or so I had several more dashes to the jungle, so bang goes the neighbourhood! Then I started to feel much better. Dumping that lot was a huge weight off my mind and, to be honest, a huge weight out of my bottom.

I called into a garage later that afternoon for a cold drink, and the cashier, commenting on my cycling trip, said "Don't you mind

166

being alone?" I thought that having shit flying out of your arse every five minutes is definitely not something you want to share with friends.

In the previous two weeks I'd dealt with armed muggers, a spectacular crash, explosive diarrhoea and been admitted to hospital with exhaustion. Who knew what excitement the next few weeks would bring – maybe I'd get struck by lightning or abducted by aliens. Let the good times roll, baby!

Anyway, back to the cycling. Daily in Malaysia, and before it in Indonesia, I was stunned by the lack of interest parents showed in the safety of their children. Toddlers were just perched onto mopeds and expected to hang on as mum or dad rode around at top speed over bumpy, dangerous roads. For example, I saw a man riding fast, one-handed on a wet, muddy road, with plenty of other traffic zooming about, while holding a baby under his arm. What did he think would happen if he skidded, hit a pothole or had to make an emergency stop? He didn't even pay attention to the road, but rubber-necked to stare at me. This lack of concern for the welfare and lives of their own children was something I saw a hundred times per day, and I found it very unsettling. I suspected it was probably the same in all the other Asian countries, but although it bothered me a lot, I won't mention it again.

There had been several days of torrential rain. Snorkel and flippers might be an easier form of transport than a bike. I texted my friend Greg at Southend Hospital and asked him to save me a bed because I might be in with trench foot.

I'd nearly reached the northern-most point of Malaysia. The hotel I'd stayed the night before provided an unusual breakfast. They served spag bol, which may sound odd, but was perfect cycling fuel, so I had two platefuls.

I was due to cross into Thailand the next day. Sharon had said watch out for the ladyboys! They didn't even use the Roman alphabet in Thailand, so god only knew how I was going to work out the road signs. If I asked any ladyboys for directions and they said "I'll show you the way" or "Come with me" I wasn't too sure how to respond. I'd heard some of the girls in Thai bars had an unusual way to play ping-pong.

Anyway, my last evening in Malaysia. My initial impression had been Warm, Clean and Modern, and so it proved to be. One odd thing I noticed was that they docked the tails of all the cats, which seemed unnecessary and pointlessly cruel, a bit like circumcision. I wondered if the Imam did both jobs. If so, he was a busy boy.

Before crossing the border, I want to say thanks one more time to Murti. I hope your wood yard prospers, and you are a millionaire by Christmas. *Terima kasih.*

18 – Thailand

Won't you help me sing
These songs of freedom?

'Redemption Song'
Bob Marley

Coming over the border from Malaysia the first thing I noticed about Thailand was that the army was everywhere. They had had a military dictatorship since a coup the previous year. The military bosses had given themselves the cuddly title of The National Council for Peace and Order and promptly abolished free speech, a free press, political protest, democracy and any other niceties of freedom that we regard as inalienable human rights.

People had been arrested for holding up three fingers, a reference to the gesture of silent defiance in *The Hunger Games* films. Wearing a T-shirt referring to Orwell's *Nineteen Eighty-Four* or displaying the words 'Respect my Vote' or 'Peace Please' had resulted in arrest. Someone giving out 'Sandwiches For Democracy' was chucked in prison for 'Possessing sandwiches with ill intent' (no pun intended, presumably). A student playing *La Marseillaise* was arrested, the French national anthem being considered too evocative of liberty, equality and fraternity. If five or more people gathered together they could be arrested as an illegal assembly. The pettiness of the dictatorship knew no bounds – a man was arrested for holding up a paper with the words 'Holding up a paper is not a crime'. Some people who posted comments on social media critical of the regime were sentenced to thirty years in prison. I could have been in trouble if the cops found me writing about these things in my diary.

169

There were roadblocks every mile or two, with loads of strutting soldiers with assault rifles, heavy machine guns and armoured vehicles. Have you ever carried a serious gun? It feels *good*, better than taking drugs. Suddenly you are transformed from being a weedy loser who has difficulty making friends into a badass Clint Eastwood or an even badder-ass Tupac – Mean, Moody and Magnificent. (Actually Tupac was shot in the balls, so it's probably more accurate to call him Onepac). My mum was right – "Take the toys from the boys." It was slightly ridiculous seeing the soldiers in their new camouflage uniforms (the better for hiding) stopping traffic while wearing a hi-vis vest on top (the better to be seen).

After the coup in Thailand all the countries in Europe and North and South America, plus China, Japan, Australia and others all condemned the military takeover. Only Vietnam sent messages of support, the weirdos.

The military top brass now, of course, controlled the national budget. Who were they going to spend the money on first? Themselves! People in those positions always develop an inflated view of their own importance. In a dictatorship there is no open accountability, so the door is wide open for corruption. Anybody who complains, or rocks the boat, gets banged up.

Putting these thoughts aside, I should get on with the cycling. On my first night in Thailand I decided to treat myself to a posh hotel to settle myself in. The Imperial in Narathiwat fitted the bill, and the receptionist asked if I'd like a standard or deluxe room. Deluxe was only £40, so what the heck. It turned out to be the best place I'd ever stayed. Basically it was the Presidential Suite, with luxury furnishings, parquet flooring, plenty of complimentary freebies and four different rooms. I felt like the King of Siam. The only let down was turning on the taps to see the water coming out brown for five minutes before running clear.

After lounging around like royalty for a while I decided to investigate the restaurant downstairs. On the menu was 'Rosted Duck', 'Gordon Bleu Chicken', and vegetable soup. I figured I'd be safe with the veg soup, but it contained several types of meat and prawns anyway, plus some black stuff which I think might have been seaweed. Whatever, it all went down the hatch, and was not too bad.

Next night, another fabulous hotel, and only £22. I took my wife to the Park Lane Hilton in London once, for a treat, and it was over £550 per night. It was a pokey little room, the heating didn't work and the staff were snobby. The upmarket hotels in Thailand were much better in every respect, and a fraction of the price.

The Thai language was so confusing. A page of text looked like a plate of worms. Apparently schoolchildren had to learn five distinct versions of Thai:

1. Street – for normal conversation
2. Formal – for polite/respectful occasions
3. Rhetorical – for public speaking
4. Religious – for dealing with the 'God Squad'
5. Royal – for talking to 'The Owners'

*

In Thailand there was a grim irony that the world's oldest profession was focused on the youngest members of society. The number of boys and girls coerced into prostitution has been estimated between 70,000 and one million. Paedophiles from Europe, America and Australia are drawn there like a magnet. Gary Glitter lived there, as did Ray Teret, Jimmy Saville's chauffeur. In theory, child prostitution was illegal in Thailand, but it was common knowledge that the police and government officials got a cut of the profits so nothing would be changing soon.

I suppose it doesn't help that the age of consent in Thailand is 15 (it's 14 in China, 13 in Japan). During those years, kids should

171

be doing sport, reading books, hanging out with their school friends and arguing with their parents about the washing-up.

I had been in Thailand for three days and my diary did not contain many laughs. There was not much to laugh about concerning paedophiles, prostitution and a police state.

Anyway, let's move on to more cheerful things, like dogs. I recalled that in Argentina the prevailing dog culture was – 1: See a cyclist. 2: Chase the cyclist. 3: Try to eat the cyclist. However, so far in Thailand, I didn't know why, dog culture was – 1: See a cyclist. 2: Look kindly at cyclist. 3: Wag tail at cyclist. How could it be so different? I had lived in fear of those four-legged bastards in Argentina, but in Thailand I had not been chased by a single dog. Were all Thai dogs peace-loving Buddhists? It was strange, because they were all the same species. In-fact, they were all the same breed – mongrel.

As I progressed north up through Thailand I discovered I had spoken too soon. For some reason as I went north the dogs changed and every damn mutt I saw gave chase and snapped at my ankles. I still tried to kick them in the teeth, whether they were Buddhist or not. I booted one right on the nose and gave him the shock of his life.

Pressing on, I passed some towns with marvellous names – Pong, Fang, Bang Man, Ban Thi Wang and Khaosuankwangwittayanukul and Chumporn, where I stayed one night. It was only £11, but it was quite rough. I think it was a converted office block, or prison for all I know. There were no sheets on the bed. The mosquitos were delighted to see me for a good meal. The tap water was brown all the time – so I decided to wash the next day, thank you very much. A sign in the lift advertised a Thai massage for £6, but it looked a bit pervy. I shouldn't moan about the hotel though, it was cheap and a roof is a roof, which was very welcome because as usual it was lashing with rain outside.

I went to the restaurant for a bite to eat. I tried to pick up a cup with what I thought was the handle, but it was a large insect on the side of the mug. After ordering a meal the waiter kindly brought over some magazines for me. He gave me *Paris Match* (French) and *Hola* (Spanish). That's the trouble with us non-Orientals, we all look the same.

On the subject of insects, there were some very big ones in Thailand. There was a large blue/black creature which seemed like a mouse with wings. The following day I was zooming downhill, admiring the countryside, when one of them hit me (or I hit it) in my neck. It gave me quite a shock. Four of them grilled on a skewer with some satay sauce might be a tasty snack. Insects are packed with protein and nutrients.

I went past a bullfighting ring. Not man v. bull, but bull v. bull. By coincidence it came on the TV later that evening. The bulls bashed heads for ages. Lots of blood was spilt, until eventually one gave up, and the other was declared the winner. I think the purpose of it all was for gambling.

I'd only met two other cyclists since Singapore. The first man was a deaf mute so we communicated with nods, smiles and finger pointing, which is pretty much how I communicated with all the Thai people anyway. I knew some British Sign Language from home, but that was about as much use in Thailand as a chocolate teapot. The other cyclist I met was a German called Tomas. He had a superb custom-built bike of which I was very jealous. He was a Buddhist or something and what a miserable git! We cycled together for about 50km, and I tried to chat, but he was very hard work and eventually he just buggered off without saying a word. I wasn't sorry to see him go. By coincidence, I passed him the next day. I shouted "Hello" but he was studying a Buddhist statue, or ignoring me, the wanker.

Apart from the Buddhist statues and temples everywhere in Thailand I saw lots of photos, paintings and statues of the royals. The King, Bhumipol Adulyadoj, had a penchant for gold coats, the vain bastard. In nearly every image he was wearing one of the coats plus large spectacles and a morose expression. Appearing to be a twentysomething, he looked like a student who has just failed his exams. In fact, he was in his eighties, and had been the monarch longer than Betty had been in England. Edward Snowden revealed via *Wikileaks* that the King had Parkinson's Disease. One curious photo, often displayed, showed the King in profile, hand on chin, looking pensive. What was strange was the drop of sweat or snot always dangling from the end of his nose.

Bhumipol was born in the USA and educated in Switzerland. His older brother was crowned King but soon afterwards was shot dead in mysterious circumstances. The evidence suggests Bhumipol shot him, either by accident or on purpose, but officially the blame fell on two palace aides (witnesses, perhaps?) who were executed, just to keep up appearances. Bhumipol didn't bother with the tradition of going into mourning for 100 days and instead went off to Europe. He lost one eye in Switzerland soon after that when he crashed (pissed?) a little Fiat into the back of a lorry.

The King's fortune was estimated at US $30 billion. With that amount of money he could have ended child prostitution in Thailand overnight by giving all the kids attendance money to go to school. Did he do that? Of course not.

I'm not sure how his wife became the Queen, but I don't think she won a beauty contest. (Ooh, I'm such a bitch). She was more Dame Edna Everage than Duchess of Cambridge. The Queen obviously had her photos touched-up because it looked like the King was with a different woman each time.

The sycophantic grovelling that accompanies monarchies in Britain, Thailand and elsewhere is embarrassing and backwards and should be consigned to the dustbin of history. Meanwhile please can you explain to me why the royals all over the world always have a chest full of medals, as if they have been in the trenches?

Enough soap-boxing Besly! Get on with the pedalling! Outside Tesco near Nung Chik I came across a Polish boy and a Danish

174

girl who were hitch-hiking. They had acquired a puppy recently, Christ knows why, and had already been denied entry to Malaysia because of the dog, so had decided to head north to Mongolia. The thought of crossing the borders of Vietnam and China with the puppy didn't seem to faze them. They were a bit delusional if you ask me.

The puppy kept jumping up and licking the sweat from my legs and its claws nearly tore my Lycra shorts. Why do so many dog owners think people don't mind their pooch licking and scratching you? For all I knew it could have had rabies. If I had just licked my arse and salty balls, then licked you, you would probably not be very impressed. Mind you, that might bring us back to the subject of specialist services in the more discerning Amsterdam sex shops.

On the road the next day I noticed that the bottom crank on my bike was starting to make a grinding noise, and the back wheel had a buckle again. I was in a car park making some adjustments when a coach stopped right next to me and fifty Thai pensioners got out and surrounded me. They really enjoyed themselves, as if I was providing a spectator sport.

Later I checked into a nice hotel in Phetchaburi and as usual wheeled my bike upstairs to the bedroom. After dumping my belongings, I came down to the reception area where a house band was playing a few slow songs. To call them dreary would nearly be a compliment. I'd been to some dull gigs in my time where I'd seen the audience yawn, but here the actual members of the band were yawning! Before I slipped into a coma I decided to go back upstairs to my room for a shower. Some hotels had large wet room-type showers, so I liked to take the bike in with me to give that a wash too.

After me and The Rack had showered I went across the road to a restaurant/pub for supper. I was the only customer, but after about half an hour four beautiful girls arrived. They had very high heels and very low cleavages. They were so scantily-dressed that vajazzling was probably less an option than a necessity. I was

175

happily watching football on the TV and tucking into a massive green curry washed down with several bottles of *Chang* lager, when one of the girls, who was absolutely stunning, came up to my table and asked if she could sit and talk with me. She seemed charming and wore the world's shortest mini-skirt. I am happily married, so declined and got out of there double quick. I don't know if she was a ladyboy.

On the 9th of November 2015 I'd been away exactly six months to the day, so I marked the occasion by having another crash. That made four. It was pouring with rain as usual and I pulled into a car park that had such a smooth surface it was like an ice rink. The bike went right while I went left. I landed face down, bruising my left hip this time. It was so slippery I was floundering around like Bambi on the frozen lake. However, the main injury was to my ego, because everyone in McDonald's was watching. The crash also bent all the derailleur gear mechanism, which I tried to straighten, but I couldn't quite get it working perfectly. Apart from that little hitch I was making good progress cycling the length of Thailand. I was hoping to have a few days' rest in Vientiane, Laos and wash my clothes. They did whiff a bit.

Getting towards the northern end of Thailand, I rode into Nakhon Ratchisami and I spotted the Sami Thani Hotel. As was usually the case, the hotel was clean, modern, luxurious and cheap. The reception manageress was very impressed that I was cycling around the world, and took photos to show her family. She gave me a free upgrade to a premium deluxe suite. She was a lovely lady with the slightly unfortunate name of Mrs Supaporn. To be fair, I've no idea what Besly means in Thai. Perhaps it means Pigsbreath, Shagnasty or Superporn. You can imagine Mrs Supaporn showing her husband the photos that evening and saying "Here's that cyclist I was telling you about, dear. Shame he has the slightly unfortunate name of Mr Shagnasty."

I was on the road again at dawn, as always, next day. After a few miles there was a huge snake, about eight feet long, stretched across the hard shoulder. Its body was about as fat as my leg, although having come second in an argument with a motor vehicle, its head was as flat as a pancake. Alive, it must have been a formidable beast. With snakes like that around there I suspect camping could get quite exciting!

I couldn't understand Thai business practices. For example, there would be a hundred stalls in a row along the road all selling water melons, with none of them getting much custom. Then next day I'd pass a hundred stalls all selling chickens, or ladders, or religious artefacts, or sausages or pineapples. The first person who thought to mix it up a bit would make a fortune.

On my last evening in Thailand I thought I would go to an outdoor bar for a few bottles of Chang. The neon sign at the entrance should have said Beer Garden, but it was not working properly and spelt Leer Garden. There was a group of a dozen contractors from England, Italy and Germany flirting with the pretty waitresses who were half their age and half their weight. It was all a bit cringe-worthy. Perhaps Leer Garden was an appropriate name after all. Another wooden sign, nailed onto a tree, said "Beware of falling coconuts." That's one you are unlikely to see in Southend.

I'd had a bad impression of Thailand for the first few days, with the soldiers pointing guns at everyone, but that turned out to be only in the south where there is an armed Muslim separatist movement. I had been given free tea, cakes, orange juice and room upgrades. The majority of the country had been a pleasure to cycle through. The roads and drivers had been quite good, and unlike many male visitors to Thailand I was leaving without an STD.

Photo Album #2

"Those squirrels are big out there!"

"You should see their nuts!"

"Is that an opera house in your pocket dear? Or are you just pleased to see me?"

The crocs try to eat your dog... or you

Crash number three

Mrs Supaporn and Mr Shagnasty

Everyone is equal, but some are more equal than others

With Kan,
the coach
at the
Vientiane
Judo Club

The only
nice
place in
Vietnam

Cockfight - the RSPCA wouldn't like it

Cat butchers

Ghosts of war

The daily near-death experience was over

Do it, done it

14,000 miles, 28 countries, and possibly the
world's sorest arse

19 – Laos

I've been lost I've been found
But I don't feel down

'Half the World Away'
Oasis

Crossing the wide Mekong River was pretty nice the first time. The second time, I was cheesed off. By the third time, I was sick of that damn river. The Laos border guards kept sending me back over the Mekong to the Thai border because I didn't have the right stamps in my passport. The guards, with their little bit of power, thought my inconvenience was hilarious. I thought "Don't be a bureaucratic jerk all your life. Take today off." One of the guards was convinced I had a second passport secreted about my person. SFB - Shit For Brains.

Eventually I got into Laos and my heart sank more. Why was I dragging myself across all these poor countries? Raw meat and fish were on sale in the blistering sun. The only shade the food got was when the flies were walking about on it.

Most of the roads were knackered and the houses looked quite run down. Conversely, there were some big smart mansions, complete with Doric columns. These usually had a Hammer & Sickle communist flag hanging outside, and most had a Mercedes, Porche, Range Rover or even a Bentley in the driveway. Karl Marx would turn in his North London grave. State-communism is working very nicely for some people. As the pigs said in *Animal Farm* "Everyone is equal but some are more equal than others."

The Americans took a murderous dislike to Laos from 1964-73, suspecting that it was being used as a supply route for the *Viet Cong* during the Vietnam War, and dropped more bombs on the country than were used in the whole of WW2. Epic levels of terrorism, delivered by B-52's, naturally make people seek radical solutions.

Consequently, the communist Lao People's Revolutionary Party, which was really just a puppet of Vietnam, stepped into the void and had ruled Laos since 1975. It was the only legal political party. Laos is a Marxist/Leninist single party state mostly run by the military generals. Apparently anybody who protested received a visit from the secret police and was never seen again. According to the World Trade Organisation corruption was endemic.

I pedalled into the tiny capital city of Vientiane and was pleasantly surprised. Vientiane seems even smaller than Southend, but it was very lively, safe, friendly, relaxed and international, a bit like Southend. There were a lot of blond people there for some reason. Being an ex-French colony meant there were fresh croissants and baguettes for sale from the heavenly-smelling boulangeries. There were French, Italian, Swedish and Lebanese restaurants and bars full of happy folks from all over the world. Vientiane was one of the best and most cosmopolitan places I'd been in Asia.

There was a Japanese Festival with an open air pop concert in the centre of town on my first evening. Hundreds of people enjoyed themselves listening to the music and watching the dancing. Around the main square a few dozen stalls had been set up, mostly selling snacks, but I noticed one stall only sold tomatoes, another only sold tractors, and a third only sold ballpoint pens. I kid you not. Onwards with the Revolution brothers and sisters, towards Peace, Prosperity and a Plenitude of Pens!

Next day I found the judo club, so I was happy. I was itching to have a go, but I'd got no *judogi* there so had to be content just to watch. I really missed the training. Most of the *judoka's* were Lao, but there were also people from Ukraine, France and America. There were only half a dozen judo clubs in Laos so it was difficult for the *judoka's* to get the tough training sessions necessary to be successful internationally, but they had a go.

While watching the judo I had a long chat with an American, TJ, about Laos. He had been there twenty years and he said it had improved fantastically, from the previously grim, oppressive times to now, when there was much more freedom, better healthcare and education, and the infrastructure had improved by leaps and bounds. He really liked the people, who he described as calm, tolerant and fatalistic.

TJ said one of the best things to do was an underground river boat ride near Lak Sao. It sounded magical. However, there were so many things I would liked to have seen on my trip that I didn't have the time or money for. In the final analysis, it was a cycling trip, not a sightseeing trip, although in reality I bet I came to understand more about each country I went through than package tourists who were just led from one highlight to the next.

On the way back from the judo club I was accosted by three ladyboys. They seemed remarkably keen to exchange body fluids. I think they were on heat or something. I was moments away from a fate worse than death, but with some nimble footwork I managed to escape their clutches, and escape their crotches. I think for those guys any hole was a goal. The phrase 'comfortable with your own sexuality' always makes me smile because it makes me think of trying out a sofa at the DFS superstore.

Arriving safely back at the hotel I checked the internet and saw that the British Foreign & Commonwealth Office advised that some roads in Laos were still prone to bandits. There was particular warning about Highway 13. Next job was to check my map for the best route to Vietnam. What road would I be taking? Highway 13, of course. However, I figured if I could survive hot pursuit from the sex-mad ladyboy posse of Vientiane then dealing with a few bandits on Highway 13 should be a doddle.

Before leaving the capital I bought my friend John a Hammer & Sickle flag. He would like that – John has a wicked sense of humour and likes to confuse people by describing himself as an anarcho-Stalinist. I expect Jeremy Clarkson thinks it is no coincidence that the initials of Hammer & Sickle are the same as Health and Safety.

After a day's rest in Vientiane I set off again. I met a Russian cyclist who had pedalled from Siberia. He was severely sunburnt. (Predominately traveling west, I tended to get sunburn on my right ear in the Southern Hemisphere, and on my left ear in the Northern Hemisphere). He said his name was Yura, named after the cosmonaut Yuri Gagarin. He told me he had been arrested cycling across China, but I think what he meant was he had been escorted off the motorway by the police.

I spent the following night in Muang Paksan, where everyone was preparing for the biggest wedding I have ever seen. There must have been more than two hundred tables, each with six chairs, laid out on the grass in front of my hotel. As I wasn't a friend of the bride or the groom I had to go across the street to a roadside café for a bite to eat. I started off with a few bottles of *Beerlao* and a nice big bowl of chicken soup. While scoffing my soup a large insect fell from the ceiling onto my head. Instinctively I brushed it off, accidentally into my soup. I hooked it out onto the table. It was about three inches long and looked like a fish with legs. After a few minutes it casually walked away, as if it was in a strop with me. It was an IWA – Insect With Attitude.

I was making steady progress across Laos, so I'll tell you about a species of rodent, with a bushy tail like a squirrel, and a distinctive skull shape, called the Laotian Rock Rat. It had been believed to be extinct for the last eleven million years. However, in 1996 some American wildlife experts found three of them on sale in the meat market in Thakhek, about to be turned into kebabs.

I found a restaurant that evening, and, as often was the case, I was the only customer. They had 'beef steck' and fried potatoes on the menu which sounded good. I asked if they had some vegetables but they only had minced octopus! So, beef and spuds it was for me then.

The four women running the place made sure I was fed and watered (actually kept topped-up with Beerlao) then they sat down at the table in front of the restaurant and cracked open a bottle of whiskey. Before long they were screaming with laughter the way women do when they are really enjoying themselves and a bit tipsy together – probably talking about sex. Within an hour the whiskey bottle was empty. They raised their glasses in a cheers-like gesture to me several times and came over to chat. During all this, I noticed granddad had been allocated the job of looking after the kids. He took them across the road to the Buddhist temple. Short straw.

Next morning, I was off at dawn, as always. I cycled past a petrol station that had some huge military rockets on display on the forecourt. I couldn't read the Laotian inscription, but no doubt it was something patriotic and profound like 'Missiles For Peace', 'Bombs For Socialism' or 'Kiss My Chuddies, Uncle Sam'.

Heading for Vietnam I had to cross the Laos mountains. There were swarms of pretty butterflies that looked cute, but from a cyclist's point of view were a bit of a nuisance because they kept fluttering into my face.

The little road weaved its way through a series of quiet valleys with tiny villages, wooden houses, water buffalo pulling carts and women working in the fields wearing those conical Chinese hats. It made me think of *The Land That Time Forgot*. I noticed that the Premier League had not forgotten the area though. The fashion for kids there, as in most of Asia, was Manchester United shirts or sometimes Liverpool, Chelsea or Arsenal. As I cycled along when kids shouted out "Hello!" I shouted back "Manchester," or whatever shirt they were wearing, which made them smile.

Close to the Vietnam border I met a very tall couple from Holland pedalling along (the Dutch are the tallest nationality) who were doing research for a cycling touring company they had started called AWOL. They had a fantastic little book called *Point It* which contained several hundred photos, no text, of everything a traveller might need – different foods, accommodation, transport, etc. The book was a simple but effective aid to help anyone get by in any country. I wished I had one.

I spent my last night in Laos in Lak Sao. The hotel had an interesting plumbing system. The basin where I brushed my teeth drained straight onto my feet. In the hotels in Laos it was usually possible to watch TV beamed in from other countries, which was just as well, because there were only two Laotian channels – one for soaps and one for the military. On the lamp posts in the village, like others in the country, there were loudspeakers blaring out communist propaganda and patriotic music. Laos was a strange country, but in many ways I liked it.

20 – Vietnam

Sent me off to a foreign land
To go and kill the yellow man

'Born in the U.S.A.'
Bruce Springsteen

Within a few days it became blatantly obvious that the Americans and Australians could never have won the war in Vietnam. Half the country was virtually impenetrable mountainous jungle, perfect for guerrilla warfare. The other half of Vietnam consisted of densely populated towns and cities which would have been impossible to control. Why the Western politicians and Generals thought they could win is a mystery. (Probably because the bosses get very rich by war, while the poor schmucks at the bottom do the dying). 60,000 Americans, 521 Australians and 1,000,000 Vietnamese died.

It could be quite daunting for the first few hours after crossing into a new country; as a cyclist I was thrown in at the deep end. There were the problems of language, traffic, money and understanding normal social mores. Vietnam, in particular, was quite a shock because it was all so noisy, crowded, dirty and alien. They had extra loud horns on the trucks and buses which they used so much it hurt my ears and really got on my nerves. Added to which I got the shits again, meaning I had to dash into the jungle on occasions. It had not been an easy welcome to Vietnam.

Judging by all the flags outside, the biggest and smartest building in every town was something to do with the Communist Party. Speaking of which, I passed the town of Tan Ky, which made me smile because 'Tankies' were the old-school Stalinists in

191

Britain (they supported the Soviet tanks which crushed the Prague rebellion in 1968).

The Vietnamese soldiers had smart uniforms, but often wore flip-flops. Western military top brass, when referring to an impending conflict say "Let's put some boots on the ground." The Vietnamese military possibly have an impending conflict with China soon over the Paracel and Spratly Islands, but it doesn't have the same gravitas if they say "Let's put some flip-flops on the ground."

Hundreds and hundreds of people, mostly kids, shouted out "Hello" and waved every day, which was nice. Often people wanted their photo taken with me. I stopped at one little shop for a drink and the lady there gestured to ask if I would like some food. I was starving, so said yes. She gave me some delicious soup and rice and refused payment afterwards, but I left 50,000 dong (about £3) on the table anyway. Next day, at another little shop a young girl offered me a bunch of flowers, which was lovely.

On the other hand, some people clearly didn't like me and didn't hide it. One woman flatly refused to serve me in her restaurant, although other customers were eating. Perhaps she thought I was a Yankee Capitalist Oppressor Pigdog.

Cycling along near Du Luong, a dozen teenagers on six mopeds surrounded me. They were friendly at first and we laughed and chatted as we rode along together. Then when we were further out into the countryside the mood changed, and they kept repeating phrases such as "Money, money" and "I want to fuck you." I made a quick mental check as to where my Maglite was, and noted where their bike keys were – in case it all kicked off I planned to grab their keys and throw them into the next paddy field. They were on both sides and behind me, but the oldest must only have been about 18, so I wasn't too bothered. I like a bit of action. With teenagers I would only have had to really hurt one or two of them and the others would have bottled it. They stayed with me for a few miles, repeating their phrases then, perhaps sensing I was not inclined to giving in, got fed up and turned back.

It was difficult to get any food and at one point I was so hungry I thought I might die of starvation by the afternoon. I thought "Please tell my wife and kids that I loved them 'till the end!" There were no proper shops, only roadside shacks selling crisps and coke, which I was sick of. I came to realise that when I saw a restaurant in Vietnam I just had to walk straight into the kitchen, open the fridge, if they had one, and point at what I wanted, then indicate for them to cook it.

Another notable thing about the country was that people pushed in. If I was standing at a counter, for example, someone would push around me and stand right in front with absolutely no shame. That would cause fights in Britain, and most of the world. Also, when customers wanted to buy something no words were exchanged either way. No "Please," "Thank you," "You're welcome," or "Goodbye." Buying stuff was a completely silent process in which the shop assistant gave the goods and the customer threw down the money then walked away. It was as inhuman as dealing with an ATM.

As I rode towards Thanh Hoa I stumbled upon a group of a dozen or so men in a circle watching a cockfight. They didn't seem to mind me taking a few photos. The roosters mainly ripped at each other's neck. If the fight strayed out a bit one of the men would boot the birds back into the middle. The RSPB wouldn't like it.

I said previously that I wasn't going to mention mopeds again, but I must tell you about two I saw near Ha Long. The first interesting man I saw riding along had about twenty live ducks, feet strapped together, tied onto his bike. There were three on each side of the handlebars, and others tied to the saddle, suspension, mudguard, etc. I couldn't help thinking that if all the ducks flapped in unison they could take off to freedom. The second man was riding around selling sausages with a large fully-lit barbeque in progress on the back of his moped. The fact that naked flames were just near his petrol tank didn't seem to bother him.

Cycling in Vietnam, I concluded, was one of the most unpleasant experiences on this earth. It was unbearably noisy, what with the extra loud honking all day right in my ears. The climate was sweltering, sometimes with torrential rain. Communication was incredibly difficult, partly because the language shared no common ground with any European language, nor did we share any common sign language for simple things like food, drink or directions. Camping would have been impossible because all the land was either urban or else dense jungle or paddy fields. Trash was thrown everywhere, like Indonesia. The only thing that made it better in Vietnam than Indonesia was that you could get a Saigon or Hanoi beer, to wash down your meal of dog.

Speaking of dogs (you may have guessed this subject would come up), I went into a roadside café for lunch and asked the lady, who had a face like thunder, for some food. After five minutes Mrs Thunderface brought out a large bowl of soup which contained noodles, vegetables and meat. It was tasty enough, although the meat was a mystery. I finished it, paid, and on the way out noticed they had several dogs in cages behind the café. The dogs weren't waiting for walkies or din-dins. They *were* the din-dins. For the next couple of hours I felt a bit queasy, although that might have been psychological.

The Vietnamese ate dog because they believed it increased their virility. They also ate cat – perhaps they believed it will help them to land on their feet. (Switzerland is the only country in Europe where they eat dog and cat).

Later that afternoon, by coincidence, I heard a lot of yelping and a lorry loaded up with dogs passed me. The dogs, of every breed, were in cages smaller than the size of a washing machine. There were four or five live adult dogs, rammed higgledy-piggledy, in each cage and at least one hundred cages on the lorry. Five million dogs are killed for their meat or fur in Vietnam every year.

194

Back home my Laura had an interview for a job at Battersea Dogs Home that same week – what a different world we lived in.

My last day in Vietnam was the most interesting. It was more pleasant because I went through some peaceful countryside, away from all the full on horn blasting, which was really starting to 'Hanoi' me. A bus did pass me, however, and a man had his head out of the window puking his guts up. Thankfully he missed me. Perhaps he had the same dog I had.

In another village there was a smartly-dressed man, drunk as a lord, walking in circles as if going around an imaginary table. It would take him a long time to get home at that rate. Then I passed the cat butchers. There were lots of cages, each about the size of a suitcase, with a dozen or more cats piled into every one. They were in the sun, so the cats were panting hard, and mewing as they climbed on each other. Maybe the ones at the bottom had suffocated. A man was taking them out by the scruff of the neck and putting them into sacks for some reason, perhaps to drown them. He put five or six in each sack, which was the size of a pillow case.

I was leaving this horrible country the next day, but I was still slightly embarrassed to admit that after a week I had only learnt seven words of Vietnamese. Those seven do, however, reflect my primary interests and concerns regarding the country:

Beer = Bia
Yes = Vang
Thank you = Camon
Dog = Cho
Cat = Meo
Meat = Thit
No = Khong

21 – China

There are nine million bicycles in Bejing
…It's a thing we can't deny

'Nine Million Bicycles'
Katie Melua

So, there I was, China. Wow! I never thought in my life I would go there. Before this trip the Far East for me usually referred to Shoeburyness. At the customs, for some reason the nurse took me out of the queue and checked my blood pressure.

The standard of living appeared to be reasonable, and apart from the Chinese writing everywhere this country immediately reminded me of Europe. Most people were well dressed, at least compared to Vietnam, though apparently it was possible for girls to buy hairy-legged tights here to avoid unwanted male attention!

Since the communist government whole-heartedly adopted a capitalist economy about twenty years before the rate of poverty had gone from 85% to 13%. But there was no democracy. All the main government decisions were made by the Communist Party politburo in Beijing. Beijing, incidentally, simply translates as Capital, as does Tokyo and Seoul in their respective languages.

I saw on the news that the politburo had banned golf for party members recently because, quote "It provides opportunities for shady deals." The politburo was, among many things, also responsible for the Confucius Peace Prize, designed to counteract what was seen as the Western bias of the Nobel Peace Prize. Recent winners included Fidel Castro, Vladimir Putin and Robert Mugabe, all of whom have a reputation for being cold-blooded killers.

The Japanese Army used 50,000 bicycles to successfully invade China in 1937 (and later to invade British colonies). This demonstrated that the humble bike can be a devastatingly effective weapon of war. Whole armies can move 50-100 miles per day, across almost any terrain, carrying heavy loads, silently, with little maintenance and no concerns about fuel. You could describe it as cycle-logical warfare.

After WW2 the Communist Party Chairman, Mao, took control of China. Among his other brainwaves was a campaign in the 1960s to get rid of the Four Great Pests – flies, mosquitos, rats and sparrows. Sparrows were targeted because they were known to nibble some crops. Status and rewards were offered to people to kill as many of the Four Pests as possible. All went well initially, but unfortunately nobody realised beforehand that the sparrows also ate millions of insects. When the sparrow population was almost eradicated the insects had no predators and so flourished. Plagues of locusts devastated crops and twenty million people died of starvation. Belatedly, Chairman Mao decided the Four Great Pests should be flies, mosquitos, rats and cockroaches. Personally I think Simon Cowell should be in that list somewhere. Even today, some Chinese cities run fly-killing campaigns, offering the equivalent of 10p for each dead fly handed in. (Did you hear about the two flies talking to each other? One said to the other "Your humans are undone!")

On my first night in China, it was difficult to find a hotel because all the writing was in Chinese characters, and I didn't have a Scooby what they meant. I just went up to a building that *looked* like it might have been a hotel, and asked. Anyway, I found a lovely hotel in Fang Cheng for only £10. During the night a prostitute's card was slipped under the door. I'd stayed in hundreds of places on this trip, but that was a first. Maybe the Chinese characters at the front of the building didn't say 'Hotel' but 'Knocking Shop'.

The next day I noticed that the stitching on my shorts was starting to fall apart. My milky white bum shone through the black

197

shorts like a torch on a dark night. I tried sewing them up but made a hash of it.

Luckily while riding into Lianzhou the following afternoon I spotted a proper bike shop, so I found a hotel nearby, showered and changed, then walked back to the shop, taking my shorts to show them what I wanted. The man in the bike shop more or less grabbed the shorts out of my hands to examine them. Unfortunately, earlier that day I had had a visit to the woods and the shorts still had skid marks in them. My face went red as the man poked his finger all through the padding and brown stains. Did he think I had dropped chocolate down my pants? Anyway, they had some top quality professional cycling shorts, at a fraction of the price we pay in Europe, so I bought them and exited quickly, still blushing.

Back at the hotel, I realised that it was a pretty rough place. The toilet was the squat hole in the floor type. I'd no problem with squatting because that's what I did in the woods anyway. What was a problem was the stench. It was not possible to flush that squat toilet properly, so there was about fifty years of shit in those pipes. The smell was overpowering and made it difficult to sleep. Every hour or two, all night, the toilet would also suddenly make a loud gurgling noise like a giant's bowels. Cockroaches scattered when I turned on the light. It would have been a contradiction in terms to go to that toilet and describe the experience as a comfort break.

Next morning, as I was pedalling along in my smart new shorts, the legs kept riding up giving the impression I was wearing hot pants. Pedestrians did double-takes as it looked like a member of Village People had just cycled past. It's fun to stay at the YMCA, apparently.

A new day brought a new plan! I would wear double shorts! This spared my modesty and provided a really comfy seat, with the added bonus that if I was incontinent nobody would ever know, unless they had a good sense of smell. However, after a couple of hours, double shorts proved to be too tight in the goolie

198

department, so I was soon back to wearing hot pants and giving all the girls a treat. Or nausea.

Navigating in China was quite a challenge. There were very few road signs, and most are only in Chinese (although 'town centre' was sometimes indicated as 'cityproper'). I forced myself to memorise the Chinese characters for the next town. I had picked up a Cantonese phrasebook in Sydney, but that proved to be a complete waste of time. It was absolutely useless to ask anybody for directions, partly because my pronunciation just drew blank looks, and partly because many Asian people just pointed in any direction, either to make me go away or so as not to lose face. I tended to navigate by the sun, like Christopher Columbus, and hoped it didn't turn cloudy. This was the twenty-first century but the old methods of finding the way from A to B still came in handy!

During early mornings in Chinese towns I frequently saw groups of men and women doing Tai Chi in the park, sometimes to the tune of 'Auld Lang Syne'. Like many things about China, I had no understanding regarding Tai Chi, but it looks like a rewarding bit of exercise, and they clearly made it into quite a social event, so good luck to them.

Cycling across China could be very interesting. In one rural area that I went through the farmers put all their crops on the road for cars and lorries to drive over, presumably as a kind of threshing procedure. That would not have been a problem for the motor vehicles, but necessitated some nifty steering by Yours Truly on my humble bicycle. I had already had four crashes on the trip, and I had no desire to use my elbows/hips/face as a brake again!

After cycling all day I would find a place to stay, have a wash and brush-up, then go to sniff out somewhere nice to eat. The default food in the restaurants seemed to be canine or feline. I would prefer bovine or chickine. You could try ordering chicken in a restaurant, but that too could be lucky dip. I requested chicken in one place and what came out sort of tasted like chicken, but it

199

had fish bones. Perhaps the Chinese have done some genetic modification and created a chickenfish.

If possible I usually plumped for the seafood, because it was probably not dog or cat. The year before, when we went to Scotland, I spoke to a local fisherman who caught prawns which got packed into a refrigerated container, sent to China for peeling, then returned to Britain in another refrigerated container. Apparently that was cheaper than paying Scottish people to peel them.

It is so ironic that the Western countries had, in Korea and Vietnam, two bitter wars by proxy against China, plus the Cold War, to get them to adopt capitalism, and now that they have they whinge about cheap Chinese products. Western countries don't like it that the Chinese are more ruthless capitalists than themselves and take their jobs and profits.

*

I rolled into the town of Suixi one evening and spotted a hotel – I was getting good at that by now. The receptionist had a room but when she saw my passport, and was unable to read it, she indicated that I couldn't stay. She said the Chinese equivalent of "On yer bike, Sunshine" or "Sling your hook" or "Vamoose." Down the street was another hotel which also made a big song and dance about my passport, but eventually accepted it.

The room was only £10 per night, but I noticed they also had an hourly rate. During the protracted shenanigans over my passport two young gay men roared right into the reception on a motorbike in a cloud of dust and smoke, smelling strongly of drink, threw some money on the counter, grabbed a key, and dashed upstairs, giggling, and gagging for it.

When I eventually got settled in my room I noticed there were about 900 TV channels. How could anyone possibly decide which one to watch? The government TV channels were called CCTV, which was kind of spooky.

Social mores in China seemed so different to ours. In the rest of the world if you pass somebody in the countryside it would be normal to nod, wave or say "Hi". I had done these things dozens of times in China and the only reply I got was complete blank incomprehension. The people who I did communicate with, in shops, hotels and elsewhere, were clearly very friendly, and the whole country seemed very safe. In some circumstances the people are more touchy-feely than we are, although they didn't shake hands or kiss friends like we do. The drivers were not too bad, although they had that ridiculous Indonesian style of pulling out from side roads without looking. Spitting in the street and smoking indoors were normal.

To pay for things I just took out a bunch of notes (there were no coins in China) from my wallet and let them help themselves. The shopkeeper or hotel receptionist might have shown three fingers, for example, indicating thirty yuan, then he or she would just take the correct money. People were amazingly honest. Rarely, I noticed that some people took a bit more than expected, but I didn't really mind because prices were so unbelievably low anyway.

I could confidently recognize the two Chinese characters for hotel by now, so checked into a place in Dianbai. First, though, the receptionist went through a large lever-arch file of mugshots to see if I was on the Wanted list. After a shower I went out to explore and noticed a fancy hotel along the street which had a smart restaurant upstairs that advertised 'Western' food. Needless to say, I was over there quicker than a rat up a drain. For weeks I'd mostly survived on crisps, coke and the occasional meal of dog or cat, and was feeling pretty run down. I ordered soup and an Australian steak, fairly optimistic that it would be beef, not dog. The meat arrived on a bed of spaghetti, and it was actually beef, and was actually delicious, and I fuelled up with excessive amounts of actual German lager. I was as happy as a pig in shit. After polishing

201

off the steak I waited a while then the soup arrived together with the dessert, but, face bothered?

On the way back to my hotel was a 'gentleman's' club. It was a chilly evening but they had eight scantily-clad girls, four on each side, standing outside in the cold, freezing their tits off, to give a sort of guard of honour welcome to the expected male punters. It was tragically sad, and a symptom of a low-wage economy.

I knew they had desperately poor wages so I liked to leave a decent tip for waitresses, chambermaids and others. However, several times I noticed that there seemed to be no concept of tipping and members of staff would call after me to come and get my change. Twice women sprinted fifty yards down the road to catch me up to give me the money I had left on the table for them. (No woman previously had ever sprinted after me, so my plan was working.)

One day I stopped to check the map near a woman who was waiting at a bus stop. At her feet was a sack, which, out of the corner of my eye, I noticed seemed to be moving. Then I heard the mewing. It was a bag of cats.

The towns and villages were hives of activity with a million small enterprises working feverishly away. Riding through China I could hear the screeching and squealing which might have been people working on sheet metal, or might be a pig being slaughtered.

At home I had read the statistic that half the deaths in the world caused by pollution occurred in China. Bear in mind that, as Disraeli said, "There are three kinds of lies: lies, damned lies, and statistics," I have cycled over 500 miles across southern China, not a small distance, and seen no evidence of any more pollution than we have in Britain. Maybe the polluting industries are somewhere else in China, or maybe the problem is exaggerated by the Western media to set China up as an evil bogeyman, following the logic that if you make someone else look bad it makes you look good.

I spent a night in Yangjiang, in a lovely hotel which cost peanuts.

Like other Chinese hotels I stayed in, they didn't provide a mini-bar containing drinks and snacks, but they did provide a tray of sex aids. There were exotic styles of condoms, lotions, potions, aphrodisiac pills and some other gadgets which I wasn't too sure about. Seeing as none of it was any good to me unless Sharon made a surprise visit I decided to go to the restaurant. The menu had photos of chicken and noodles, which I pointed to, and the waitress agreed and noted my choices down. It didn't matter, they still brought me dog and rice. I had the rice, but I couldn't face any more dog. It was tasty enough, but I must be too English, and still found the idea of eating dog repulsive.

In the morning, riding out of Yangjiang I passed 1st Yudong Road, 2nd Yudong Road, 3rd Yudong Road and 4rd Yudong Road, which made me smile. Then I ran over a lizard. Sorry mate. In the afternoon I cycled with a Chinese man, I think his name was Izhou, for about 40 km which was very enjoyable and really made my day.

It was my last night in China, and I stayed in a fine hotel in Kaiping on Floor 3A. They didn't like to have a Floor 4 because in China 4 is considered to be an unlucky number. (Likewise, in America most skyscrapers don't have a 13th Floor).

Kaiping had an ancient leaning tower, like Pisa. Near the hotel was a 'Wild West' restaurant which I made a beeline for. The waiters and waitresses were required to dress as cowboys/cowgirls, complete with Stetson. I spent the evening enjoying the good food, tanking up on lager, and people watching. There were the four women quaffing cocktails on a girls' night out, and laughing uproariously. There was the grumpy group who sent their steaks back (never send your food back, the chef will spit in it). There was the young married couple who didn't talk much, possibly because the bloke was stuffing his face as if his life depended on it, while his wife was very demure. There was the romantic couple who looked sweet, in the first flush of love. Another couple were continually on their mobiles. My Laura had taught me the etiquette that this was very rude when out with someone at a restaurant. Last, as I had noticed in all the communist countries – Laos, Vietnam and China – the staff all sat down to eat at the same time as the customers, because we are all equal, comrade.

The last forty miles into Macau was a nightmare maze of motorways, with no bikes allowed. The few road signs were in Chinese. There must have been some way into Macau by bike, but I couldn't find it. If I'd kept looking I'd have been there until Christmas. So I took the front wheel off my bike, jumped in a taxi and arrived at Macau customs on four motorised wheels. Sorry if this upsets any cycling purists, but I had just cycled about 3000 miles from Singapore (like Land's End to John O'Groats three-and-a-half times) with only one sick day and one rest day, so I didn't begrudge myself a little pampering at the end. The truth is, for the sake of completeness I would have loved to cycle into Macau. It would only have taken half a day, but it didn't seem possible. If you can find a bike route, then you are a better man than I am.

Actually, the taxi driver was useless and we kept going round in circles. Twice we stopped in gloomy back alleys for him to check his Sat Nav, where I thought either he had taken me there to get me murdered horrifically by the Triads, or he has the world's worst sense of direction. After an age we made it to the customs post at the border with Macau. If I'd known a route, it would have been quicker to cycle.

22 – Macau

Las Vegas + Beijing + Lisbon = Macau. It was a Portuguese colony until 1999, when sovereignty was handed over to China, but it remained independent in every other respect apart from foreign policy and defence. I was in the most densely populated country on earth, although it was still possible to find some open spaces and quiet places. There were 21,000 people per square kilometre in the country. If the same density of people lived in Britain we would have a population of 5.1 billion people.

The currency was the Macanese *pataca*, which was pegged to the Hong Kong dollar. By a quirk of history, the previous currency in Macau was the Mexican dollar, which I thought was pretty funny.

The Portuguese architecture, language and culture meant mainland Chinese people flocked to Macau to get a feeling of visiting Europe I think, but gambling was how Macau made its big money. Macau had more gambling income than Las Vegas apparently. If you have never walked around a casino you should put it on your to-do list so you can see the fools pouring money down the drain. The bookie always wins.

I stayed at the London Hotel, which was on the rougher side of town, but everywhere in Macau I witnessed conspicuous consumption with plenty of people driving Porches, Aston Martins and Bentleys. It was definitely a car loving place --they had the glamourous Macau Grand Prix the week before I arrived, which I would have loved to have seen.

Across the west bay was the Chinese mainland province of Guangdong. I wasn't sure if the Chinese resented Macau's prosperity and wanted a gesture of defiance, but directly opposite they had built a tall skyscraper which, abutted by two lower buildings, gave the distinct impression of an erect cock and balls.

I went all over Macau trying to get the feel of it. I got a shock cycling down the road when a bus came straight at me – coming from China, I hadn't realised they had switched to driving on the left! Later it made me smile when I saw a tourist talking on his mobile which still had his selfie stick attached, as if he was chatting into a golf club.

This was only a flying visit for me. In the morning I was going to catch the ferry over the east bay to Hong Kong. I was really looking forward to that English-speaking, iconic destination – a significant milestone towards home. My heart was filled with antici...................................pation.

23 – Hong Kong

Hong Kong's up for grabs
London is full of Arabs

Oliver's Army
Elvis Costello

As agreed by treaty, in 1997 the sovereignty of Hong Kong was handed over from Britain to China. Some people told me that not much had changed since then, apart from the Beijing government encouraging lots of mainland Mandarin-speakers to move there to counteract the prevailing preponderance of Cantonese speakers. Hong Kong, like Macau, retained a great deal of independence in all matters of government apart from foreign policy and defence.

I got a stiff neck from looking up at the awe-inspiring skyscrapers. Some were 88 floors high, which is considered a lucky number in Chinese culture. What was surprising is that they had such a small footprint, looking like a pencil standing on its end. It looked like a strong gust of wind would knock them over like dominoes.

Hong Kong is one of the safest cities in the world, cosmopolitan, expensive and clean. Rubbish wasn't collected once a week, but twice per day! There was no graffiti.

Lots of shops sold ivory and other animal products which were undoubtedly from endangered species. Hong Kong has the highest number of Rolls Royces in relation to its population, seven-and-a-half million, anywhere in the world. Added to which, the city trams were ancient, slow and rattlely, but cute. There was a pod of rare pink dolphins that lived in the bay, which seemed very metrosexual. It was illegal to eat dog, which made visiting restaurants a more relaxing experience. Speaking of relaxing, on the TV news one day there was an item about an old lady who initially was thought to be having a little snooze in one of Hong Kong's McDonald's. She was in fact dead, and security camera footage showed she had not moved a muscle for at least seven hours.

In Hong Kong I found I could get an excellent pint of Guinness. In 1980 I had a summer job at the Guinness brewery in Dublin and everyone was given three pints at lunchtime every day, so naturally we developed a fondness for it. After those three pints we also developed a fondness for sitting in the sun and not doing any work. Can you name a better job?

Central Hong Kong was small enough to explore on foot, so it wasn't long before I tracked down the judo club, which had a first-class dojo on the 12th floor of one of the towers. I really enjoyed watching and the standard was very good.

After the judo I shared a few beers and had a great chat with some of the ex-pats who had lived there for decades. Paul, one of the coaches, told me his first apartment had measured twelve feet by five. It had a slimline bed, a tiny kitchenette and a shower over the toilet. However, they generally all loved it in Hong Kong – the people, climate and lifestyle.

The Judo lads said that Hong Kong's main source of income was importing goods from China then exporting them straight back again, enabling Chinese companies to evade tax. Hong Kong is the second busiest port in Asia, after Singapore, and it is all based on a scam. The richest man in Hong Kong, and the 8th richest in the world, Li Ka Shing, not surprisingly owns the container terminal. He also owns the Panama Canal.

The judo boys said that when Hong Kong was a British colony some of the Brits were racist snobs who put down the locals, but now the Hong Kongers had come alive and were blossoming culturally, socially and even, with demonstrations the year before, politically. Democracy was slowly gaining a toehold.

Myself and one of the judoka's (let's call him Fred) decided to hit the town. First Fred taught me how to body-swerve the fake Buddhist monks who asked for money. Then we went for a classic Hong Kong meal at one of the numerous all night restaurants. Like a lot of lonely people, Fred talked and talked and talked. Then he gave me an extensive tour of the red-light district, with which he seemed extremely familiar. Fred said girls from all over the world, but mostly Filipinos, sometimes university educated, were brought there and told they would get 50% of the price of the drinks they encourage the punters to buy. The snag was their managers (read: pimps) charged them a fortune for accommodation and other expenses, so that within a few days the girls realised that they could not survive unless they got their kit off. Thus started their descent into prostitution.

Moving swiftly on, Fred and I ended up in a tiny bar called The Wanch, and enjoyed one of the best live bands I've ever seen. We fell out of The Wanch at about two o'clock in the morning, I said goodbye to Fred, and staggered back to my 19th floor hotel room. Fortunately, they had a lift, otherwise I would still be climbing the stairs now.

On my last day in Hong Kong I found a lovely Indian restaurant near the waterfront, so I went there for a proper English meal. After my fix of chicken curry, I wandered around and discovered a lesbian bar on Hollywood Road. Anywhere that played The Sex Pistols was alright by me. In the morning I was due to be flying over India to Israel. I knew I should go to bed early but, "bollocks", I thought, let's have another beer and carry on trying to work out who is male and who is female.

24 – Israel

Go out and smash it
Like oh my God
...Fill up my cup
Mazel Tov

'I Gotta Feeling'
Black Eyed Peas

The flight from Hong Kong to Israel was with Turkish Airlines. The food was excellent, and there was lots of it. On arrival almost all the passengers headed for the toilet. I can't speak for the Ladies, but in the Gents the cacophony of farting was phenomenal. It sounded like a 21-gun salute, or the Grimethorpe Colliery Band attempting to play New Age jazz.

For centuries Israel had been synonymous with citrus fruit, in particular oranges from Jaffa (the old port near Tel Aviv). Now no citrus fruits are grown in Israel for export, because they use too much water. In this part of the Middle East water is a more precious resource than oil.

Israel receives $10 million *every day* in military aid from the USA. Israel also receives huge sums of money from other individual, corporate, national and charitable sources. I have heard detractors in England call the MFI furniture store "Money For Israel." Without this support Israel would implode tomorrow.

Whatever. Israel holds such fond memories for me. When I was 18 and 19 years old I worked at Kibbutz Sasa for four months, and Moshav Pazael for another four. There are about 300 *kibbutzim* in Israel. They are communal settlements, normally agricultural, originally founded to promote socialism and Zionism. *Moshavs* are slightly different, but work along the same broad lines.

The *kibbutzim* aimed to 'make the desert bloom' and to provide a safe and egalitarian place for Jews to settle in the Holy Land. They encouraged volunteers from all over the world to come and work with them, which is what I did. Each day we would do 5-6 hours work in the fields or the kitchen then spend the rest of the time at the swimming pool, mixing with young people of every nationality, getting rat-arsed and having a ball.

Things didn't always turn out as well as intended. The *kibbutzim* and *moshavs* were sometimes used to take Palestinian land, or as fortified military settlements. Religious fanatics, often new immigrants, are not known for their skills in delicate diplomacy when dealing with the locals. Rash aggressive language from one side causes rash aggressive language from the other side, causes stone throwing, causes shooting, causes suicide bombing. It all ends in tears.

It was December 6th 2015 and I was delighted to be back in Israel. In its own way it is very cosmopolitan, lively and modern, yet with fantastic history all around. It's not too rich and it's not too poor. The Israelis have a reputation for being rude like Parisians and New Yorkers, and unfortunately some people conform to the stereotype. Israelis proudly give themselves the sobriquet of Prickly Pears ie prickly on the outside but sweet on the inside. But when an Israeli is rude to you for no good reason, which is often, it's more tempting just to drop the '-ly Pear' part of the description. Almost all languages of the world are spoken in Israel and many people are tri-lingual, able to speak Hebrew, Russian and English. The population was three-and-a-half million when I was there last. Now it was eight-and-a-half million.

*

On my first full day in Israel there were hundreds and hundreds of young soldiers, equal numbers of men and women, on a sort of cultural exercise along the seafront in Tel Aviv, and as usual many of them were heavily armed. It was kind of unexpected to see pretty soldiers with lovely long hair wearing lipstick. The girls looked nice too. (You saw that one coming!) What mildly surprised me was that about half of the soldiers were of African origin, I think because a lot of Ethiopian Jews live in Israel now.

I spent a couple of days in Tel Aviv getting some work done on the bike, then cycled to Acre. On the way, beside the road in Haifa, I came to the Commonwealth War Graves Cemetery. There were rows and rows of British dead, no soldiers, only members of the Palestine Police Force. They all had quintessentially English names like Arthur Higginbottom, Harold Stokes, and there may even have been a Tommy Atkins.

The Israelis have had a revolving door attitude towards the British. They liked the British following the Balfour Declaration in 1917, but circumstances changed and by the 1930s they were shooting and bombing us. By 1940 they realised the Nazis were a worse enemy than Britain, so the policy became to join the British Army and fight against Germany. After the war they returned to shooting the British until Independence in 1948. By 1956 we were all friends again, united in shooting Egyptians during the Suez Crisis.

The old fortified city of Acre was one of the most impressive places I visited on my whole cycling journey. It is a maze of ancient alleyways and staircases leading to little squares and mosques, or opening out to views of the sparkling blue Mediterranean. It was late afternoon in the warm sun so I found a bar and sat overlooking the beach, sipping an ice-cold beer and feeling like Shirley Valentine.

In the Acre Youth Hostel they had a normal elevator and a *Shabbat* elevator. I asked the manager what the difference was. She explained that Orthodox Jews don't work on *Shabbat* (the Sabbath) from Friday sunset until Saturday sunset. They even consider turning on a light switch, or pressing an elevator button, as work. Therefore, during these times, the *Shabbat* elevator was

212

programmed to go up and down, stopping at every floor, automatically, so there was no need for anyone to press any buttons. If there was no *Shabbat* elevator presumably Orthodox Jews would climb the stairs which, of course, is a lot harder work than pushing a little button. The lunacy of religion was captured perfectly in *Monty Python's Life of Brian* when, for no apparent reason, the crowd decided "We must follow the man with one shoe!"

Next day, cycling along near the Lebanese border I called into Kibbutz Sasa for a trip down memory lane. Sasa, incidentally, is the only word I can recognize in Hebrew – it looks a bit like NONO, but it's read from right to left.

When I was there over 35 years before the economy of Sasa was almost exclusively based on growing and exporting apples. Now they had diversified and made armoured vehicles for the U.S. military. A classic case of ploughshares into swords. However, the Kibbutz members still operated on communistic values, and all adults received the same wage. Cars were shared. Children were brought up in social groups of ten, in their own house, just visiting their parents every afternoon and all day Saturday. Delicious food was provided free for everyone in the communal hall.

The only two Israelis I could remember from 1978 were Schmuleck and Shimshon. Schmuleck had died of cancer. Shimshon was tasked with organising us international volunteers, and trying to curb our excesses. That was an unenviable job, like trying to run up a down escalator. The Kibbutz secretary told me that Shimshon had left Sasa in 1982 to go and live in Florida.

Shimshon had fought just down the road in the Golan Heights in the Yom Kippur War of 1973. Syria, Egypt, six other Arab countries, plus Cuba, amassed a force of one million men and thousands of tanks and launched a surprise attack. Israel was within a whisker of being overrun. That must have been a desperately frightening time both in Sasa and all over Israel.

Now there were what seemed like thousands of public shelters

213

for protection against Israel's hostile neighbours. I soon got used to seeing normal people, not just soldiers, armed with assault rifles or handguns waiting at bus stops, outside schools, in shops, and everywhere else. All Israelis must learn to use guns, and train in unarmed combat in the army.

(When I visited a museum in Tel Aviv the security guard, while searching me, asked matter-of-factly, "Do you normally carry a gun?" I should have replied "Only when I go to Romford.")

I can remember some of the volunteers from my time at Sasa. There was Irish Eddie, Scottish Eddie and his Glaswegian buddy the submariner, there was Jesus (because he looked the part), American Dave who was sex-mad, and plenty of attractive girls from Sweden, Italy, Canada and elsewhere. I was very cosy with a Jewish girl from Liverpool. By an amazing coincidence my best friend John was also a volunteer at Sasa, although slightly after my time there.

One day a Japanese lad rocked up to the shacks where we lived and introduced himself as Yoshimura Fukumoto. The charismatic Irish Eddie pondered this for a few moments while he supped his *Nesher* lager, then announced in his strong Dublin accent "Well, we'll just call you Josh." Thus he became part of the family.

I took some photos to show John back home, although not that much had changed at Sasa. The shacks were still there, still with the graffiti above the doors – Hotel California, Riot Squad etc., though they were used for storage now. I chatted with some of the *kibbutzniks* over a few cups of coffee, and they gave me a bag of apples, which was the perfect gift to send me on my way.

Onwards and upwards! (That, in fact, is the English translation of *El Al* the name of the Israeli national airline). From the forested mountainous area in the north of the country I cycled down to Lake Kinneret. Christians prefer to call it the Sea of Galilee, but it's just a lake really. Loch Ness is longer, although not as wide. The Apostles' texts about Jesus walking on water there seems to have been a mistranslation from the original Aramaic

214

where "walking on" is the same as "walking by". Clearly, to boost his messianic image, the translators preferred to write that Jesus walked *on* water at the Sea of Galilee rather than just walked *by*, like you or me could have done!

I stayed in the Youth Hostel overlooking the lake. Next door was the Church of Bread and Fishes. It would be a great place to open a bakery, and a fish and chip shop. You could advertise 'Salvation with every Saveloy' or 'A Taste of Heaven with Every Haddock'. On that thought I decided to press on. I still had more places to go and more people to annoy.

25 – Palestine

We ban that boogie sound
Degenerate the faithful

'Rock the Casbah'
The Clash

Pedalling down the Jordan Valley I crossed into the West Bank, which was partially under the control of the Palestinian Authority, and so went from *Shalom* to *Salaam*, and from *Toda* to *Shukran*.

There were blue skies, a warm sun, a cool breeze and some breathtaking scenery. Three Israeli Hercules transport planes flew so low I thought I could jump up and touch them. I passed a knocked-out tank, which I presume must have been there since the Six Day War in 1967. There were quite a few Israeli settlements, which were easy to spot due to the rolls of barbed wire, fortifications, watch towers and soldiers on guard. Even bus stops along the main road had concrete shelters as protection against snipers.

I was on my way now to one of those settlements, Moshav Pazael, where I worked in 1979. As I cycled up to the checkpoint entrance four young girl soldiers were also arriving. They each carried an M16 assault rifle and a handgun. These four young women, who told me they were eighteen-years-old, were assigned to guard and look after the Moshav day and night until they were relieved in seven days' time. Israeli soldiers were given huge responsibilities from a very early age. When I was eighteen I could barely look after myself, and vaguely recall spending most days trying to achieve some sort of world record for masturbation.

Anyway, with a stroke of luck I found the farmer, Haim, and his wife Miriam, who I worked for at Pazael all those years ago. I

216

was so pleased to meet them again. Haim gave me a tour, but I could hardly recognise anything.

We talked about the old days, like the time we got shot at. The tractors used to have armour as protection against snipers and landmines. If we were working in the fields and Haim needed something back at the Moshav he would leave us with a gun, not that we knew how to use it. Because of the heat we started work at 4.30 twice a day, ie from 4.30 until 9 in the morning, and 4.30 until 6 in the afternoon. The time in between was spent mucking about in the swimming pool. Miriam reminded me about Victoria, a stunning girl from Tyttenhanger Green in Hertfordshire, who all the boys, me included, were in love, or lust, with.

After that wonderful visit I said goodbye to Haim and Miriam and carried on pedalling south. I began to notice that the West Bank was so much dirtier than Israel. Trash was just fly-tipped beside the road. There seemed to be more flies than any other country I'd been in. I got chased by dogs, which hadn't happened for a while. The drivers were shit too. Three times within an hour I had to swerve or brake hard to avoid being hit. In hindsight I think those close shaves were not accidental. Groups of young men shouted at me as I passed and, correct me if I am wrong Dr Watson, but I don't think their motives were very friendly. I knew the Palestinians often got a raw deal (which is the understatement of the year) from the Israeli's, but I just found it so unpleasant and backwards there.

I was looking for somewhere to stay the night in Jericho, and luckily I found the Oasis Hotel, which was appropriately named, being a very good hotel in the midst of a dump of a town. Jericho was founded 5000 years ago, and is the oldest continuously inhabited city in the world, but in my opinion it's time they knocked it down and built a new one.

Near the centre of Jericho was a large concrete compound with a big sign outside saying 'This project was donated as a gift from

217

the American people to the Palestinian people'. What was it? A prison.

Next morning, pedalling from Jericho to Jerusalem I went through a moonscape from 1000 feet below sea level to 2400 feet above, so it was a bit of a slog. Halfway up the very long hill three Israeli lads in a pick-up truck offered me a lift. That had not happened since New Zealand, so I was quite impressed. Did I decline? Is the Pope Catholic? Ironically, or with perfect timing, about two miles further up the hill was the Church of the Good Samaritan. The penny dropped – the area was Samaria.

Five miles before Jerusalem the road forked. After studying the map, I thought it would be more interesting to fork left and take the old road through Palestinian East Jerusalem. It turned out to be worse than Indonesia. There was garbage thrown everywhere. Broken buildings and abandoned, smashed-up cars. Butchers with meat in the direct sun, including a fresh cow's head, covered in flies. Small fires burned on waste ground. Worst of all were the people, who were openly hostile. Men and women spat on the ground as I passed. Lots of young men shouted at me in Arabic and I don't suppose it was "Have a nice day!"

While I was stationary in traffic one man, cursing, barged into me, nearly knocking me and the bike over. Further on, kids on BMX bikes rode along beside me demanding "One dollar. One dollar." Later, two young men drove their car straight at me and screeched to a halt, in a cloud of dust, only about five feet away. I thought they might jump out and attempt an ISIS-style beheading, so that I would suffer a fate like the cow I had seen ten minutes earlier.

I carried on pedalling thinking "I must get to the nice part of Jerusalem soon" until I came up against the graffitied, burnt, ugly and coyly-named Separation Wall. The road was blocked, of course, and I had to turn around and pedal back the five miles I had just come. The return journey was all downhill and so was much faster. The only hold-up was when, because it was a Friday and loads of people had double-parked their cars outside the mosque, a lorry blocked the road – so groups of men bounced the parked cars sideways out of the way to let the lorry through. Anyway, I thought, *Salaam* to East Jerusalem, and let's get the fuck outta here.

26 – Israel (Again)

Get up in the morning, slaving for bread, Sir
So that every mouth can be fed

'Israelites'
Desmond Dekker

West Jerusalem – clean, prosperous, friendly, efficient, happy, modern – in other words, *breathe*. Nearly everywhere was closed because of Shabbat, but eventually I found a bar and got fish and chips and some holy water (ie Guinness). I got chatting to an Israeli called Dan. He told me the latest desperate tactic by Palestinians to get revenge on the Jews was not bullets or bombs, but random stabbings. He said the media try to play it down, but sometimes there are 3-4 stabbings per day in the Jerusalem area. Dan said it is extremely dangerous for Israelis to walk into East Jerusalem or the Old City, and he wouldn't go to either. The Palestinian attacker was usually shot dead, so essentially it was a suicide mission. It seemed like I have had a lucky escape pedalling all through East Jerusalem twice that morning.

In its 4000-year history Jerusalem has been captured or recaptured 44 times. This is way more than any other city in the world. In second place is Jaffa, also in Israel, which has been conquered a mere 14 times. So, by that record, the current Jewish control over Jerusalem is probably only temporary. The normal *modus operandi* in these parts is "Praise the Lord, and pass the ammunition." You could buy T-shirts that said 'Guns 'n' Moses'.

By International law, if you address a letter to 'God, Jerusalem' all postal services around the world are obliged to deliver it to the city. The Jerusalem sorting office has a special box marked 'To God'. They get about 1000 letters per year, which often ask for

220

something carnal or financial, such as assistance in getting to sleep with a certain Hollywood actress, or next week's lottery numbers. Speaking of which, in 2010 the same numbers – 13,14,26,32,33 and 36 – came up in the Israeli lottery twice within three weeks.

Ignoring Dan's advice, I had a meander all over the Old City, and saw the Wailing Wall, Dome of the Rock, Via Dolorosa and all that jazz. The Church of the Holy Sepulchre stands over Calvary, where Jesus was supposedly crucified. Crucifixion seems like a peculiarly ancient and barbaric form of capital punishment, but it is still used regularly in Sudan, the UAE and elsewhere. In 2014 Saudi Arabia even sentenced a 17-year old boy, Ali Mohammed Baqir al-Nimr, to crucifixion for taking part in an anti-government protest.

Religious clothing styles in Jerusalem made me think that everyone must be on their way to a fancy-dress party. Christian and Muslim men wore dresses. The Armenian monks swished about like black ghosts. Russian orthodox Jews walked the streets wearing white tights, a silk dressing gown and something like a furry car wheel on their heads. Another man I saw had grown his beard so extensively he looked like he was wearing a balaclava. I think it's funny that you can get a *kipa*, the Jewish skullcap, with any design on it, including your favourite football team such as Liverpool or Manchester United. Does dressing-up in eccentric outfits get these people closer to god? By that logic Screaming Lord Sutch is on a fast-track to heaven.

Due to the kosher rules which say don't mix dairy and meat it was difficult to get a cheeseburger in Jerusalem, but I didn't care because in the evening I discovered Jerusalem's main Irish bar, The Dublin, had a steak and met the crème of the local alcoholic community. Worryingly, I fitted in perfectly, and we got on like a house on fire. Many of them had been in car crashes for some reason. You could put two and two together. (All my family drive now so when we go out one person stays sober and everyone else are the designated drunks). It's ironic that in bars in Ireland

221

smoking is illegal, but there in Jerusalem both staff and customers virtually chain-smoked in the Irish bar.

My original plan was to get to Tel Aviv the next day to watch Hapoel Tel Aviv play Beitar Jerusalem at The Bloomfield Stadium. Unfortunately, I got my days mixed up and they were playing that night, so we watched it on TV in The Dublin there in Jerusalem.

Hapoel was traditionally a trade union sponsored left-wing football club, which played in red (what a surprise). It is nicknamed The Workers, and fans hold up posters of Karl Marx and Che Guevara while singing "The workers, united, shall never be defeated!" Beitar are associated with right-wing Israeli nationalism, so we were all set for a ding-dong fiery battle. However, the standard of football was slightly worse than when a group of blokes put down jumpers for goalposts and have a kickabout in Southend's Priory Park. Hapoel vs. Beitar finished as a 0-0 snoozefest.

Nursing a hangover, I pedalled out to Bethlehem in the morning. I had to cross the Separation Wall again, and it was nearly impossible not to be reminded of Belfast's Peace Wall or the Warsaw Ghetto. Bethlehem means House of Meat in Arabic and House of Bread in Hebrew and it was not intimidating like Palestinian East Jerusalem, although I did see two lads walking along wearing jihad T-shirts. It was full of tourists and pilgrims going to the Church of the Nativity and buying tacky souvenirs in Manger Square. Bethlehem is twinned with Glasgow and 56, yes 56, other cities around the world, which is quite impressive considering as it is basically just a large village.

It was Christmas the following week for most Catholics and Protestants, which is a busy time for Bethlehem, with the hotels and gift shops doing brisk business. This Christmas bonanza doesn't just happen once a year in Bethlehem but three times! After December 25th has passed the Eastern Orthodox crew show up to celebrate the birth of Jesus on 7th January. Just as the folks in Bethlehem are planning to put away the fairy lights and thinking

"I couldn't possibly eat another mince pie" the Armenians turn up mob-handed to celebrate Christmas on January 19th. Make your minds up you lot – on which day was Jesus born? (As an aside, the word 'Bedlam' meaning crazy is a cockney derivation from the 'Bethlehem' lunatic asylum, which was on the site now occupied by the Imperial War Museum in South London).

I had hoped to get the ferry from Haifa, Israel to Piraeus, Greece but that service had been discontinued. I'd taken that ferry a long time ago and will never forget the rolls of barbed wire on board to keep us, the third-class passengers, separate from the second and first-class passengers. On the ship I met a Jewish lady who still had a serial number tattooed on her forearm from when she was in a Nazi concentration camp.

Back to today, and I dismantled my bike for the last time and put it in the bike bag for a flight from Tel Aviv to Athens. At the security check at the airport the guard commented that my Maglite looked more like a weapon than a torch, which of course, is true.

Overall it had been an absolute pleasure visiting Israel again. The nice people outweigh the bad. There is fantastic history to soak up, the weather had been perfect for cycling, and the food was fabulous. However, if you want the world's best bagels you still need to go to the Brick Lane bakery in London's East End.

27 – Greece

She came from Greece with a thirst for knowledge
She studied sculpture at St.Martins College

'Common People'
Pulp

Judging by recent grim TV reports you would think that Greece must be beset with murder and mayhem. Arriving by plane I was expecting to see the Airport in flames, hear the sounds of screaming and gunshots, and maybe witness the occasional bit of cannibalism. In fact I could hardly tell the difference between Greece and any other European country. Apparently the Greek economy was struggling, but the bosses say that in every country to try to prevent the workers from striking for better wages.

I was so pleased to be back in Europe, although geographically-speaking Europe is really just West Asia. People are invariably friendly and polite, you can drink the water, there is toilet paper, drivers rarely use the horn, and best of all, I was on the last leg before home.

In the 1960s and 70s Mum and Dad drove my sisters Shiel and Gill and me all over Europe in their Vee Dub camper van for three weeks every summer. The deal was that they would drive through the night until about 3 or 4 in the morning, then park up, settle down and sleep somewhere in the countryside. My sisters and I were under strict instructions not to wake Mum and Dad until about 9 or 10, while our early morning task was to go out and find a village, get milk and a loaf of bread for breakfast, and work out which country we were in! Wow! What a wonderful, innocent, trusting world we lived in, with parents who encouraged our independence, even though Shiel, the oldest, was only about 10.

224

Nowadays, the delights of Europe mean that about 5000 desperate refugees escaping the wars in Syria, Iraq, Afghanistan and Africa arrive on Greece's shores every day. They want to share our peace, prosperity and liberalism. The European Union has thus become a victim of its own success.

Greece has world-class historical sites of course, and it was here that the foundation stones for all Western art, literature, science, medicine, philosophy and sport were laid. The ancient Greeks even invented a steam engine in Alexandria, but could not find a practical use for it, such as going from Stockton to Darlington. The ancient Greeks may have been brainy but they didn't have all the answers, because nobody knew then, or now, what doner kebabs are made from. In modern times this wonderful country has given us Greek yoghurt, Greek dancing, Greek salad, computer Greeks (shouldn't this be geeks? - Ed.), and Peter Andre.

Sharon and I had come to Athens for a city break the previous April. We found it lovely and warm so on the first day we got changed into our swimming togs and headed for the pool. Luckily we didn't jump straight in because there was no water. April is too cold for the Greeks to swim.

Later we visited a very ornate Greek Orthodox cathedral, and for some reason neither of us could stop giggling. Other people were frowning and tut-tutting. After ten minutes Sharon uttered the memorable words "That's enough Jesus!" and we left, still giggling.

We toured the Acropolis and ran a lap at the ancient Olympic stadium. Athletes in those days competed in the nude. *Gymnos*, from where we get the word gymnastics, means 'naked'. Apart from athletics the ancient Olympics also included poetry-reading and a kissing competition, which was only for boys.

Back to 15 December 2015. Only ten days to Christmas. Normally I hate the insipid Christmas songs, but I was sitting in a restaurant near Athens and felt contented and reassured to hear Paul McCartney, Slade and The Pogues. I'd just polished off a huge and delicious meal and was wondering whether I should smash the plates on the floor. Apparently Greek people do that kind of thing, so they would probably have quite liked it if I did the same as a show of appreciation for their culture. Maybe next time.

So, I got started, on the long ride from Athens to Calais. I passed the regional HQ of Golden Dawn the neo-Nazi party which got about 7% of the vote in the most recent election. Their logo is a variation on the swastika. Some of their members joined the Serbian fascists during the Bosnian War of 1995 and were implicated in the murder of 8373 men and boys in the Srebrenica massacre. The wilful ignorance of Golden Dawn is staggering given that Greeks fought and died in large numbers fighting against the German Nazis in WW2, and there are plenty of war memorials reminding them of this fact. Local anarchists had done quite a good job of vandalising and paint-bombing their HQ. They didn't muck about, there had been some assassinations too. (I am reminded of the old phrase "Anarchists are socialists who mean it!")

Moving on, I passed road signs in the mountains warning of bears, but I think I would prefer a bear to the pack of feral dogs that stormed out of a derelict building and chased me. There were five or six big dogs, dirty, ugly bastards, possibly rabid, and they meant business. Luckily the road was slightly downhill so I managed to cycle very fast. You could say that I went quicker than Greeced Lightning! They were really going for me, but I'd learnt a few tricks over the past seven months so managed to stay out of their jaws, but only just. To be honest with you, my heart was really pounding for about fifteen minutes after that close shave.

The dogs were turning out to be a serious problem. Better song lyrics to start this chapter might have been *Who Let the Dogs Out?* I met a French couple, Thomas and Claire, who were cycling to China, and they had been chased by a pack of twenty dogs a few days before. I was chased up to ten times every day. It was like Argentina again. Consequently, like Argentina, I gave a little cheer

226

when I saw one of them run over. You would too if you'd been terrorised by those vicious four-legged fleabags. One day I saw a roadkill dog being eaten by one of his erstwhile buddies. It's a dog-eat-dog world out there, literally.

Within a day I learnt the Greek alphabet sufficiently well to read the town names on the road signs. The trouble with learning something fast is that you forget it fast too, which was my experience of Esperanto.

Greece is very mountainous and spectacularly beautiful. On my first day out of Athens I was pedalling up and up and up and eventually got to a high col. There was a solitary house with a large boat in the garden, which reminded me of Noah's Ark. Heavy dark rainclouds hung overhead. The concept of clouds, ie hundreds of tons of water suspended above us is difficult to understand, but thankfully that lot didn't pour onto my head. The Greek Noah, with his Ark, seemed to be preparing for all eventualities though.

The food in Greece is delicious, and I was putting on weight. Lots of Greek deserts involve large amounts of honey, which suited me fine because I have a sweet tooth. Did you know that it takes the entire lifetime of twelve bees to make just one teaspoon of honey?

You've seen the photos in the travel agents - blue skies, charming white-washed houses and windmills gently turning beside an enticing turquoise sea. Yes, Greece can look lovely, but bloody hell, not the next day it didn't, crossing the mountains between Amfissa and Lamia in December. It was cold, wet, windy and I had to cycle through a blizzard. My teeth were chattering and my whole body was shaking so uncontrollably it was difficult to stay on the bike. I was soaked through and caked in wet snow. I think my face basically had its suntan sandblasted off by strong winds and stinging sleet. I'd bought expensive ski gloves the day before, but they had already disintegrated and my hands were painful and numb from the cold. It'd been a tough day at the office.

227

Eventually I made it to Lamia, found a hotel, stripped *gymnos-style* (not in the reception), and put all my stuff on the radiators and chairs to dry. When I was warm and dry enough I headed out to a nearby bar to cheer myself up.

Panathenikos were playing AOK Corfu on the TV. AOK scored very early then Panathenikos attacked for the next 89 minutes. The ball visited row Z behind the AOK goal a dozen times and the woodwork took a battering. At one stage Panathenikos had six players offside – count 'em one, two, three, four, five, six. Is that a world record? With the last touch of the game, at 93 minutes, Panathenikos equalised with a scrappy header. Not classy football, but I enjoyed it. They get a lot of football violence in Greece, but boys will be boys.

The weather was better the following day and in the afternoon I saw my first European magpies. I ducked out of habit from dealing with their viscous Australian kin, but I needn't have bothered because our ones are cute and only interested in nicking shiny stuff.

I had found a friend. He didn't talk much, but he was a good listener. In fact, he was dead. It was a sun-bleached sheep skull, or maybe a goat, that was lying next to the road. I attached him to my handlebars to ward off evil spirits and to frighten small children. Obviously I named him Yorick, although Duggery was also on the shortlist.

After slogging to the top of a spectacular mountain pass a cosy cafe tempted me inside. All around were snow-covered peaks and forests. The air was very cold but the sky was deep blue. Half-a-dozen cheerful locals were warming their toes in front of the log fire. Most of the men had hunting rifles propped against their chairs. Even a Greek Orthodox priest was in there, wearing his blackout curtain dress, having a sneaky brandy. The cafe owner had to keep dashing out to shoo goats off the roofs of the parked cars, which I thought was hilarious. Priests, rifles, snow, mountains, log

228

fires, goats on cars – this was Europe, not far from England, but what a world away from Southend!

It was bitterly cold at night in Greece, and I knew it would only get colder as I travelled north towards England, so to save weight I decided to dump my tent. If I'd camped in that weather I would have frozen to death. I was glad I had carried the tent around the world, for emergencies, but had never actually had to use it. In many places it would not have been possible to camp anyway. For example, in Indonesia nearly all the land was occupied and any spare patches had heaps of rotting trash thrown on them. In other more suitable countries such as Australia, I had been pedalling along in the late afternoon and told myself "OK Besly, from now on look for a spot to camp." Then, lo and behold, over the next hill or around the next corner, there would be a hostel, hotel, pub, guesthouse or bed and breakfast. They were usually lovely and cheap. I had spent more on food and drink than accommodation anyway. Sometimes I saved money by sleeping in planes, ferries or airports, or stayed with friends and family. I spent my youth camping in a thousand muddy fields. Been there, done that, got the smelly T-shirt. I was 55 now, still just a kid, I know, but if there was the opportunity of a comfy bed and a warm shower then I was going to take it. I am not a masochist, well, no more than any other cyclist. I had met some cyclists over the last eight months who were camping. However, they normally had so much equipment that they had to walk up steep hills. Their camping gear cost them thousands of pounds, money which I would prefer to spend on hotels. Plus, they hardly meet any local people, because, by definition they have to find somewhere quiet to camp *away* from people.

As I mentioned, based on the TV News coverage we get in England, I had been expecting Greece to be on the brink of economic collapse. I saw a small shanty town near Amfissa, and another near Karditsa, but we have similar places – Traveler sites – in Britain. In the Greek towns and cities, the shops seemed busy,

229

Marks & Spencer were doing a roaring trade, the bars and restaurants were buzzing and everyone appeared to be having a whale of a time. Crisis? What crisis?

Greece had been a pleasant surprise. All the people had been polite, friendly and welcoming. The history and the scenery were inspiring and gorgeous. I was particularly impressed by the lovely little towns of Archova, Delphi and the ski resort of Metsovo. The weather had been a bit pants, but one of my favourite books, *Captain Correlli's Mandolin*, is partly set in a bitter Greek winter, so I had an inkling of what to expect. All-in-all everything about Greece is good – apart from the dogs, Golden Dawn and Peter Andre.

28 – Albania

Dog chases stopped the moment I crossed the border into Albania, which was a relief. At the customs post was the first car with English plates, a top-of-the-range BMW, that I had seen since Gibraltar. I got talking to the driver, who lived in Barking, Essex but was, I think, Albanian. He was pleasant enough, but something didn't quite seem right, which was maybe why the guards were totally stripping the car out. Albania has the reputation for being one of the drug capitals of Europe.

As with all the Balkan countries, Albania had a brief heyday of glory and independence, but mostly has been under the cosh of Greeks, Romans, Serbs, Bulgarians, Ottomans, Italians, Germans and a few others. They had eleven years under their own exotically-named King Zog. Funnily enough, Albania is one of the old names for Scotland, possibly derived from the Greek name for Britain, Albion.

Albania had the communist dictator Enver Hoxha in charge for over forty years (1944-85), which resulted in excellent standards of literacy and healthcare, good wages, but no freedom or human rights. If you disagreed you were locked up, tortured and/or killed. In 1967 Hoxha declared Albania to be the world's first atheist state. (With a stroke of brilliance, when my father was a headmaster in Bognor Regis, he appointed an atheist to teach R.E!)

In his paranoia Hoxha ordered over 700,000 concrete bunkers to be built as defence against an invasion that never came, and they were still visible all over the country. Some have been blown up for their scrap metal value, and I saw others which had been converted into churches or petrol stations. Hoxha also had a slightly peculiar fixation with the English comedian Norman Wisdom, which meant that Wisdom was a huge star in Albania decades after he'd faded from celebrity back home.

They got rid of communism in 1991. Albania joined NATO, which immediately insisted that they increase their military budget, scrap all their Chinese weapons and buy Western hardware. I'm not sure if it was related to joining NATO but there is a George W. Bush Street in the capital, Tirana. Presumably at the time they hadn't realised that Dubya was such a divvy-bollocks.

In 1997 the economy nose-dived when a government-sponsored Ponzi banking scheme collapsed. The army and police deserted leaving the armouries open, which were promptly looted by all the local crims. Mysteriously, Albanian gang-bosses suddenly 'escaped' from Greek high security prisons and turned up in Albania to settle blood feuds and terrorise the locals. Over half-a-million guns and three-and-a-half million hand-grenades went missing. Criminal gangs seized naval ships, 19 MiG fighter planes and artillery and took over whole towns and cities. About 2000 people were killed.

On my first night I found the stunning and cheap Hotel Kalemi in Gjirokaster. I was absolutely gobsmacked how spectacular the hotel and town were. Perched high above the town was a huge castle that made Jerusalem look provincial. I wandered all around the castle in awe, and only two other French tourists were there. During the communist era the castle was used as a prison. In the grounds there is a captured American spy plane from 1957, that people had broken bits off for souvenirs and had written graffiti on. There was also a large collection of German and Italian artillery captured during WW2, and even a tiny FIAT tank which reminded me of a FIAT 500 car with a little gun on the roof. Four strong blokes could have turned it over. Nobody ever won a war in a FIAT 500. (My favourite tank story was from the Hungarian Uprising in 1956. Kids jumped onto the Soviet tanks and smeared strawberry jam onto the tiny driver's windows, thus immobilising them!)

Like Thailand, I spoke too soon about the dogs. While I was pedalling past a farm near Tepelene two big, ugly dogs tore down the track then after me, snapping at my legs. I managed to boot one of them in the teeth. Where is a Vietnamese chef when you need one?

I decided to get rid of poor Yorick. I suppose it was a bit strange having a skull on my handlebars. I left him beside the road and waved goodbye. It was a shame really, I knew him well.

Riding through Albania it was quite noticeable how few women there appeared to be. Apparently Albania has a high rate of sex-selective abortions, which is a dopey idea, resulting in far more boys than girls being born. So lots of men of all ages just seemed to hang about beside the road, possibly because they didn't have a nice woman to cuddle up to at home.

There were no actual bus stops, so men would wait by the road to cadge a lift. Some others were herding sheep, goats and turkeys, even in the town centre. I don't know why all the other men were hanging about. They seemed harmless enough I think, but the truth is they looked like a bunch of thugs, or a football firm just about to kick your head in.

Homer Simpson thought all Albanian people had white hair and pink eyes, and because I had heard there are 27 words for moustache in the Albanian language I expected all the men to have moustaches. We were both wrong. The fashion was leather jackets, designer stubble and an attempt to look like Marlon Brando.

Albania is the place to go if you like nature; they have bears, wolves, deer, wild boar and golden eagles. It is also very cheap. For example, I stopped for lunch and got a large packet of peanuts,

two large chocolate bars, a banana and a fizzy drink for 180 leke –
less than £1. That evening I had a meal of cabbage pie, goat's
cheese, fried dough, toast, soup, stew and two bottles of *Tirana*
lager for less than £5. An unusual meal, but delicious!

So, only a short stay in Albania for me. It was an interesting
place but a bit rough at the edges. Blokes sold home-made hooch
at the roadside. Kids threw stones at me one day, but they were
only playing. A man offered me a live rabbit. My comedy-hero,
John Belushi, of *Blues Brothers* fame, was Albanian, so that
straightaway makes me look favourably towards the country.

Bari in Italy was only 45 miles away across the Strait of Otranto,
so I was planning to jump on the ferry later that day and head
across. I toddled down to the ferry port in Durres, but had to wait
eight hours for the next one. The receptionist was a young lady
with large breasts wearing a top which said "Give the world good
energy". Unfortunately, she didn't follow her own advice and was
a fantastically miserable bugger.

29 – Italy

Most Italians clearly take pride in their appearance, and dress well, which was nice to see. In contrast, as the days passed, I looked more and more like a bag lady who had rolled into town on a bike that I found in a river. Anybody would think I'd been round the world or summink. It wouldn't have surprised me if someone, with a kindly smile, pressed a few coins into my palm, offered me half a sandwich or asked me for a copy of the *Big Issue*. I thought, when I get back to Southend I'm going to treat myself to a sharp Italian-style suit, take Sharon out for a romantic evening, and knock 'em dead. I love wearing a smart whistle.

Bali to Bari had taken exactly three months. I believed I'd barely left Bali before I was barrelling into Bari. Try saying that quickly. Oh stop messing about Besly and get on with the story! So, apart from the well-dressed folks in Italy, three other things struck me within an hour of getting off the ferry. First, there was a newish ferry in port which looked like the sister ship of the one I was on, except that it had been engulfed in flames, the starboard side receiving the worst damage. I could see through the stern doors all the trucks and cars burnt to a crisp. Second, there were loads of proper cyclists in Italy! That cheered me up. Third, you could buy 2016 calendars of Mussolini in the shops. Were these people retarded? Mussolini was an idiotic, nasty, megalomaniac, even worse than Simon Cowell.

I planned to cycle the whole length of the Italian east coast beside the Adriatic Sea, along a road called the Via Adriatica. My name means 'From the Adriatic' apparently, not that my Mum or Dad had ever been there before I was born. The vast majority of the people who I have met called Adrian were all born in the same year as me. Clearly the name was only briefly fashionable for one summer. I have never liked my name, and you will find that lots of people don't like their given name either. I want to be called Elvis. Elvis Besly has a certain ring to it. (In 2014 I ran the Southend Half Marathon dressed as *The King* and had a great laugh.)

Each town I passed through in Italy impressed me more. Trani combined modern elegant shops and bars with ancient cobbled streets and a well-preserved castle. I wasn't sure if it was a coincidence, but there were lots of LGBT rainbow flags on display in Trani. The next town was Barletta, and that was even more impressive. It was Christmas Eve and Barletta had an old-fashioned Nativity scene display in the town centre, which is not my cup of tea, but reminded me that present-day Nativity plays in England sometimes include spacemen, footballers and even Elvis Presley. Yes, I said *Presley*.

Christmas Day 2015. I sent and received a million texts. I really missed my family. I was even missing my nephew George's wedding. Our cat got a little elf coat! It was a normal cycling day for me, though, because there is no peace for the wicked. Buses and trains were running, and dustmen and farmers were working, but every shop, bar or restaurant I passed was closed. Late in the afternoon I found a hotel open near San Severo, but their kitchen was closed until January.

I was so hungry after cycling all day in the cold with no lunch I was considering eating my own arm, or maybe eating the wallpaper like they did in the Siege of Leningrad. My hotel was about two miles out of town so I decided to cycle in to see what I could find. San Severo was as deserted as if there had been a nuclear war. On the brink of taking a bite out of my arm I spotted a restaurant open, and whooped with joy. I speak almost no Italian, and the waiter spoke no English, but I kept nodding whenever he said something and eventually got a delicious four-course meal. Happy Christmas! Buone Feste!

Boxing Day, and I was on the road just after dawn at 8 o'clock. It was very cold and overcast with an icy wind whipping across the flat farmland. Every mile or two along the Via Adriatica was a layby, and each one had a prostitute standing there, alone, shivering and very vunerable. They were miles from anywhere, with no car, so I assumed their pimp dropped them off. What a desperate life, just after Christmas too. Most of us whinge about our jobs at some stage, but we have it easy compared to those girls. As I cycled past each girl would stick her tongue out and draw it across her top lip in a move that was presumably meant to be sexy, but was just tragic. At least one of the 'girls' was a transvestite touting for one of the more atypical Italian gentlemen. Just don't tell your *mama*.

*

Consistency is not the strong point of Italian road signs. Many times I arrived at a junction and there would be a sign saying, for example, Foggia left, and also, Foggia right. At other times I had been riding along towards, say, Ancona and a sign would indicate 20 km to go. So I carried on pedalling for about half-an-hour and then a sign would say 24 km to go. Five minutes later another sign might say 9 km to go. These misjudged distances happened all day every day, which annoyed me at first, but eventually I came to find hilarious. My favourite was 'Ravenna 35 km'. One day, no matter how far I travelled, I saw those signs from morning till afternoon; and they were often pointed in completely random directions. I came to the conclusion that the factory where they make the Italian road signs (it might be a prison, which is where they make some English road signs) made a large batch of 'Ravenna 35 km' signs and someone decided to just nail them up anywhere around Italy to make some space in the warehouse. Finally, to clear up one misconception, not all roads lead to Rome, although one helluva lot seem to lead to Ravenna.

Incidentally, in the 1880s it was the Cyclists' Touring Club in England which were the first organisation to put up road signs, long before the government twigged that it was a good idea. Speaking of the history of cycling, when bikes were initially mass-produced over 100 years ago it enabled large numbers of normal workers to get out to the countryside, and in particular to genteel seaside resorts. *The Daily Mail*, among others, ranted and raved against the uppity unwashed invading their precious middle class resorts and the cyclists were derogatorily christened 'Scorchers'. Consequently, working class cyclists produced their own newspaper and, of course, called it *The Scorcher*. At the same time, and in the same rebellious spirit, socialist cycling clubs sprang up all over Britain. They united to form the Clarion Cycling Club which is still going today and has 1200 members. I'm not sure if they have a slogan, but an obvious shoe-in would be 'Cyclists of the world unite! You have nothing to lose but your chains!'

Enough history, let's get back to the present. All day there was thick freezing fog giving visibility of only 5-10 metres. The Italian drivers did not seem to reduce their speed at all despite the fog, so on stretches of road with no hard shoulder I felt I could be hit from behind and killed at any moment. I had some near misses. Eight hours of that and my nerves felt shredded. The heavy wet fog also meant I got soaked through and chilled to the bone. I saw hundreds of cyclists on every dry, clear day in Italy, but I was the only one braving the bad weather. That's because I'm hard, or stupid.

All up the east coast of Italy, between the towns, I saw numerous Commonwealth War Grave cemeteries from WW2. There were separate cemeteries for British, Canadians and Gurkhas. There was also a very large Polish military cemetery at

Bologna. I found these cemeteries very moving.

My efforts to speak Italian were pitiful, I'm ashamed to say. I more or less resorted to speaking English with an Italian accent and adding an 'o' to every other word. So the next dayo I plannedo a little detouro off the Adriatico coasto to visito San Marino. O.

30 – San Marino

bought a toothbrush, some toothpaste
...said to my reflection
Let's get out of this place

'Tempted'
Squeeze

Founded in 301, San Marino is the oldest surviving sovereign state and republic in the world. It is like a tiny island totally surrounded by Italy, with a population of just 30,000. It is one of the wealthiest countries in the world, and the only one where the number of cars exceeds the number of people.

They have an interesting political system which is directly related to the ancient Roman Republic. There are two Heads of State, to maintain balance, one from each of the main political parties, and they are only in office for six months before there are new elections. San Marino is not part of the European Union, but they use the Euro.

When Napoleon conquered the Italian peninsular he respected San Marino's independence, as did Garibaldi when the unified Italian state was formed. In 1944 the RAF bombed San Marino, mistakenly thinking the Germans were there. 35 civilians died.

San Marino's sporting trophy cabinets are not jam-packed. The national football team have had over 70 defeats, two draws and just one win (1-0 against Liechtenstein in 2004). San Marino has never won an Olympic medal, although one of their shooters came fourth at London 2012. So near, and yet so far. It's the taking part that counts.

Pedalling up to San Marino, it was obviously quite a Mecca for cyclists. I think they enjoy the challenge of cycling up 2900 feet.

They flashed past me on my carthorse of a bike.

Getting to the top was worth it. There was a fairytale castle and a sublime little town. As mist shrouded the rest of Italy below us San Marino enjoyed bright blue skies so it felt like a magical land up above the clouds. Fe, fi, fo, fum. I smell....

I was only staying one night. I had a pizza in the evening, which was a waste of ten euros. No matter how big a dinner you have there always seems to be enough room for a little something sweet afterwards. My Laura says we have a separate stomach for dessert! So, I finished with tiramisu which the waitress translated as 'double lift' because it contains both chocolate *and* coffee. In the morning I headed back down the beanstalk, sorry, road, to Italy.

31 – Italy (Again)

How does it feel
To be on your own
Like a complete unknown

'Like a Rolling Stone'
Bob Dylan

On New Year's Eve I waved goodbye to San Marino, pedalled north-west for about 60 miles and eventually found a hotel in Imola, back in Italy. Imola has the track where the San Marino Grand Prix was held for many years. I don't think it ever shook off the stigma of Ayrton Senna dying there, so in 2007 they cancelled the Grand Prix. As a kid, my hero was Graham Hill, who spent all his adult life racing cars at 150 mph around Grand Prix circuits like Imola, then died in a plane crash.

To welcome in the New Year I decided to have a big fat steak plus a few Peronis. I must have had more to drink than I realised because when I got back to my hotel room I found myself pissing in the hand basin.

Next day I crossed the Apennine mountains, which was hard work, but it was a charming area and easy on the eye. (The slippery Tony Blair had a house around there somewhere.)

I checked into a hotel in Aulla. They had brown toilet paper. I wasn't sure if that was a good idea or bad. After dealing with all those mountains I rewarded myself with a big meal in the hotel restaurant. On the table opposite was an Italian man with quite a few miles on the clock. He was dressed by his local charity shop, picked his teeth, picked his nose, talked to himself, drank like a fish, kept walking about and was a nuisance to the waitresses. I thought, Christ, that's me in twenty-year's time. Probably less than twenty.

The weather had been brutal in Italy – very cold, windy, fog, torrential rain – which was bad enough, but it created other problems, such as when I needed to go for a pee. Cycling along, eventually I couldn't hold it anymore and I had to find a quiet field or woods. Then came the problem of trying to get the one-eyed trouser snake out from under several layers of wet clothing using numb, frozen hands that didn't work properly. After much wrestling and cursing, and just before I pissed myself, I managed to unleash the beast and stood there in a cloud of steam with my face a picture of serenity, like when you see a dog having a poo.

I'd developed bags under my eyes over the past few weeks. I got enough sleep, so perhaps it was because my face was getting such a battering from the weather and I was squinting so much.

My route took me over the Col di Bracco. Sweating profusely despite the cold, I crested with great satisfaction, then discovered I had no brakes. I'd fitted new brake pads in Greece only a couple of weeks previously, but they were worn out because I'd been up and down so many mountains since. So feeling cheated I had to walk down from the Col, thousands of feet, which really hacked me off.

It had been raining heavily all day and I was soaked through. My cycling shorts were good for cycling, but walking a long way, while wet caused a red-raw, painful rash and blisters in the undercarriage department. At the foot of the mountain I found a hotel in Sestri Levante where I could try to recover, but when I went for supper in town it looked like I was walking with pineapple lodged up my rectum. Actually, it *felt* like I'd got a pineapple lodged up my rectum. Ah yes, the romance of travel....

In the morning, with an unrideable bike, I decided to put it into a taxi and go to the next town, Genoa, where there was a Decathlon bike store. (If you say "Do you know her?" quickly it comes out as "Genoa.") I bought new brakes and a new rear wheel (no.4!) and got back on the road again riding along the Italian Riviera.

While the bike was getting repaired, Christine Sexton from the *Southend Echo* texted and said she would arrange for a photographer to meet me when I got back to the BASILDON sign. Sharon has a big homecoming party planned. Shiel was organising Faversham Cycling Club to accompany me from Dover to Faversham, if I could arrive on a weekend. All exciting stuff! I was so happy and looking forward to England!

Pedalling on, I arrived in the little port of Savonna. Towering above us was the cruise liner *Costa Diadema*. The enormous size of the ship – it was 306 metres long and taller than a 20-story tower block – dwarfed the town. This was the sister ship of the *Costa Concordia* that ran aground and capsized in 2012 on its way to Savonna while the captain was trying to impress his girlfriend (a very young Moldovan dancer not officially aboard). 25 died from drowning and 7 from jumping. Captain Schettino left on a lifeboat while 300 passengers were still on the ship. The Coast Guard officer, desperately trying to rescue people, famously and repeatedly shouted at him *"Vada a bordo, cazzo!"* which roughly translates as "Get the fuck back on board!" You could buy T-shirts in Savonna adorned with the words 'Vada a bordo, cazzo!' Schettino was sentenced to 16 years' prison. Spookily, when in 2005 the ship was launched by the model Eva Herzigova the champagne bottle failed to smash, which sailors consider to be a bad omen.

It was my last day in Italy and I was riding around the spectacular rocky coast towards France and Monaco. Italy is quite a cycle-friendly country which was good and the people had been charming, well, apart from the weirdos buying *Il Duce* calendars. So, *grazie, ciao e arrivederci!*

32 – France (Again)

It's a crack, I'm back
Yeah, I'm standing on the rooftops

'Ready to Go'
Republica

Well, there I was back in the lovely France, one of my favourite countries. If I was in charge of town planning every city would have a *Rue de Remarques!* I'd done more than a *Tour de France*, I'd done a *Tour du Monde*. Now I could dazzle the locals with my word-perfect command of French again. Sorry, I just drifted off into a dream there for a moment. You would think us English would be better at speaking French, seeing as it was the official language of England until the sixteenth century, which was really not that long ago.

I'd pedalled over the border from Italy and had considered staying in Monte Carlo, just down the road, until I saw the prices, which would have broken my bank, and yours probably, so I checked into one of the IBIS (my brother calls it the Abyss) hotels in Menton. Only 1256 km to Calais.

The nickname the French give us English is *Les Rosbifs* ie 'The Roast Beefs'. However, when we thrash them at any particular sport – I'm thinking of Gemma Gibbons in the judo at London 2012 – they probably have some stronger nicknames for us.

Around six in the evening I went out for supper. I walked into a Chinese restaurant and the chef had his foot on the table. He had some diabolical skin disease and the waitress was slapping a

245

thick layer of white cream on his heal and ankle. I was very relieved when they said they didn't open until 7 o'clock, giving me the opportunity to politely escape.

Next day, passing through Monaco, which is roughly the size of Regent's Park in London, it occurred to me that it's strange how the super-rich all huddle together. This was the second most densely populated country on Earth, after Macau. These rich scoundrels like Philip Green have enough money to buy acres of land almost anywhere else in the world, yet they live in Monaco like sardines. I went through the tunnel where the F1 drivers do about 120 mph at my more sedate pace of about 12 mph. Nelson Piquet described the Monaco Grand Prix as like riding a bicycle around your living room, which I thought was pretty cute, and strangely appropriate.

On the road next day waves were crashing over the seawall near Cannes but generally the weather was better in France than Italy so I was making good progress. That gave me time to stop most days and rip down a few posters of the fascist party *Le Front Nationale*. There were thousands of them, but they came off very easily when they were wet from the rain. That was my little contribution to 'fighting the good fight'. Actually, Laura and I spent many productive evenings ripping down or defacing BNP (the British fascists) posters when they tried to get elected in Dagenham in 2010.

I was staying in a dive of a motel near Frejus. Cheap, but not cheerful. The only toilet, down the corridor, had a flooded floor, so going for a pee also involved a paddle. To compensate I treated myself to a big steak at the restaurant just along the road. While waiting I had four baskets of bread and four large beers, which cheered me up. There were only two other customers, and their main interest was not food or drink but chain-smoking. As she walked out carrying my steak the waitress had a hacking smoker's cough as well. I had asked for it to be cooked medium but it came out very rare, which actually I didn't mind. It did make me wonder

246

if I had asked for it rare what would it have been like? Alive?

The chef, Allan, came and sat with me and we had a good talk about family stuff, travel, work and *Les Anglais*. His sister lived in Bromley, Kent. Allan said lots of English people lived down the road in St. Tropez. I asked why they choose to live there and he said "Because they are rich!"

Talking to Allan jogged my memory back to when I was sixteen and working as a kitchen porter at the Sunshine Holiday Camp on Hayling Island. That was when I'd seen a really ugly episode of bullying which involved a Frenchman. There were about fifty of us who prepared and dished out the meals. Dominating the kitchen porters was a fat bastard, I don't remember his name, but he made a big thing of being a Manchester City supporter. In that little pond he wanted to be a big fish, and he was a nasty scumbag. He didn't pick on me but there was a harmless French lad working there and one day this bully battered him, for no particular reason other than the fact that being French is different, then held him down on the floor and using his teeth made a circular cut around the French lad's nose. Then he stood up, smiling, with blood on his teeth and proudly said "That's my speciality!"

Lying in bed next morning I could hear the rain pelting down outside and against the window. It was very difficult to get motivated to go out into that deluge knowing I would be cold and wet all day. In the army, to get the soldiers out of bed, the sergeant apparently shouts "Hands off cocks! On with socks!" With that in mind I gave myself a kick up *Le derriere* and leapt out of bed.

Pedalling along in the rain I passed Aix-en-Provence. That town is the main base of the French Foreign Legion. I happen to know this because when I was 17 I went to join. It was one of those romantic and adventurous things to do. It was quite a mission back then to find out how to join, but I'd read a book about the Legion from the library and discovered you could go to Fort de Nogent near Paris and sign up. It's a lot easier these days, just surf the web. There was the prospect of foreign travel, learning a language and plenty of action – just what I fancied. I made my way to Paris, found Fort de Nogent, went up to the heavy wooden door which said *Légion Étrangère* and I stood there, and I stood there, I was going to knock but I bottled it. I've often looked back and regretted not joining. C'est la vie. (Isn't it strange that you can join the Army at the age of 16, but you must be over 18 to play the *Call of Duty* video game.)

*

Dripping wet, I found a little hotel that evening. In my panniers I carried one smart(ish) shirt and one pair of trousers and, basically, no other clothes. It made me smile to arrive at a hotel in my stinking, weather-beaten sodden cycling gear, have a shower and change, and later walk regally past the receptionist. In my head I felt like James Bond when he emerges from the ocean in his scuba diving gear, unzips it, and underneath is wearing a white dinner jacket, a black bow tie and a cheeky grin, as he heads off for a thrilling rendezvous with Pussy Galore. A man can dream.

Avignon was on the route, but unfortunately I didn't see *Le Pont*. Still, I couldn't get that song that we learnt at school out of my head all day. Further on and I arrived in Orange, an ancient town named after the mobile phone company.

Pressing on, I made it to Villefranche and started to search for a place to lay my head and rest my weary bones. A manger would suffice. Luckily I found a proper Irish pub which served perfect Guinness, tasty food and had rooms to rent upstairs. That ticked all the right boxes, so I got in there quicker than you can say *sláinte!* All around the world I always left a couple of pounds' worth of change in the hotel room for the chambermaid when I left in the morning. They would be the lowest paid workers in the building, so if a few quid made them smile then I was happy too. I don't have a lot of money, but compared to anyone who has to clean hotel rooms for a living I'm sure I'm rich.

The next plan was to cycle to Troyes, but the freezing crosswind over the exposed French countryside was so fierce and blustery that it nearly blew me off the bike several times. Scary stuff when traffic is close by. Sudden gale force draughts from the trucks roaring past made me wobble even more, so I decided to finish early and find myself somewhere to stay ASAP so I could live to fight another day.

In Saint-Seine-l'Abbaye there was an ancient stone hotel, with oak panelling, wonky floors, wonkier walls and a heart-warming and toe-warming log fire. After a hot shower I headed for the bar. I had three pints before the restaurant opened and quite a few during dinner. An English man, Roger, was staying there, having flown in from Birmingham that morning for work. He said he was doing construction but he couldn't tell me anymore because it was all military, hush, hush. 'Secret squirrel' and all that. Oops! I've just blown his cover, Rog from Cov. We talked about being away from our family and he said he had a partner. "Does she mind?" I asked. Just too late I realised that the partner might be a 'he'. Besly fucks up again. By this time, I was a bit worse for wear due to the drink and was slurring my speech so I thought I'd better say goodnight and head off to my room.

Sometimes I think a more accurate title for this diary would be *Drink It* –

Drinking My Way Around The World For A Laugh. To be honest, I have a certain distrust for people who don't drink – those who are afraid to let their hair down and make a tit of themselves at least once a year.

Back on the road near Macon I met Marnix (I'm not sure of the spelling), a Dutch lad cycling from Holland to Morocco. His bike was very heavily laden with camping gear and even a guitar, and everything was getting soaked in the rain. The previous night he'd found a cave and slept there. Marnix said he had seen the Chinese cyclist, Tiler, who I had met in Spain, on *YouTube*. I didn't ask if it was a clip of Tiler pissing in a plant pot.

It was a tough cycling day again with nine hours of strong crosswinds, lashing rain and hailstones. Luckily the hailstones were only small, unlike the ones in Bangladesh on 14 April 1986, which were bigger than cricket balls and killed 92 people. Cycling in such bad weather was so exhausting that when I got off the bike in the evening I had difficulty merely standing up.

The weather improved a bit the next day, there was only 290 km to Calais and I was feeling very excited. I had been texting my good friend and workmate at Southend Hospital every couple of days saying 'Only 1100 km to Calais!' 'Only 640 km to Calais!' 'Only 290 km to Calais!' etc. and each time she seemed as happy and excited as me. Then she texted me back and said 'Where is Calais?'

The area of France I was cycling through was wide open rolling farmland with lots of wind turbines and 'nodding donkeys' pumping oil. The fields were green now, but exactly one hundred years before they would have been red because the Battle of the Somme raged here. In 1916 Harold MacMillan and Signalling Officer JRR Tolkien were in the trenches over on my left, while in the trenches on my right were Otto Frank (Anne's father), and Corporal Adolf Hitler. I saw a sign for *Le Monument des Fraternisations* reminding us of Christmas Day 1914 and other occasional episodes of fraternisation during the First World War. It's a shame Hitler didn't adopt more of that spirit. Nearly one-and-a-quarter million men were killed or wounded during the Battle of the Somme. I passed dozens of military cemeteries for British, French, Canadians and South Africans. Why were there no German cemeteries? They died in huge numbers too. Were their bodies just ploughed in?

On a more cheerful note, I was cycling through a little windswept village when a young boy, about 8 years old, rode across the road on his scooter shouting "Bonjour Monsieur!" and cheerfully babbling a load of other stuff in French. He held on to my panniers, still yakking away happily, for a free tow along the

250

high street. It was a nice moment but I was glad when he got fed up and let go because I was knackered.

I arrived that evening in Saint-Omer, checked into a cheap motel, and I was too tired to walk the 1 km into town for a meal. The receptionist kindly phoned for a takeaway for me. It arrived and I scoffed it down using the plastic cutlery. After five minutes I noticed that one of the fork tines was missing. It had four when I started eating but now it only had three. When I was a kid I accidentally swallowed a thruppenny bit and had a poo in the garden next day and got it back. However, I wasn't going to be poking around in my shit the next day looking for that fork tine!

This area was called Pas-de-Calais and was under English rule until 1558 (I don't mean just before four o'clock). It had taken five weeks of cycling, without a rest day, to get there from Athens. In Europe I had had rain, wind, cold, snow, fog, hail, and a few warm days. My arse was blistered and painful and resembled the rear end of a Mandrill monkey. It was the part of me most pleased to be arriving in Calais!

From Calais you can easily see England. Dozens of times when I was battling up hills or against inclement weather in South America, Australia or Asia the lyric that would invariably pop into my mind would be –

There'll be bluebirds over
The white cliffs of Dover
Tomorrow when the world is free

So you can imagine I was delighted to be there at last looking at the white cliffs in the distance. It was difficult to believe. The English Channel is only 22 miles wide, a swimmable distance, although it is illegal to swim it in this direction from France to England. My *BGT* ex-mate, David Walliams swam from Dover to Calais in 10 hours, 34 minutes. One of the judo boys, John Goodbody, from the Budokwai club in London, attempted to swim across but after 11 hours was suffering from hypothermia and exhaustion and had to be pulled into the support boat. Being a slim chap he decided to eat a lot, put on 3 kilos, train harder, and have another attempt two weeks later, when he succeeded in crossing the Channel in 15 hours. Swimming *La Manche*... mmm... maybe my next challenge? In 1673 you could have walked across the Channel because it froze over. (As an aside, in 2015, 338 people died from drowning in the UK, but only 133 died from cycling.)

Enough of this frivolous chit-chat, I couldn't wait to get on the first available ferry and across to Dover! Yabba Dabba Doo!

33 – England (Again)

It's coming home
It's coming
Football's coming home

'Three Lions'
Skinner and Baddiel

After skirting around all the East European men smoking under the No Smoking signs and taking several deep lungfuls of salty air from the outside deck of the Dover-bound car ferry it was time to head down to the restaurant.

Tucking into fish, chips, mushy peas and a proper cup of tea was a moment I had looked forward to for nearly a year – heaven! Still within Calais harbour, it took about ten minutes for the ferry to slowly turn around. A boy on the next table asked his Mum "Are we there yet?" I thought there was a strange smell in the restaurant, then I realised it was me. I'd not washed my clothes for over two weeks. When I worked at Oldchurch Hospital we admitted a man who lived in a skip. I smelt like him.

Kevin and Laura met me at Dover and we held on and greeted each other with a tighter grip than a wrestler giving a bearhug. A thousand times I had nearly been under the wheels of a truck, and I'd faced plenty of other dangers and worries, so I was quite overwhelmed that the daily near-death experiences were over. Well, they would be in two days.

Sharon cried when she heard about the attempted mugging in Indonesia. In the morning Shiel, my cousin Ian and his wife Judy, and cyclists from Faversham accompanied me the 30 or so miles to The Freewheel, a brilliant cyclists' pub in Graveney. The mayor of Faversham was there to welcome me. Adrian, the pub landlord, a.k.a. Doctor Bike had laid on food, international bunting and decorations, a world map for me to sign and a reception party. We spent the afternoon there, followed by a big family meal at the Spice Lounge curry house, then on to another pub afterwards. I never bought a drink all night, and by about 11 o'clock I was hammered, but so happy. I was easy to spot – I was the one with the biggest grin.

I stayed with my sister Juliet in Faversham, gave an interview and had photos taken for the local paper in the morning, then hit the road for the last leg to Essex. I was going to catch the foot ferry again from Gravesend to Tilbury. Gravesend is the point where I forked west, and nearly nine months later I had arrived back there from the east.

*

Across the Thames I could see glorious sunshine bathing glorious Essex. The ferry chugged over to Tilbury. I asked if I could cross for free because I had just cycled around the world, but the crewman wasn't in a generous mood twice. Ten miles more and I was at the BASILDON sign, my 'official' starting and finishing point. My family were there with a banner and a reporter and photographer from the *Southend Echo*. After photos and an interview, and with an enormous (big!) feeling of relief, it was time to go home to the bosom of my family, or to be precise, soon between the bosoms of Sharon.

34 – Home (Again)

Imagine there's no countries
It isn't hard to do
Nothing to kill or die for

'Imagine'
John Lennon

So what profound lessons have I learnt from cycling around the world? When Edmund Hilary conquered Everest he had an epiphany to help the Nepalese people, which he did for the rest of his life. Unfortunately, I am not as altruistic as him. I have returned simply with a renewed love and appreciation for my family, friends, Essex and England. The more I travel the more I realise I like home. That is my guilty secret.

At my homecoming party we danced the night away, the celebration interspersed with some of Tezza's rude pub games. For one of the forfeits I had to eat a whole garlic. Another forfeit meant one of my mates had a whole pint of ice cubes poured down his pants. He carried on dancing as if nothing had happened. After a skinful, just before closing time, I found myself riding my bike around inside the pub doing stunts. (Some quite cunning.)

It was strange arriving home and being treated like a minor hero or celebrity, especially when my previous daily existence as a cyclist was being treated as a nobody, a nuisance to the traffic, or, by some car and truck drivers, a target for intimidation. Every cyclist knows what I am talking about. Without exception every single day for nearly a year I had had close shaves, people shouting abuse at me, throwing things, or honking their horn aggressively. Those motorists think they are tough and important, from the comfort and safety of their car or truck, but I just think they are effing tossers. Having said that, on the days when the sky was blue, the sun was warm, the birds were singing and everything was going well I loved the freedom of the cycling life, and didn't want it to end.

Strangely enough I still don't really consider myself as a cyclist, even though I have just cycled around the world. Real cyclists have racing bikes, all the right gear and a passionate interest in everything two-wheeled. My real sporting passion is judo, although, as I've said before, cycling ticks all the right boxes for lovely fresh air, seeing new places and the whiff of adventure. After nine sweaty months on the road that was not the only thing that whiffed.

The *Guinness World Records* book only recognises RTW trips if you travel a minimum of 18,000 miles (the distance around the equator is 24,901 miles). I have read Mark Beaumont's book *The Man Who Cycled the World*. He covered 18,297 miles in 194 days, which was a world record at the time. Since 2010 Alan Byte holds the world record at 125 days. I read another cycling book (I can't remember the author) and the guy only went across Australia, the thin bit of Southern Africa, and the thin bit of South America, and he described that as going around the world although he probably only covered about 5000 miles. Some RTW sailors just loop around Antarctica, and call that a round the world voyage. On my trip I had pedalled about 14,000 miles across twenty-eight countries and five continents, which is not good enough for the *Guinness World Records*, but it's enough in my humble opinion to be called a RTW cycling trip.

It had taken me 254 days to go around the world. (That's 255 days for you because I cycled west). I estimate I have pressed each pedal six million times. The *Guinness World Records* still would not be interested in my achievement, unless there is a record for the world's sorest arse.

To cycle around the world does not feel like one big achievement, like winning Olympic gold or discovering penicillin.

It's a thousand small challenges – such as slogging up the next hill, going hungry, coping with fear, worrying where you will sleep, or being soaked by the rain. Any of these things individually you can do. Put your mind to it and you can conquer all the challenges to achieve your chosen goal.

I hope this modest diary helps motivate you to stop watching TV and go out and live a life less ordinary. Aspire to becoming, as Billy Connolly would say, "Windswept and Interesting." I made this trip for the price of a Ford Fiesta. What do you want to tell your grandchildren – that you had an epic adventure or that you bought a new car?

Over a pint in the King Harold with Larry Ralph, aged 82, survivor of the Blitz, 6th Dan in judo, World Masters bronze medallist and fit as a fiddle, we discussed cycling around the world.

Without hesitation I said "Done it!"

Nightly Stops

Start date: 9 May 2015

England Basildon, Brockham, Portsmouth
France Reminiac, Nantes, Fontenay, Angouleme,
Cadouin, Agen, St.Suplice, Tarascon (2).
Andorra Andorra La Vella
Spain Tarruga, Miami Beach, Benicassim, Sueca,
Yecla, Pueblo del don Fadrique, Guadix, Alhama,
Benalmadena, La Linea.
Gibraltar (4) Town
Spain Ronda, Camas, Rosal de la Frontera.
Portugal Grandôla, Lisbon (4).
Brazil Rio de Janeiro (4), Mangaratiba, Paraty,
Ubatuba, São Sebastião, Guaruja, Miracatu, Rio
Pardinho, Curitiba, Joinville, Paulo Lopez,
Ararangua, Orasio, Guaiba, Camaqua, Pelotas.
Uruguay Rio Branco, Treinta y Tres, Mariscala,
Minas.
Argentina Buenos Aires (3), San Antonio de Areco,
Pergamino, Venado Tuerto, La Carlotta, Rio Cuarto,
Villa Mercedes, San Luis, La Dormida, Mendoza.
Chile Santiago (5), Easter Island (2), Santiago
(3).
New Zealand Auckland (3), Cambridge, Rotorua,
Taupo, Taihape, Ashhurst, Paraparaumu, Wellington,
Anakiwa, Ward, Kaikoura, Cheviot, Christchurch.
Australia Melbourne, Warragul, Stratford, Orbost,
Cann River, Pambula, Narooma, Ulladulla, Shell
Harbour, Heathcote, Parramatta (20),Wyong, Karuah,
Coopernock, Macksville, Grafton, Bangalow, Surfers
Paradise, Brisbane, Dicky Beach, Gympie, Childers,
Gin Gin, Benaraby, Rockhampton, Marlborough,
Carmila, Mackay, Proserpine, Home Hill,
Townsville, Ingham, Mourilyan, Cairns (4).
Indonesia Gilimanuk, Besuki, Sidoarjo, Tuban,
Kudus, Batang, Cirebon, Losarang, Bekasi (3).
Singapore City (5).
Malaysia Mersing, Kuala Rompal, Kuantan (2),
Dungun, Kuala Terengganu, Kota Bahru.

Thailand Narathiwat, Pattani, Hat Yai, Thung Song, Surat Thani, Chumporn, Prachuap Khiri Khan, Phetchaburi, Nakhon Pathom, Saraburi, Nakhon Ratchasima, Ban Phai, Udon Thani.
Laos Vientienne (2), Muang Pakxan, Vieng Kham, Lak Sao.
Vietnam Pho Chau, Dien Chau, Thanh Hoa, Ha Long, Mong Cai.
China Fang Cheng, Lianzhou, Suixi, Dianbai, Yangjiang, Kaiping.
Macau City
Hong Kong City (3)
Israel Tel Aviv (2), Acre, Karei Deshe,
Palestine Jericho
Israel Jerusalem (2), Tel Aviv.
Greece Rafina, Thiva, Amfissa, Lamia, Trikala, Metsovo, Ioannina.
Albania Gjirokaster, Fier, Durres.
Italy Barletta, San Severo, Ortona, San Benedetto del Tronto, Senegallia.
San Marino Town
Italy Imola, Reggio Nell'Emilia, Aulla, Sestri Levante, Savona.
France Menton, Frejus, Aix-en-Provence, Orange, Tain l'Hermitage, Villefranche-sur-Saone, Chagny, St.Seine Abbaye, Troyes, Château-Thierry, Cambrai, St.Omer.
England Dover, Faversham, Basildon.

End date: 18 Jan 2016

Adrian Besly left home at 16 and has done dozens of jobs. He has worked on farms, in factories, been a driver, kitchen porter, circus worker, film extra, drug tester, printer, pest controller, door-to-door salesman, courier and most recently, a staff nurse at Southend Hospital Accident & Emergency Department.

He has had two booklets published; *Bash The Fash* about fighting against the BNP and NF, and *The Couriers Are Revolting* about organising a trade union for motorcycle despatch riders. Despite being a hard worker he has the unusual distinction of having been on strike in four different industries.

Apart from following QPR, his sporting passion is judo. He is a 3rd Dan black belt and still trains, coaches and competes. He has represented Great Britain. Adrian performs Britain's most talented harmonica/comedy routine, although Simon Cowell did not agree. He has two wonderful children, Kevin and Laura, and is married to the gorgeous Sharon.

Printed in Great Britain
by Amazon